Tolkien and the Classics

Tolkien and the Classics

edited by
Roberto Arduini,
Giampaolo Canzonieri
& Claudio A. Testi

2019

Cormarë Series No. 42

Series Editors:
Peter Buchs • Thomas Honegger • Andrew Moglestue • Johanna Schön • Doreen Triebel

Series Editor responsible for this volume: Thomas Honegger

Library of Congress Cataloguing-in-Publication Data

Roberto Arduini, Giampaolo Canzonieri & Claudio A. Testi (eds.):
Tolkien and the Classics
ISBN 978-3-905703-42-9

Subject headings:
Tolkien, J.R.R. (John Ronald Reuel), 1892-1973
Comparative Literature
Fantasy
Interdisciplinary Perspectives
Middle-earth
The Lord of the Rings
The Hobbit
The Silmarillion

Cormarë Series No. 42

First published 2019

© Walking Tree Publishers, Zurich and Jena, 2019

All rights reserved. No portion of this book may be reproduced, by any process or technique, without the express written consent of the publisher

Set in Adobe Garamond Pro and Shannon by Walking Tree Publishers

Cover by Anke Eissmann (copyright by the artist, published by permission of the artist)

Board of Advisors

Academic Advisors

Douglas A. Anderson (independent scholar)

Patrick Curry (independent scholar)

Michael D.C. Drout (Wheaton College)

Vincent Ferré (Université de Paris-Est Créteil UPEC)

Dimitra Fimi (University of Glasgow)

Verlyn Flieger (University of Maryland)

Thomas Fornet-Ponse (Rheinische Friedrich-Wilhelms-Universität Bonn)

Christopher Garbowski (University of Lublin, Poland)

Mark T. Hooker (Indiana University)

Andrew James Johnston (Freie Universität Berlin)

Rainer Nagel (Johannes Gutenberg-Universität Mainz)

Helmut W. Pesch (independent scholar)

Tom Shippey (University of Winchester)

Allan Turner (Friedrich-Schiller-Universität Jena)

Frank Weinreich (independent scholar)

General Readers

Johan Boots

Jean Chausse

Friedhelm Schneidewind

Isaac Juan Tomas

Patrick Van den hole

Johan Vanhecke (Letterenhuis, Antwerp)

Acknowledgments

This volume is part of Walking Tree Publishers' continued endeavour to support the academic dialogue and exchange between the different national research efforts in matters Tolkien. Although most of the texts were translated from one language (Italian) into another (English), they have been allowed to keep most of the characteristics of their original academic tradition. The translation, then, does not deny its origin in the Italian tradition and especially in the scholarly study-group which met to discuss, criticise and comment on each other's essays (see the Introduction by the volume editors on this) and thus offers a fascinating insight into the rapid development that Italian Tolkien studies have taken under the auspices of AIST (Italian Association of Tolkien Studies).

Our thanks go to all those who worked with us to make this volume possible – most prominently, of course, the contributors, but also the three volume editors, Roberto Arduini, Giampaolo Canzonieri and Claudio A. Testi, who initiated this project with their AIST study seminar on the topic and who proved conscientious and enthusiastic collaborators.

A great 'thank you' also to Larissa Zoller and Sophia Mehlhausen who were in charge of the layouting and proofreading of the text, respectively. The cover art is the work of Anke Eissmann, whose illustrations to the works of Tolkien and other authors have gained international recognition. Also, I want to thank my colleagues at Walking Tree Publishers, Andrew Moglestue, Peter Buchs, Johanna Schön, and Doreen Triebel, who did a great job with the quality management of the layout, the proofing, and who made sure that all the numerous administrative tasks involved in producing a book were taken care of efficiently and responsibly.

Jena on the Saale, May 2019
Thomas Honegger, Series Editor

Contents

About the Authors i
Abbreviations vii
Roberto Arduini,
Giampaolo Canzonieri, & Claudio A. Testi
Introduction xvii

TOLKIEN AND AUTHORS FROM ANTIQUITY

Gloria Larini
Giant, Solitary, and Anarchist.
The Trolls in *The Hobbit* and Polyphemus in the *Odyssey* 3

Leonardo Mantovani
Renewing the Epic: Tolkien and Apollonius Rhodius 13

Gloria Larini
To Die for Love. Female Archetypes in Tolkien and Euripides 25

Lavinia Scolari
Tolkien and Virgil, Ancient Lore and Literary Inspiration 35

TOLKIEN AND AUTHORS FROM THE MIDDLE AGES

Valérie Morisi
Stories of Wonders and Wanderings:
The Hobbit and *The Travels of Marco Polo* 47

Claudio A. Testi
Tolkien and Aquinas 57

Elisa Sicuri
Tolkien and Malory: Writing a Mythology for England 73

Chiara Bertoglio
Dante, Tolkien, and the Supreme Harmony 83

Tânia P. Azevedo
Gawain vs. Gauvain: Tolkien and Chrétien de Troyes   97

Roberto Arduini
The Innkeeper and the Miller: Common Folks in Chaucer and Tolkien   105

Tolkien and Authors from the Modern Period

Amelia A. Rutledge
Tolkien and Sir Walter Scott:
Critiques of the Chivalric/Heroic Imaginary   123

Luisa Paglieri
Tolkien and Shakespeare: Debtor Against His Will   131

Sara Gianotto
Tolkien and Alfieri. Fëanor and the Characters of Alfierian Tragedy   143

Cecilia Barella
Tolkien and Grahame   155

Andrea Monda
Tolkien and Manzoni   167

Melissa Ruth Arul
The Yoke of Pride and Shame:
Joseph Conrad's Lord Jim and J.R.R. Tolkien's Túrin Turambar   175

Chiara Nejrotti
From Neverland to Middle-earth   185

Giampaolo Canzonieri
The Hobbit and the Puppet:
Two Protagonists Journeying into Opposite Directions   197

Simone Bonechi
Tolkien and the War Poets   205

Barbara Sanguineti
With Light Step Through the Threshold:
Female characters, the Gothic, and the *meditatio mortis* in Tolkien and Poe   217

Tom Shippey
William Morris and Tolkien: Some Unexpected Connections   229

About the Authors

ROBERTO ARDUINI, is the President of the Tolkien Society of Italy (Italian Association of Tolkien Studies, AIST). He is a journalist and independent scholar, and a member of the Scientific Review Committee of *Tolkien e Dintorni* (Tolkien and his Surroundings), a book series published in Italy by Marietti 1820. He contributed to the *J.R.R. Tolkien Encyclopedia* (edited by Michael Drout, Routledge, 2006) and, together with Claudio Antonio Testi, he has edited for Marietti, among others, *La Falce Spezzata. Morte e immortalità in J.R.R. Tolkien* and *Tolkien e la Filosofia*, both published in English by Walking Tree Publishers (*The Broken Scythe*, 2012; *Tolkien and Philosophy*, 2014).

MELISSA RUTH ARUL teaches Literature in English at the IGCSE level at Sri Kuala Lumpur, a private school. Besides Tolkien, her interests include fairy tales, folklore and fantasy. She graduated with a Master's degree in English Literature from the University of Malaya, Malaysia. Completing her dissertation, *A Critical Study of the Self and the Other in Selected Texts of J.R.R. Tolkien*, led in 2010 to her presenting a paper on "Elvish Identity – A Journey" at the *Festival in the Shire* in Wales. Her paper "Silmarils and Obsessions: The Undoing of Fëanor" has been published in *Tolkien and Alterity* (edited by Christopher Vaccaro and Yvette Kisor, 2017).

TÂNIA P. AZEVEDO is presently a lecturer at Instituto de Letras e Ciências Humanas (ILCH), Minho University, Braga, Portugal. She has a four-years degree in Modern Languages and Literatures (Portugese and English Studies) from the Faculty of Arts at the University of Lisbon, and a two-years degree in Education qualifying her to teach Portuguese and English in schools. Her Master's degree in English Literature was also completed in Lisbon, and explored the re-writing of Christian myth in the works of J.R.R. Tolkien. She holds a PhD in English Literature, for which she worked on *Sir Gawain and the Green Knight* and translated it into Portugese.

CECILIA BARELLA graduated from the University La Sapienza, Rome, in English Literature. Her research interests deal mainly with British XIX century literature, fairy tales and folklore, and children's literature. She has collaborated with several publishing houses and cultural magazines since the early '90s and written numerous articles, reviews, introductions, and translations. For the last fifteen years she has been taking part in a study group on Tolkien's work and related topics. In this area, she has written several essays and (co-)edited collections of essays such as *Tolkien e i Classici I* and *Tolkien e i Classici II*.

CHIARA BERTOGLIO is a concert pianist, musicologist and theologian. She has got a Ph.D. in Music Performance Practice (Birmingham, 2012), and a Master's degree in Piano (Accademia di Santa Cecilia, 2003), Musicology (Venice, 2006; Rome, 2004) and Theology (Rome, 2008; Nottingham, 2016). She performs worldwide as a soloist, including concerts at Carnegie Hall and other venues such as the Concertgebouw, Santa Cecilia, The Royal Academy, etc. She is the author of several books, the latest of which is the award-winning *Reforming Music* (De Gruyter, 2017). One of her essays on Tolkien and music has been published in *Tolkien Studies*, while another is forthcoming in the volume *Music in Middle-earth and Beyond* (Walking Tree Publishers, 2019).

SIMONE BONECHI graduated in Modern History at the University of Florence and received a Ph.D. in History from the Sacro Cuore University of Milan. He regularly collaborates as author and translator with the Italian Tolkien magazine *Endóre*, and is a member of the Italian Association of Tolkien Studies (AIST). He also collaborated on some Italian translations of Tolkien criticism published in *Tolkien e Dintorni*, and his essay "In the Mounds of Mundburg: Death, War and Memory in Middle-earth" appeared in *The Broken Scythe. Death and Immortality in the Works of J.R.R. Tolkien* (WTP, 2012).

GIAMPAOLO CANZONIERI graduated in Computer Science and now earns his living in the financial sector. He discovered *The Lord of the Rings* at the age of fifteen and Tolkien has been part of his life ever since. He is a member of the Scientific Review Committee of *Tolkien e Dintorni*, has written a few essays and translated, co-translated or supervised the translation of many essays and writings by various authors, among which Verlyn Flieger, Tom Shippey, John Garth, Dimitra Fimi and J.R.R. Tolkien himself. In 2018 he translated J.R.R.

Tolkien's *The Return of Beorhtnoth Beorhthelm's son* (Bompiani 2019). He is a founding member of Italian Association of Tolkien Studies (AIST).

SARA GIANOTTO graduated in Historical and Librarian Sciences from the University of Turin, with a thesis centred on a digital bibliography of Tolkien's works. She later completed a Master's course in Publishing, Journalism and Cultural Management at La Sapienza University, Rome. She is a member of the Italian Association of Tolkien Studies (AIST) and founder of Eterea Edizioni. For both AIST and Eterea she is social media manager and editor. She published two essays in *Tolkien e i Classici I* and *Tolkien e i Classici II*, and the book *Scrivere in Tengwar* ("Writing in Tengwar"), Eterea Edizioni.

GLORIA LARINI graduated in Greek Language and Literature first, and then in Philosophy, from the University of Pisa. She received a Ph.D. *summa cum laude* in Ancient, Medieval and Renaissance Studies at the Italian Institute of Human Sciences/Scuola Normale Superiore. As a scholar she has written a dozen papers, published in national and international academic journals and books. She also edited two volumes (the last with Franco Cardini, *Professor Emeritus* of Medieval History) and is a member of the Italian Association of Tolkien Studies (AIST).

LEONARDO MANTOVANI graduated in Literature from the University of Trento, where he is conducting further studies for a Ph.D. in Classic Philology. His fields of research comprise J.R.R. Tolkien and epic Greek poetry and its reception during Hellenism. He is a member of the Italian Association of Tolkien Studies (AIST) and has given various speeches on his research in Lucca, Modena, and Mantova. Currently, he is focussing his research on the connection between Tolkien's *Legendarium* and Classic and Norse mythologies.

ANDREA MONDA graduated in Religious Science from the Pontifical Gregorian University of Rome. His thesis on the theological meanings of *The Lord of the Rings* was published in 2008 by Rubbettino Editore under the title *L'Anello e la Croce*. He worked as a teacher of Catholic religion in the high schools of Rome, the Pontifical Gregorian University, and the Pontifical Lateran University. Since 18th December 2018 he has been editor-in-chief of the daily newspaper of the Holy See, *L'Osservatore Romano*. Together with Saverio Simonelli, he has published *Tolkien, il Signore della Fantasia* (Frassinelli, 2002) and *Gli Anelli della Fantasia* (Frassinelli, 2004).

VALÉRIE MORISI has a Bachelor's degree in Foreign Languages and Literature, 110/110 *cum laude*, and a Master's degree in Modern, Post-colonial and Comparative Literatures, 110/110 *cum laude*, both from the University of Bologna. She is the editor-in-chief of the Italian Association of Tolkien Studies (AIST) website, and as a scholar has organised for AIST many conferences on Tolkien, the last one at the Festival del Medioevo, the greatest cultural event on Middle Ages in Italy.

CHIARA NEJROTTI graduated in Philosophy and Pedagogy from the University of Turin and is currently teaching Philosophy in a High School. As a scholar she has written several essays on J.R.R. Tolkien and C.S. Lewis, as well as on myth, fairy tales, and fantastic creatures. She regularly participates in conferences and events about fantastic literature and contributed to the expanded re-edition of *Dizionario dell'Universo di Tolkien* (Bompiani 2016) and to *Tolkien e i Classici I* and *Tolkien e i Classici II*. She is a member of the Association "Sentieri Tolkieniani".

LUISA PAGLIERI graduated in Languages and in Italian Literature from the University of Turin. She is a translator, a novelist, and an essayist. She wrote numerous essays about J.R.R. Tolkien, C.S. Lewis, and the marvellous element in medieval literature (published, among others, by Brepols, Messaggero, and the Dutch Tolkien Society Unquendor). She is a member of the Italian Association "Sentieri Tolkieniani".

AMELIA A. RUTLEDGE, a medievalist, retired from George Mason University (Fairfax, Virginia) where she taught courses in medieval literature (especially Arthurian legend) and intellectual history, science fiction, fantasy, and children's literature. Her research focuses on contemporary fantasy, and she has published articles about Robin McKinley's *Deerskin*, on the construction of masculinities in two contemporary novel sequences based on Arthurian legend, and on elements of Pauline theology in J.R.R. Tolkien's *Legendarium*. She is currently working on a study of Patricia A. McKillip's Arthurian-based novel, *Kingfisher*.

About the Authors

Barbara Sanguineti graduated in Italian Literature and Language from the University of Turin with a dissertation about the influences of Gothic literary villains on 19th-century Italian novels. She lived for many years in London, studying English and teaching Italian. She is the author of several fantasy short stories. Since 2014 she has cooperated with the Italian Association of Tolkien Studies (AIST), which she joined in 2016. She has published essays in *Tolkien e i Classici I* and *Tolkien e i Classici II* as well as in other thematic publications.

Lavinia Scolari graduated in Classics from the University of Palermo. She received a Ph.D. in Anthropology of the Ancient World at the University of Siena and her current research focuses on reciprocity in Latin literature and in Greek and Roman mythical lore. As a scholar, she has written 17 papers (4 concerning Tolkien's works) and 2 books. Together with Giusto Picone she has edited *J.R.R. Tolkien: Viaggio ed Eroismo ne* Il Signore degli Anelli. *Atti del Convegno di Studi* (Palumbo Editore 2016).

Tom Shippey is Professor Emeritus of Saint Louis University, Missouri. He has lectured and published widely not only on all matters medieval, but also on Fantasy and Science Fiction. His books include *J.R.R. Tolkien: Author of the Century* (2001), *The Road to Middle-earth* (4th revised edition 2004), *Roots and Branches: Selected Papers on Tolkien* (2007), *Hard Reading: Learning from Science Fiction* (2016), and, most recently, *Laughing Shall I Die: Lives and Deaths of the Great Vikings* (2018).

Elisa Sicuri graduated in Modern Literature (BA in 2014, MA in 2016) from the University of Parma. Since 2016 she has been a member of the Italian Association of Tolkien Studies (AIST) and her interests focus on Tolkien's constructed languages. Besides Tolkien, she is also interested in the study of medieval Latin philology and linguistics. She took part to various seminars and she authored several papers in journals (*Spolia – Journal of Medieval Studies*) and books (*Il ruolo delle lingue e delle letterature germaniche nella formazione dell'Europa medievale*).

Claudio Antonio Testi graduated in Philosophy from the University of Bologna and received a Ph.D. *summa cum laude* from the Pontificia Università Lateranense. He is co-founder of the Italian Association of Tolkien Studies and

President of the Philosophical Institute of Thomistic Studies. He holds courses on Tolkien and on formal logic at the Dominican Philosophical Study of Bologna. He has written 43 papers (published, among others, in *Tolkien Studies, Hither Shore* and *Journal of Tolkien Research*) and edited 15 volumes. He authored, most recently, *Pagan Saints in Middle-earth* (Walking Tree Publishers, 2018).

Abbreviations

Abbreviations for Tolkien's works

ATB *The Adventures of Tom Bombadil and Other Verses from the Red Book*, London: George Allen & Unwin, 1962; reprinted in *Tales*, 61-118.

AW '*Ancrene Wisse* and *Hali Meiðhad.*' *Essays and Studies* 14 (1929): 104-126.

BL *Beren and Lúthien*. Edited by Christopher Tolkien. London: HarperCollins, 2017.

BLT 1 *The Book of Lost Tales, Part One*. Edited by Christopher Tolkien. London: HarperCollins, 2002.

BLT 2 *The Book of Lost Tales, Part Two*. Edited by Christopher Tolkien, London: HarperCollins, 2002.

B&C *Beowulf and the Critics by J.R.R. Tolkien*. Ed. Michael D.C. Drout. Medieval and Renaissance Texts and Studies 48. Tempe AZ: Arizona Center for Medieval and Renaissance Studies, 2002.

BMC *Beowulf: The Monster and the Critics*. Proceedings of the British Academy 22 (for 1936), 1937. Reprinted in *MC*.

CH *The Children of Húrin*. Edited by Christopher Tolkien. London: HarperCollins, 2007.

EW 'English and Welsh.' *Angles and Britons: O'Donnell Lectures*. Cardiff: University of Wales Press, 1963, 1-41. Reprinted in *MC*.

FA *The Fall of Arthur*. Edited by Christopher Tolkien. London: HarperCollins, 2013.

FCL *The Father Christmas Letters*. London: HarperCollins, 2004.

FFW 'Fate and Free Will.' Two annotations written in 1968 and published in *Tolkien Studies* 6 (2009): 183-188.

FGH *Farmer Giles of Ham*. Edited by Christina Scull and Wayne G. Hammond. London: HarperCollins, 1999.

FH *Finn and Hengest: The Fragment and the Episode*. Edited by Alan Bliss, London: George Allen & Unwin, 1982.

GN   'Guide to the Names in *The Lord of the Rings*.' *A Tolkien Compass*. Edited by Jared Lobdell. La Salle ,IL: Open Court, 1975, 153-201.

H   *The Hobbit: or, There and Back Again*. Edited by Douglas A. Anderson. London: HarperCollins, 2001.

HBBS   'The Homecoming of Beorhtnoth Beorhthelm's Son.' *Essays and Studies* N.S. vol. 6 (1953): 1-18. Reprinted in *Tree*.

HoMe   *The History of Middle-earth*. Twelve volumes edited by Christopher Tolkien, containing: *LT I-II, LB, SME, LR, RS, TI, WR, SD, MR, WJ, PME*.

Letters   *The Letters of J.R.R. Tolkien*. Edited by Humphrey Carpenter, with the assistance of Christopher Tolkien. London: HarperCollins, 1999.

LB   *The Lays of Beleriand*. (*The History of Middle-earth* 3). Edited by Christopher Tolkien. London: HarperCollins, 2002.

LN   "Leaf by Niggle." *Dublin Review* (January 1945): 46-61. Reprinted in *Tree*.

LotR   *The Lord of The Rings*. 50th anniversary edition. Boston: Houghton Mifflin, 2004.

LR   *The Lost Road and Other Writings: Language and Legend before The Lord of the Rings*. (*The History of Middle-earth* 5). Edited by Christopher Tolkien, London: HarperCollins, 2002.

LSG   *The Legend of Sigurd & Gudrún*. Edited by Christopher Tolkien. London: HarperCollins, 2009.

MC   *The Monsters and the Critics and Other Essays*. Edited by Christopher Tolkien, London: HarperCollins, 1997.

MR   *Morgoth's Ring*. (*The History of Middle-earth* 10). Edited by Christopher Tolkien, London: HarperCollins, 2002.

OOE   *The Old English Exodus: Text, Translation, and Commentary*. Edited by Joan Turville-Petre. Oxford: Clarendon, 1981.

P   *Pictures by J.R.R. Tolkien*. Edited by Christopher Tolkien. London: George Allen & Unwin, 1979; republished London: HarperCollins, 1991.

PME   *The Peoples of Middle-earth*. (*The History of Middle-earth* 12). Edited by Christopher Tolkien. London: HarperCollins, 2002.

Preface   'Prefatory Remarks' to *Beowulf and the Finnesburg Fragment: A Translation into Modern English* by J.R. Clark Hall. London: George Allen & Unwin, 1940, ix-xliii. Reprinted in *MC* as 'On Translating *Beowulf*, 49-71.

RGEO   *The Road Goes Ever On: A Song Cycle*. Poems by J.R.R. Tolkien, music by Donald Swann. London: HarperCollins, 2002.

RS   *The Return of the Shadow.* (*The History of Middle-earth* 6). Edited by Christopher Tolkien, London: HarperCollins, 2002.

S   *The Silmarillion.* Edited by Christopher Tolkien. London: George Allen & Unwin, 1977; reprinted London: HarperCollins, 2001.

SD   *Sauron Defeated.* (*The History of Middle-earth* 9). Edited by Christopher Tolkien, London: HarperCollins, 1992.

SGGK   'Sir Gawain and the Green Knight.' (W.P. Ker Memorial Lecture given on 15 April 1953.) Reprinted in *MC,* 109-161.

SGPO   *Sir Gawain and the Green Knight, Pearl and Sir Orfeo.* Translated by J.R.R. Tolkien, edited by Christopher Tolkien. London: HarperCollins, 1995.

SME   *The Shaping of Middle-earth.* (*The History of Middle-earth* 4). Edited by Christopher Tolkien, London: HarperCollins, 2002.

SP   *Songs for the Philologists.* By J.R.R. Tolkien, E.V. Gordon and others, printed by the Dept. of English. London: University College, 1936.

SWM   *Smith of Wootton Major.* Edited by Verlyn Flieger. London: HarperCollins, 2005.

Tales   *Tales from the Perilous Realm.* Containing *Giles, TB,* and *Smith.* London: HarperCollins, 2002.

TI   *The Treason of Isengard.* (*The History of Middle-earth* 7). Edited by Christopher Tolkien. London: HarperCollins, 2002.

TOFS   *Tolkien On Fairy-Stories.* Edited by Verlyn Flieger and Douglas A. Anderson. London: HarperCollins. 2008. Originally published as 'On Fairy-Stories.' *Essays Presented to Charles Williams.* Edited by C.S. Lewis. London: Oxford University Press, 1947, 38-89.

Tree   *Tree and Leaf.* London: HarperCollins, 2001; containing: HBBS, OFS and LN.

UT   *Unfinished Tales of Númenor and Middle-earth.* Edited by Christopher Tolkien. London: HarperCollins, 2001.

WJ   *The War of the Jewels.* (*The History of Middle-earth* 11). Edited by Christopher Tolkien. London: HarperCollins, 2002.

WR   *The War of the Ring.* (*The History of Middle-earth* 8). Edited by Christopher Tolkien. London: HarperCollins, 2002.

YWES   *The Year's Work in English Studies.* Containing the chapter 'Philology, General Works.' Vols. 4-6 (1923-1925), cited by no. of volume and page.

Abbreviations for some parts of *S* and *LotR*:

Ainul	'Ainulindalë'
Val	'Valaquenta'
Qu	'Quenta Silmarillion'
Ak	'Akallabêth'
RiPo	'Of the Rings of Power and the Third Age'
FR	*The Fellowship of the Rings*
TT	*The Two Towers*
RK	*The Return of the King*
App	'Appendix'
TAA	'The Tale of Aragorn and Arwen'

Abbreviations connected with *The History of Middle-earth*

AAm1	Annals of Aman', written in 1951-52 as revision of AV2, chronology for LQ, published in *MR*.
AAm2	Typescript written in 1957-58 of the 'Annals of Aman', published in *MR*.
AB1	'Annals of Beleriand', written in 1930 as a chronology for Q, published in *Shaping*.
AB2	Second version of AB1, written in 1930-37 as a chronology for QS, published in *LR*.
AB3	See GA1. 'Aman', written about in 1959, before 'Athrabeth', published in *MR*. 'Athrabeth Finrod ah Andreth', manuscript written in 1959-60, published in *MR*.
Athrabeth B-C	Amanuensis typescripts of 'Athrabeth Finrod ah Andreth', written in 1959-60, cited in *MR*.
AV1	'Annals of Valinor', written in 1930 as a chronology for Q, published in *Shaping*.
AV2	Second version of AV1, written in 1930-37 as a chronology for QS, published in *LR*.
Commentary	'Commentary to Athrabeth' written in 1960, published in *MR*.

Abbreviations

Converse A-B-C   Three different versions of 'Converse' published in Michaël Devaux. *J.R.R. Tolkien, l'effigie des Elfes*. Paris: Bragelonne, 2014.

Converse   'The Converse of Manwë and Eru', written in 1959-60 and before the 'Commentary to Athrabeth', published in *MR*.

DA1   'Drowning of Anadûnê', typescript of extreme unevenness, written in 1945-46, published in *SD*.

DA2   Typescript written with care of 'The Drowning of Anadûnê', written in 1945-46, published in *SD*.

FM1   'The Tale of Finwë and Míriel', written in 1957-58 before LawsA, published in *MR*.

FM2   'The Tale of Finwë and Míriel', written in the late '50s, after FM1 and before LawsB, published in *MR*.

FM3   'The Tale of Finwë and Míriel', written in the late '50s, after LawsB, published in *MR*.

FM4   Final text of 'The Tale of Finwë and Míriel', written in the late '50s after LawsB, published in *MR*.

FN1   'Fall of Númenor', written in 1936-37, inserted in 'Lost Road' and published in *LR*.

FN2   Written in 1937-41 but after FN1 and published in *LR*.

FN3   Written in 1937-41 but after FN2 containing some corrections related to DA1-2 and NCP, published in *SD*.

GA1   'Grey Annals', written in 1951-52, revision of AB2, chronology of LQ1, published in *Jewels*.

GA2   Written in the early '50s, clean manuscript, second version of GA1, published in *Jewels*.

GA3   'Grey Annals', written 1957-58, connected to LQ2, published in *Jewels*.

LawsA   'Laws and Customs among the Eldar', manuscript written in the late '50s, published in *MR*.

LawsB   Typescript written in the late '50s, after LawsA published in *MR*.

Lost Road   'The Lost Road', unfinished tale written in 1936-37, published in *LR*.

LQ1   'Later Quenta Silmarillion', revision of QS, dated 1950-51, published in *MR*.

LQ2	'Later Quenta Silmarillion', written in 1958 as revision of QS, published in *Jewels*.
LT	*The Book of Lost Tales*, written in 1917-20 and published *LT I-II*.
MuB	'The Music of the Ainur/Ainulindalë', written in the 1930s, published in *LR*.
MuC*	'Ainulindalë' already in existence in 1948, far-reaching revision of MuB, published in *MR*.
MuC	'Ainulindalë', written after MuC* and before 1951, published in *MR*.
MuD	'Ainulindalë', written after MuC and before 1951, published in *MR*.
NCP	'The Notion Club Papers', written in 1945-46, containing FN3, published in *SD*.
NOO	'A Note on Óre', written in 1968, published in *Vinyar Tengwar* 41 (July 2000): 11-19 (translated into Italian in *LTP*).
NotesR	'Some notes on 'rebirth', reincarnation by restoration, among Elves. With a note on the Dwarves.' Draft written in 1972 and published in Michaël Devaux. *J.R.R. Tolkien, l'effigie des Elfes*. Paris: Bragelonne, 2014.
OK	'Ósanwe-kenta', written in 1959-60 as appendix of 'Quendi and Eldar', edited with introduction, glossary, and additional notes by Carl F. Hostetter and published in *Vinyar Tengwar* 39 (July 1998): 21-34 (translated in Italian in *LTP*).
Q	'Quenta Noldorinwa' written in 1930, expansion of Sk, published in *Shaping*.
Qu	'Quenta Silmarillion', written in 1930-37, expansion of Q, published in *LR*.
Reincarnation	Text written in 1960, after the 'Athrabeth' and (according to Christopher Tolkien) before 'Comment' (with a note dated 1966), cited in MR^{38} and published in Michaël Devaux. *J.R.R. Tolkien, l'effigie des Elfes*. Paris: Bragelonne, 2014 (including the text 'The Númenórean Catastrophe & End of 'Physical' Arda').
Sk	'Sketch of the Mythology', written in 1926, published in *Shaping*.

Citations

For *S*, *LotR*, and *H* the abbreviations usually refer to the part and the chapter of the part:

E.g. *S*, Qu.1 refers to the first chapter of the 'Quenta Silmarillion', contained in *The Silmarillion*;

E.g. *LotR*, FR.II.3 refers to the third chapter of Book Two of *The Fellowship of the Ring*, contained in *The Lord of the Rings*;

E.g. *LotR*, App A.5 refers to the fifth part of Appendix in *The Lord of the Rings*, that is 'The Tale of Aragorn and Arwen'.

E.g. *H* XIII refers to the thirteenth chapter of *The Hobbit*.

For the *Letters*, the reference is to the number of the letter:

E.g. *Letters* no. 131 refers to letter number 131, contained in *The Letters of J.R.R. Tolkien*.

E.g. *Letters* nos. 131, 156 refers to the letters no. 131 and no. 156, contained in *The Letters of J.R.R. Tolkien*.

For all the other references the last number indicates the number of the page:

E.g. *MR* 195 refers to p. 195 of *Morgoth's Ring*, 10th volume of *The History of Middle-earth*.

E.g. *MR*, Athrabeth 332 refers to p. 332 of 'Athrabeth Finrod ah Andreth' contained in *Morgoth's Ring*, 10th volume of *The History of Middle-earth*.

E.g. Flieger 2002, 28 refers to p. 28 of Verlyn Flieger's *Splintered Light*; *ibid.* 30 refers to the same book or text: here p. 30 of Verlyn Flieger's *Splintered Light*;

E.g., Flieger 2002, 28 ff refers to p. 28 and following of Verlyn Flieger's *Splintered Light*.

Introduction

Introduction

The origins of this collection, and of the whole "Tolkien and the Classics" project, are twofold. First, there was the ever-growing awareness of the importance of making scholars and critics realize how much J.R.R. Tolkien is, in all respects, a great literary classic, comparable to those already accepted as 'canonical'. Second, the desire to offer a publication that could be enjoyed, and made actual use of, by students and teachers alike, thus serving the growing interest and increasing number – in Italy at least – of secondary school final papers and university graduation theses centred on Tolkien's works.

Here it is, then, a collection of mainly short essays, each one exploring a parallel between Tolkien and a Classic of Western literature. The volume is divided into three sections:

- Tolkien and the classics of Antiquity (4 essays)
- Tolkien and the medieval classics (6 essays)
- Tolkien and the modern and contemporary classics (11 essays)

Taking a look at the Table of Contents, you will note that the collection includes authors explicitly mentioned by Tolkien in his letters or lectures (as is the case for Kenneth Grahame, Chaucer, or Dante), authors we are sure he knew from his studies, whether he mentioned them or not (the Greek, Latin, and the Medieval classics), and authors he almost certainly *never* read (like Alessandro Manzoni or Vittorio Alfieri). Yet, with all due consideration, even the last category is able to give valuable insights into the works of Tolkien and of the other authors, respectively. We are, for example, able to assess the parallels or differences produced by similar historical conditions such as war, or explore the common interest in a narrative theme, such as travel (Marco Polo).

It is indeed proper that the pleasure of reading an author's books be accompanied not only by the knowledge of the author him- or herself but also of his or her specific cultural world, and that the writer be considered in the broader context of the history of literature. So, it happens that, in a few pages, one can enjoy twenty-one essays, each one providing the reader with a comparison between Tolkien and another author, an approach that, we hope, will deepen the understanding of both Tolkien and the other authors.

The present volume[1] has its origin in the endeavours of the Study Group organised by the Associazione Italiana Studi Tolkieniani (Italian Association of Tolkien Studies), a team of scholars who periodically decide on a common topic of research that, as a consequence, will be the subject of meetings in which each contributor presents his or her results to the others. The criticisms, comments, and suggestions provided in these meetings are then taken into account for the revision and incorporated into the final version of the essay. The "Tolkien and the Classics" project was started in 2013 when the Study Group decided to focus their common efforts on this particular subject. This was accompanied by a public Call for Papers, which was received very positively, so that after having published the first volume,[2] it was decided to proceed in the same direction and with the same methodology – which resulted in the publication of a second volume, *Tolkien e i Classici II*.[3]

Since the earlier projects of the Study Group were already met with interest outside Italy and led to a fruitful collaboration with Walking Tree Publishers, and with Thomas Honegger in particular, we had once more had the chance to share the results of the "Tolkien and the Classics" project with non-Italian speaking readers. The publication of *Tolkien and the Classics* is the product of this collaboration. The volume comprises a selection of essays from the two Italian volumes, to which we could add, as the icing on the cake, so to speak, a brand-new essay by Tom Shippey on Tolkien and William Morris.

The intention behind this collection has not been so much as to provide a 'best of', but rather to create a collection that, without betraying its Italian origins, could be of interest also for English-speaking readers. The reader should there-

---

1 As it was for the previous volume, edited by Roberto Arduini and Claudio A. Testi, *The Broken Scythe*, Walking Tree Publishers, Zurich and Jena, 2012.
2 Roberto Arduini, Cecilia Barella, Giampaolo Canzonieri, Claudio A. Testi (eds.), *Tolkien e i Classici*, Effatà, Cantalupa 2015 (second edition: Eterea Edizioni, 2019).
3 Roberto Arduini, Cecilia Barella, Giampaolo Canzonieri, Claudio A. Testi (eds.), *Tolkien e i Classici II*, Eterea Edizioni, Savona, 2018.

fore not be surprised by the widely different backgrounds of the contributors, who range from well-known Tolkien scholars such as Amelia A. Rutledge, to junior scholars for whom this is their first publication. This is in fact due, as described above, both to the method adopted by the Study Group and the fact that there have been originally two public Calls for Papers, which attracted many participants.

Finally, we hope this book to be useful for young students and their teachers alike, as was the case for the Italian editions, and that it may contribute to a better understanding of the truly "classic" nature of J.R.R. Tolkien's works. Given the originality of the theme and the effort behind it, we also hope for a positive reception by scholars more expert in the field. We may close with the (slightly adapted) words of one of the medieval "classics" (to be read aloud preferably with the original Middle English pronunciation): "Go, littel book [...] / And kiss the steps, where thou seest pace / Shippey, Flieger, Garth, and other scholars of grace."

Roberto Arduini
Giampaolo Canzonieri
Claudio A. Testi

Tolkien and Authors from Antiquity

Gloria Larini

Giant, Solitary, and Anarchist. The Trolls in *The Hobbit* and Polyphemus in the *Odyssey*

Giambattista Vico defined Homeric poems as "the poetic manifestation of a child-like humanity."[1] Therefore, we should not be surprised if in the trolls' episode,[2] one of the most striking scenes of *The Hobbit*, we can discover themes that are found also in the story of Ulysses and Polyphemus in the *Odyssey*.[3]

The Hobbit was initially intended as a book for children, and contains *in nuce* all the conditions for the continuation of the story in *The Lord of the Rings*.[4] Tolkien himself confesses that the work "has escaped from [...] control"[5] (*Letters* no. 124), becoming twisted and boundless. Although the parallels to the *Odyssey*,[6] and more generally with the Homeric epic poems, have been often emphasized by the scholars in relation to *The Lord of the Rings*, it seems to me that nothing like that has been done about *The Hobbit*.[7] Indeed, this contribution aims to argue for the existence of some contacts with Homer also in the beginning of Tolkien's saga.[8]

---

1 Cf. Bárberi Squarotti 1998, 63. Vico's idea is also shared by Giacomo Leopardi.
2 Gulisano 2001, 89 defines them as "minor monsters".
3 In Tolkien, the myth appears to show traces of "northern paganism, in particular Celtic paganism", Gulisano 2001, 40. For biblical influences and images , see Cardini 1994, 46; Passaro & Respinti 2003, 45.
4 For the unity of Tolkien's saga see, for example, Clark & Timmons 2000, 14.
5 Cf. Tavella 2002, 43.
6 Iannucci 2007, 216 writes about the "Odyssiac structure of *The Lord of the Rings*".
7 Cf. Pienciak 1986, 43; in Bologna 2002, 113 Gulisano calls Tolkien "the Christian Homer" but does not analyse any linguistic-conceptual parallels with the Homeric poems.
8 In *Letters* no. 142 Tolkien writes to Robert Murray: "I was brought up in the Classics" and adds: "Homer was the first introduction to the appreciation of poetry" (cf. Atherton 2012, 185). The connection with the Homeric poems is therefore clearly admitted by the author himself. For the study of Latin and Greek by the young Tolkien: Atherton 2012, 183; Monda & Simonelli 2002, 46; Fisher 2011, 60 and 74f.

The Meeting with the Monstrous

Among the elements shared by both authors are references to *monstra*.[9] The trolls as well as Polyphemus are described as having enormous bodies, living in isolation, and lacking any laws. These characteristics are connected to each other in a *synolon*, which connotes the meeting with the monstrous as a terrible event not only due to the monsters' different physical connotations but also because the monsters violate the behavioural norms of human society.[10]

Bilbo, nicknamed "the burglar",[11] discovers three trolls; the event is put to the attention of the reader and the characters at the same time, when the latter, hidden in the foliage, become aware of three figures. They are "very large persons" (*H* II), and the huge size is not limited to their bodies, but includes everything that surrounds them as well. They are "sitting round a very large fire", "toasting mutton on long spits of wood", have "a barrel of good drink at hand", are "drinking out of jugs", and Bilbo would like to warn his friends that "there were three fair-sized trolls" (*H* II). Their size is also reflected in each part of their body, so Tom's leg "was thick as a young tree-trunk" (*H* II).

Although they are different from men, Bilbo calls them "persons". The diversity is thus not total, and the terror originates from their appearance and abnormal behaviour, if compared to the observer's.

Ulysses too defines the Cyclops as a *"man* with great strength" (*Od*. IX, 214; *andr'epeleusesthai megalēn epieimenon alkēn*).[12] His exceptional size stands out especially when, after drinking the wine offered to him by Ulysses, he falls asleep bending "aside the big neck" (*Od*. IX, 514; *megalēn* [...] *alkēn*). The exaggerated and frightening physicality is pointed out by the poet several times: "there a man slept, enormous" (*Od*. IX, 187; *entha d'anēr eniaue pelōrios*), and again:

---

9 The term is meant in its etymological meaning of "portents", figures that deviate from the ordinary.
10 The "Hobbits", invented by Tolkien, are sometimes called "Halflings" because they are similar to men but smaller.
11 Bilbo Baggins is nicknamed "the burglar" because he is intended to "break" into the dragon's stronghold. He is the older cousin of Frodo, who will be the protagonist of *The Lord of the Rings*. Cf. Chiavini & Pizzo 1996, 39.
12 For the *Odyssey* references see Monro & Allen 1976, *Odysseae* liber IX, Oxford. The translation from Greek is mine.

> He was a monster, enormous, who did not resemble
> a man who eats bread, but a wooded promontory
> of high mountains, which is seen alone standing out among the others
>
> kai gar thaum'etetukto pelōrion, oude eōikei
> andri ge sitophagōi, alla riōi uleēnti
> upsēlōn oreōn, ho te phainetai oion ap'allōn (*Od*. IX, 190ff.)

As we see, although Polyphemus is initially called a "man", he differs from a "man who eats bread" because of his size and his solitary life. His superhuman strength is also evident at the end of the episode when, even though he is now blind, he tries to capture Ulysses and his companions by blocking the exit of the cave with his long arms:

> he removed the big stone from the entrance,
> and sat on the threshold, arms stretched
>
> chersì psēlaphoōn apo men lithon eile thuraōn (*Od*. IX, 416)

The quantity of food that the Cyclops gulps down is also exaggerated, and his meal prepared from human flesh is disgusting to be seen:

> he filled his big belly
> eating human flesh and drinking pure milk
>
> megalēn emplēsato nēdun
> andromea kre'edōn kai ep'akrēton gala pinōn (*Od*. IX, 296f.)

While the trolls drink a lot of beer, it is interesting to note the contrast between the pure milk drunk by Polyphemus and his cannibalic meal.

Compared to Tolkien, however, Homer seems to go beyond the description of the huge physical size of the *monstrum*, underlining also the fear inspired by his "deep voice" (*Od*. IX, 257; *phthongon te barun*) and "huge figure" (*Od*. IX, 257; *auton te pelōron*). The voice, in particular, resounds terribly in the cave especially when Polyphemus cries out after having been blinded:

> He gave a cry of pain, so terrible it echoed around the rock[13]
>
> smerdaleon de meg' ōimōxen, peri d'iache petrē (*Od*. IX, 395)

---

13 Tolkien, instead, often emphasizes the trolls' quarrelsome character and quick use of their fists.

The concept of huge size is associated in both Tolkien and Homer also to objects belonging to the *monstra*. Bilbo, for instance, tries to rob something belonging to the troll called William, putting "his little hand in William's enormous pocket" and finding "a purse in it as big as a bag to Bilbo" (*H* II). The trolls' objects, like the provisions in Polyphemus' cavern, become thus further proof of their dangerous size.

The cave where the trolls dwell also testifies to their huge physical size. It is "over the hill", and there is "a big door of stone hidden by bushes", so big it cannot be opened. Even Gandalf's wizardry is of no avail: the "monstrous" can be defeated only through cunning or by what belongs to it. The key to open the door is called "largish [...] though no doubt William had thought it very small and secret", and after turning it "the stone door swung back with a big push, and they all went inside" (*H* II).

Polyphemus' cave in the *Odyssey* is made to his measure as well:

> and around there was a wall
> tall, built with stones embedded in the ground
> and with trunks of tall pines and oaks with foliage
>
> peri d'aulē
> upsēlē dedmēto katōrucheessi lithoisi
> makrēsin te pitussin ide drusin upsikomoisin (*Od.* IX, 184ff.)

Even the wine needed to make him drunk must fill a "big goatskin" (*Od.* IX, 212; *askon megan*) to be enough for the purpose. Also the cave's door, like the trolls' door, is a "heavy boulder" (*Od.* IX 240f.; *megan* [...] / *obrimon*) that takes superhuman strength to move: "a rock so big was the boulder that he placed at the entrance" (*Od.* IX, 243; *tossēn ēlibaton petrēn epethēke thurēsin*) that "not even twenty-two carts, well made, / four-wheeled, would have moved it off the ground" (*Od.* IX, 241f.; *ouk an ton ghe duō kai eikos'amaxai/esthlai tetrakukloi ap'oudeos ochlisseian*).

In Tolkien's narrative, the "big branch all on fire at one end" grabbed by Bilbo closely recalls the red-hot pine pole prepared by Ulysses; its use highlights even more the difference between the trolls' huge size and the hobbits' and dwarves' smallness (*H* II).

In both works, *Odyssey* and *The Hobbit*, the size of the *monstra* is associated with feelings of contempt for Odysseus by Polyphemus and for Bilbo by William the troll. William calls Bilbo a "poor little blighter" (*H* II), while Polyphemus recalls that a bard had prophesied their meeting some years before, but he would have expected "a great and beautiful man" (*Od.* IX, 513; *megan kai kalon*) "endowed with great strength" (*Od.* IX, 514; *megalēn epieimenon alkēn*), and not "a small man, an insignificant and weak man" (*Od.* IX 515; *nun de m'eōn oligos te kai outidanos kai akikus*), that is "that nullity of Nobody" (*Od.* IX, 460; *outidanos poren outis*).

In Homer, however, it is not only the Cyclops' exaggerated physicality that is anomalous, but also his ferocious and arrogant nature. Polyphemus replies to Ulysses "with a ruthless heart" (*Od.* IX, 272; *nēlei thumōi*), because he fears neither the gods nor even Zeus and thinks the Cyclopes are "much stronger" (*Od.* IX, 276; *polu pherteroi*). The excessive force and power are thus associated with the idea of a violent anger, and Ulysses imagines the consequences of that for a man:

> a single blow and his brain would scatter in pieces
> on the ground, here and there, in the cavern
>
> tōi ke hoi enkephalos ghe dia speos alludis allēi
> theinomenou raioito pros oudei (*Od.* IX, 458f.)

Tolkien's narrative, instead, lacks the idea of injustice and arrogance. The three trolls do not commit murder, because their plan of cooking and eating Bilbo and his companions is not successful.[14]

Homer, on the other hand, emphasizes more than once that the meal of "human flesh" (*Od.* IX, 347; *andromea krea*) is connected to an "unsustainable madness" (*Od.* IX, 350; *maineai ouket'anektōs*) and that the Cyclops is "doing something unjust" (*Od.* IX, 352; *ou kata moiran erexas*). He calls Polyphemus an "evil monster" (*Od.* IX, 428; *athemistia eidōs*) who devoured Ulysses's companions "with violent force" (*Od.* IX, 476; *kraterēphi biēphi*). His physicality and fury appear even more exceptional when viewed from a distance, as when Ulysses and his companions escape. The Cyclops, on the shore:

---

14 Olsen 2012, 51 comments on the trolls's discussion of how Bilbo should be cooked.

Got angry in his heart even more.
He ripped the top of a mountain and threw it

cholōsato kērothi mallon (*Od.* IX, 480)

He plucks off a "cliff" (*Od.* IX, 484; *hupo petrēs*), launches a "boulder in the sea" (*Od.* IX, 495; *kai nun pontonde balōn belos*) and destroys "the prow and the woods of the ship" (*Od.* IX, 498; *sun ken arax' ēmeōn [kephalas] kai nēia doura*). Ulysses's companions call him a "wild man" (*Od.* IX, 494; *agrion andra*), because he threatens them "striking with a pointed boulder. He's so strong in the launch" (*Od.* IX, 499; *marmarōi okrioenti balōn: tosson gar hiēsin*). Polyphemus's strength exhibited in his throwing boulders becomes almost an iconic image, which serves to increase the terror of the *monstrum*:

And then, once again he raised a boulder, but much larger,
He had it spin and threw it, with force immeasurable

autar ho gh'exautis polu meizona laan aeiras
hēk'epidinesas, epereise de in'apelethron (*Od.* IX, 537f.)

In addition to those aspects, both *monstra* have in common the fact of being separated from their neighbours. Trolls have descended downwards, and Polyphemus lives far from his brothers who inhabit peaks "of high mountains" (*Od.* IX, 113; *upsēlōn oreōn*) and "hollow caverns" (*Od.* IX, 114; *en spessi glaphuroisi*).[15] Polyphemus himself lives in a "hollow cavern" (*Od.* IX, 476; *en spëi glaphurōi*), a "cavity" (*Od.* IX 235; *entosthen d'antroio;* v. 236; v. 312; v. 407) or "cave" (*Od.* IX, 462; *apo speious*), but his is not inside a mountain but "near the sea" (*Od.* IX, 182; *anchi thalassēs*) where he grazes his flock "alone" (*Od.* IX, 188; *oios*). Polyphemus lives an isolated life, and Homer remarks on the lack of contacts that is a characteristic of his environment, hinting also at a sort of social and political anarchy. Cyclopes "have no assemblies to deliberate nor laws" (*Od.* IX, 112; *toisin d'oút'agorai boulephoroi*) and "everyone enforces their law about sons and wives, and they do not care about each other" (*Od.* IX, 114f.; *themistheuei de hekastos / paidōn ēd'alochōn, oud'allelōn alegousin*). Tolkien, in his account, says that in the land of the trolls they "have seldom even heard of the king" (*H* II).

---

15 It is true that the shouts of Polyphemus call forth his brother Cyclopes, but Homer clarifies that they lived on the windy tops of the mountains, at a certain distance from the sea.

Their innate nature makes both *monstra* asocial *a priori*, unable to change or improve themselves through contacts with the others. Cyclopes do not possess "ships with painted cheeks" (*Od.* IX, 125; *nees* [...] *miltopareoi*) by which to travel and learn about other kindreds, whereas "men for many reasons / with ships cross the sea with reciprocal landings" (*Od.* IX, 128f.; *hoia te polla / andres ep' allelous neusin peroōsi thalassan*). Cyclopes seem to have adapted themselves to the land where they live, i.e. a land that needs nothing; they do not "plant seeds with their hands nor plough; / but everything grows without sowing nor ploughing" (*Od.* IX, 108; *oute phuteousin chersin phuton out' aroōsin/alla ta g'asparta kai anerota panta phuontai*);[16] they harvest without work "wheat and barley and vines" (*Od.* IX, 110; *puroi kai krithai ēd'ampeloi*), and their vines produce "huge grapes and wine, with the favour and the rain of Zeus" (*Od.* IX, 111; *oinon eristaphulon, kai sphin Dios ombros aexei*).

Some hints at isolation and a sort of autarchy can also be found with reference to the trolls, albeit in a less incisive manner from the narrative point of view. Like Polyphemus, the three trolls have "come down from the mountains" (*H* II); they live in lands where there are no men because they are "too near the mountains", and "Travellers seldom come this way now" since "things have changed for the worse and the road is unguarded" (*H* II). Their change of residence has spread terror all around. Two of Elrond's people tell Gandalf "they were hurrying along for fear of the trolls" because they had come to know that "three of them had come down from the mountains and settled in the woods not far from the road", and "they had frightened everyone away from the district, and they waylaid strangers" (*H* II). The solitude of the new land of the trolls is therefore recent, caused by the recent dislocation of the *monstra* from their former homes, and not linked to the characteristics of the place as it is for the Cyclopes.[17]

The trolls meet Bilbo and his companions on "neutral" ground, far from their usual habitat, and the Company enters their cave only after the trolls have been

---

16 The difference between the society of Ithaca and the wild life of the Cyclopes is well described in Di Benedetto 2010, 82-87.
17 The theme of travel, in its different forms, is often referred to as a point of contact between Tolkien and Homer. For an analysis of the macrostructure of the work cf. Arduini & Testi 2012, 73. About Frodo as a pilgrim in *The Lord of the Rings* see for example Catà 2009. A parallel with Ulysses is mentioned in Monda 2008, 152.

turned to stone by the rays of the rising sun. Ulysses, instead, decides to explore the Cyclops' cavern out of curiosity towards anything new.[18] This represents the victory of Greek *humanitas* over the incivility of Polyphemus, who respects neither gods nor men, whereas the victory of Bilbo and the dwarves, with the help of Gandalf,[19] witnesses a superiority that does not imply any ethical or religious idea. Tolkien highlights the physical and behavioural differences exhbited by the trolls but, unlike Homer, does not take into consideration the moral or religious ones such as Polyphemus's violation of hospitality's duty and his *hybris*,[20] which are typical negative patterns of behaviour in ancient Greek society. After all, Tolkien himself explicitly states that his work is apolitical and amoral:[21]

> Certainly it has *no* allegorical intentions, general, particular or topical, moral, religious, or political. The only criticism that annoyed me was one that it 'contained no religion' […] It is a monotheistic world of 'natural theology' […] I am in any case myself a Christian; but the 'Third Age' was not a Christian world. (*Letters* no. 165)[22]

In conclusion, the contact between Tolkien and Homer starts, in my opinion, already in *The Hobbit*, and seems to go beyond the similarities with some general themes of classical epic. The presence of some specific common elements is clear, but at the same time it is also evident that Tolkien's freedom from ideology as well as his absolute loyalty towards the narrative fantasy that, even though we have to acknowledge the resonances coming from his widely varied cultural *substratum*,[23] privileges the love of the story.[24]

---

[18] This act is connected, in the *Odyssey*, with the impious violation of the principle of hospitality by Polyphemus: cf. also note 21.
[19] Gandalf is the protagonists who is responsible for making things happen. Cf. Chiavini & Pizzo 1996, 117.
[20] In the Preface to *Odyssey* written by Vincenzo Di Benedetto, 44, the curiosity of Ulysses is considered secondary to his verification of the hospitable attitude of Polyphemus.
[21] Cf. *Letters* no. 165. These terms are meant in the non-negative sense of "devoid of politics" and "devoid of morals". For a theological reading of the saga see Monda 2008.
[22] Cf. Dickerson & O'Hara 2006, 43. Hutton 2011.
[23] See Monda & Simonelli 2002, 46, 208 for a discussion of the interest in Homer. For the pleasure of the story itself see Arduini, Barella & Simonelli 2011, 10-12.
[24] This aspect is also underlined by Rosebury 2003. Cf. Shippey 1992. For a differing "ideological" reading see De Vero 1980; Purtill 1984.

Bibliography

Arduini, Roberto, Cecilia Barella, and Saverio Simonelli. *La biblioteca di Bilbo, Percorsi di lettura tolkieniani nei libri per ragazzi*. Turin: Effatà Editrice, 2011.

Arduini, Roberto and Claudio Testi (eds.). *The Broken Scythe. Death and Immortality in the Works of J.R.R. Tolkien*. Zurich & Jena: Walking Tree Publishers, 2012.

Atherton, Mark. *There and Back Again: J.R.R. Tolkien and the Origins of The Hobbit*. London: I.B. Tauris, 2012.

Bárberi Squarotti, Giorgio. *Le capricciose ambagi della letteratura*. Turin: Tirrenia Stampatori, 1998.

Bologna, Tullio et al. *La compagnia dell'anello, il potere. J.R.R. Tolkien creatore di mondi*. Rimini: Il cerchio, 2002.

Cardini, Franco. *Il limbo delle modernità*. Rome: Guaraldi, 1994.

Catà, Cesare. "Essere in cammino. Tolkien e lo statuto filosofico del concetto medievale di 'Uomo pellegrino'." *Minas Tirith* 24 (2009): 25-44.

Iannucci, Alessandro. "Achille nella 'Terra di Mezzo'. Da Tolkien a Omero." *Omero mediatico. Aspetti della ricezione omerica nella società contemporanea*. Ed. Eleonora Cavallini. *Atti delle giornate di Studio*, 18-19 January 2006. Bologna: d.u.press, 2007, 209-225.

Chiavini, Roberto and Gian Filippo Pizzo. *Dizionario dei personaggi fantastici*. Rome: Gremese Editore, 1996.

Clark, George and Daniel Timmons (eds.). *J.R.R. Tolkien and His Literary Resonances: Views of Middle-earth*. Westport CT: Greenwood Publishing, 2000.

De Vero, Gianpiero. *Ombra e mito in Tolkien*. Naples: Tempi moderni, 1980.

Dickerson, Mattew and David O'Hara. *From Homer to Harry Potter. A Handbook of Myth and Fantasy*. Grand Rapids, MI: Brazos, 2006.

Fisher, Jason (ed.). *Tolkien and the Study of His Sources: Critical Essays*. Jefferson, NC: McFarland, 2011.

Gulisano, Paolo. *Tolkien, il mito e la grazia*. Milan: Ancora, 2001.

Homer. *Odissea*. Ed. Vincenzo Di Benedetto; introduction and comment by Vincenzo Di Benedetto and Pierangelo Fabrini. Milan: Bur, 2010.

Hutton, Ron. "The Pagan Tolkien." *The Ring and the Cross. Christianity and the Writings of J.R.R. Tolkien*. Ed. Paul E. Kerry. Madison NJ: Fairleigh Dickinson University Press, 2011. 57-70.

Monda, Andrea. *L'anello e la croce: significato teologico de Il Signore degli Anelli*. Soveria Mannelli: Rubbettino, 2008.

Monda, Andrea and Saverio Simonelli. *Tolkien: il signore della fantasia*. Milan: Frassinelli, 2002.

Monro, David B. and Thomas W. Allen (eds.). *Odysseae liber IX. Homeri Opera, recognoverunt brevique adnotatione critica instruxerunt David B. Monro et Thomas W. Allen*. Oxford: Clarendon Press, 1976.

Olsen, Corey. *Exploring J.R.R. Tolkien's The Hobbit*. Boston, MA: Houghton Mifflin Harcourt, 2012.

Passaro, Errico and Marco Respinti. *Paganesimo e cristianesimo in Tolkien. Le due tesi a confronto*. Rome: Il Minotauro, 2003.

Pienciak, Anne. *J.R.R. Tolkien's Hobbit and Lord of the Rings*. New York: Barron's Educational Series, 1986.

Purtill, Richard. *J.R.R. Tolkien. Myth, Morality, and Religion*. New York: Harper & Row, 1984.

Rosebury, Brian. *Tolkien: A Cultural Phenomenon*. London: Palgrave Macmillan, 2003.

Shippey, Tom. *The Road to Middle-earth*. London: HarperCollins, 1992.

Tavella, Emanuela. *Tolkien, dalla fiaba al mito: creazione e significato dell'universo fantastico de Il Signore degli Anelli*. Florence: Firenze Libri, 2002.

Leonardo Mantovani

Renewing the Epic: Tolkien and Apollonius Rhodius

Introduction[1]

We are not sure whether Tolkien knew the epic of Apollonius, but his early familiarity with the classical languages and literatures makes it plausible that he did. He first became acquainted with the classical Greek language in 1903[2] within the framework of the syllabus of King Edward's School, Birmingham. Despite the initial fascination and a very profound knowledge of the language – he was able to hold a whole debate in Greek[3] – Tolkien showed increasingly less interest in the studies of the Classics, and his transfer to Oxford in 1911 became a turning point: the change of his literary taste together with the lack of a resident tutor in Classics during the first two terms put a serious and lasting damper on Tolkien's initial enthusiasm for the study of Greek and Latin. The situation did not improve when E.A. Barber was chosen as resident tutor since he was, as Carpenter (1977, 54) points out, "a good scholar but a dry teacher".

The acquaintance with Joseph Wright, Professor of Comparative Philology at Oxford, changed Tolkien's academic life. Under his teaching he started studying Welsh, and in 1912, on his own, Finnish;[4] classical Greek was relegated to a mere philological interest. His intellectual passions did not correspond to his duties as a student, thus, in 1913, he obtained only a "Second Class" in the Honour Moderations, the first of two exams necessary to graduate in Classical Studies; it was not a great result, but he, on the other side, achieved a "Pure Alpha" in Comparative Philology. As a consequence, he moved to the English School in the summer of the same year, thus ending his career in Classical Studies.[5]

---

1 I would like to thank Professor Fulvio Ferrari, who helped me with this translation and gave me valuable advice during the writing of these pages.
2 Cf. Carpenter 1977, 27.
3 Cf. Carpenter 1977, 48.
4 Cf. Carpenter 1977, 59.
5 Cf. Carpenter 1977, 63.

In his published letters, Tolkien mentions only three classical authors:[6] one Greek (Homer), and two Latin (Ovid and Vergil). The obituary published in *The Times* (3rd September 1973) reports that "his love for the Classics took ten years to recover from lectures on Cicero and Demosthenes."[7] There is no trace of Apollonius in his letters, but we know that in 1914 he bought a copy of *The Life and Death of Jason* by William Morris,[8] a verse adaptation of the *Argonautica* together with a description of the death of Jason. It is therefore likely that Tolkien knew the *Argonautica* and that he had made its acquaintance during the years 1910-1913, the period we could call his most "classic".

Different Times, Same Authors

Both Apollonious and Tolkien were philologists, and they both had a strong interest in epic poetry: Greek epic for Apollonius, Germanic epic for Tolkien. Apollonius was a librarian at the library of Alexandria in the third century B.C. His position meant that he worked also as preceptor to the heir to the Egyptian throne, i.e. Ptolomaeus III Euergetes. In addition to the *Argonautica*, he wrote *Ktiseis*, i.e. poems about the foundation of cities such as Alexandria, Cyrene, Naucratis, Knidos and Rhodes. Furthermore, he composed *Against Zenodotus*, a work discussing the critical edition of Homeric poems made by Zenodotus, his predecessor as librarian. As Susan Stephens notes, Alexandria, the capital of the Ptolemaic empire, did not exist before 332 B.C. Thus, compared to the other cities, Greek and otherwise, it lacked both a historical and, more importantly, also a mythic past. The Alexandrines tried to remedy this situation,[9] just like Tolkien did with regard to 20th century England,[10] which also lacked a mythology of its own.

The *Argonautica* is nothing less than the biggest realisation of an echo which passes through the entire Greek literature, starting with the Homeric poems,[11] going on through tragedy, and finally flowing into Hellenism.[12] Apollonius had

---

6 *Letters* no. 142.
7 The obituary is avaible at https://tolkieniano.blogspot.it/2014/10/la-notizia-della-scomparsa-di-jrr.html.
8 Carpenter 1977, 69.
9 Pierce 2008, 95-114.
10 *Letters* no. 131.
11 "that Argo famed of all" (*Odyssey* XII 70).
12 For a resume of the argonautic myth see Apollonius Rhodius's *Argonautica*, book 3, 12-21.

to choose between more mythological variants, sometimes combining them, and – like Tolkien did – reformulating the epic tradition and its stylistic features that he had studied for a long time, renewing and reusing them in new contexts. Already the title shows his innovative approach: *Argonautica* is what happens to the members of the ship Argo, whilst *The Lord of the Rings* means Sauron himself, the enemy. The narration is no longer focused on an eponymous hero as in the *Odyssey* or *Beowulf*. Some episodes from both works remind us of events to be found in older epic poems, but with a different ending: for example Tolkien, during the fight between Gandalf and the Balrog on the bridge of Khazad-dûm, intentionally recreates the confrontation between Byrhtnoth and the Vikings in *The Battle of Maldon*.[13] However, he inverts the original situation by letting the wizard sacrifice himself in order to make it possible for the Fellowship to go on. The narrow causeway that induced the earl to *ofermod*,[14] leading his army into ruin, is now the symbol of altruistic heroism.

Similarly, Apollonius meticulously describes, by means of a beautiful *ekphrasis*, the mythic scenes on Jason's cloak, as Homer does for Achille's shield. Yet while the son of Peleus prepares to fight Hector, the son of Aeson prepares to meet the queen Hypsipyles and manages to make her fall in love with him.[15] Finally, both Apollonius and Tolkien wrote their works in a historical period where the epic was no longer valued highly: in the 3rd century B.C. the epic lost its mimetic function of reproducing reality in a mythic framework typical of the Homeric poems; moreover, it did no longer offer any inspiration nor didactic value to its readers, finding shelter only in the academic world.[16] Apollonius was not an archaic *aoidos,* who performed the oral recitation of the epic as a feat of memory, but a *poeta doctus* at the Ptolemaic court, who wrote a poem which demonstrated his broad knowledge in the fields of etiology, geography

---

13 See the full text in HBBS.
14 Anglo-Saxon term for "overmasting pride". This meaning was proposed by Tolkien, instead of Ker's "overboldness". This changed the interpretation of the verses 89-90, which are now read as an attack on selfish heroism. Cf. HBBS 121-25.
15 *Argonautica* often calls to mind the Homeric tradition. For this specific instance, see Clauss 1993, 122.
16 "The decline of the epic is further due, in part to the absence of national pride, and in part to the academic environment. The erudition of the writers swamped their sense of poetry; narrative was sacrificed to a catalogue, and anxiety to parade the obscurest details made it impossible to sustain the interest of a poem on the scale of the *Iliad*." Cf. Apollonius Rhodius 1987, *The Argonautica,* xix.

and linguistics. Callimacus, bringer of new literary ideals such as *leptótes*[17] and *brevitas*, heavily criticized these cyclic poems.[18]

At the end of 1937, Tolkien started the sequel of *The Hobbit*, finishing it in 1949. The last volume of *The Lord of the Rings* was published in 1955, ten years after the end of WW2. In a world that was changing,[19] Tolkien remained the same. Analysed through the lens of modernism and the literary canon of his times, he seemed to be in stark contrast. Not unlike the Greek epic that came under attack by the proponents of new poetic ideas, so Tolkien's narrative – what we today call fantasy – was rejected by many literary critics.[20]

The Hero between Innovation and Tradition

After this necessary introduction, let us proceed to the topic proper of this paper. The purpose of the next pages is to show how both authors have changed the epic by chosing as their main protagonists a new kind of hero, who is no longer characterised by brutal strength, thirst for glory, or uninhibited individualism. Instead, this new hero is a bringer of modern virtues such as *pietas*, thoughtfulness, forbearance, and, if necessary, he has even the courage of sacrificing himself for the greater good. I will analyse and compare Frodo and Jason, the protagonists, and try to isolate these innovative elements.

Jason, son of Aeson, king of Iolcus, was not of divine descent, nor did he seem to have qualities that would elevate him above his fellows. He had only a cloak, a gift of Athena, with a beautiful embroidered image, and an infallible[21] spear, received by Atalanta. In his paper "The Quest Hero", W.H. synthesised the main characteristics of a quest,[22] most of which are to be found in the narrative about the Argonauts. It is therefore no surprise that he considers Jason as the paradigmatic hero of this type of story. After having successfully

---

17 Greek word for "fineness".
18 Callimacus 1996, *Aitia*. Fr. 1 Pf.
19 For an accurate and complete contextualization of Tolkien's figure and works in his historical period see Wu Ming 4 2013, 15-54.
20 See Pearce 1999, xi-xii.
21 *Argonautica* I 769. The adjective is not relevant for the purposes of the story. The lance will be used first as a support for the helmet, in which there are the dragon's teeth, and then as a tool to prod the bulls. Cf. Fantuzzi and Hunter 2002, 368.
22 Auden 1968, 44.

passed some trials, Jason comes back with the Golden Fleece and his future bride, and finally becomes the new king. However, I do not think that we can claim, as Auden (1968, 46) does, that Jason is "instantly recognizable as the kind of man who can win the Golden Fleece."[23] Throughout the whole poem, his qualities are hidden and without the constant help of an external agent, he would not have been able to continue and succeed. He is "the victim" of a conscious deceit[24] by the poet who, depicting him apparently as inadequate and weak, invites us to search beneath the many layers of characterisations to understand his true nature and, unlike Homer, without using epithets that would constantly bleach his figure.

As for Frodo, his apparently ordinary origins are the result of subtle philological work: the correct original name of Frodo would be *Froda*.[25] Now, Froda is an Anglo-Saxon name which, in its variant *Fróda*, is connected to Old Norse *Fróthi*, a legendary king who gave his kingdom a long time of peace and prosperity, known as "the peace of *Fróthi*".[26] Frodo's lineage shows a curious element: as Flieger points out,[27] he is an orphan whose parents drowned, a strange death for people who do not love water. By combining those facts with his arrival, thanks to Bilbo, in Hobbiton from Buckland, where he used to live with his maternal grandfather, we can recognize the figure of a foreign, water-bound orphan, who vaguely reminds us of Scyld,[28] the forefather of the Scyldingas in *Beowulf*. Scyld, then, is just another name of Fróthi,[29] a bringer of peace and prosperity. With the name "Frodo", Tolkien seems to seal his destiny. Like Arthur and Beowulf, Frodo also grows up without his parents. Likewise, Jason was raised until he was twenty by the centaur Chiron in order to escape Pelias.

Both Jason and Frodo start their journeys due to external reasons. Jason has to sail from Iolcus to Colchis: Pelias, after having dethroned his brother-in-law

---

23 Auden does not seem to specify which Jason he is talking about, but it does not matter: if he is talking about Apollonius' Jason, he would not have understood him correctly, if not, he would not consider the Hellenistic work.
24 Vian 1978, 1037.
25 Tolkien explains the passage from a>o as follows: in the Hobbits' names -*a* marks the male name and -*e*/-*a* the female one. Tolkien maintained the original names changing only the final vowel. Cf. *LotR*, RK. App.F.II.1135.
26 See Shippey 2005, 233-34.
27 Flieger 2012, 150-51.
28 Scyld, as a child, arrived in Denmark in a boat. See also the parallel to Moses in the Old Testament.
29 Flieger 2012, 151.

Aeson, is warned by Apollo's oracle that his ruin will be caused by a man with only one shoe. As Jason comes back from exile with only one shoe, having lost the other while wading through the Anavros river,[30] Pelias, mindful of the prophecy, sends him on the suicidal quest for the Golden Fleece.[31]

Frodo inherits the One Ring and, advised by Gandalf, goes first to Rivendell to prevent the Nazgûl to find him in the Shire. Later, during the Council of Elrond, he states his intention to bring the Ring to Mordor in order to destroy it, thus defining his mission as an *anti-quest*. Both characters are therefore aware of their sad destiny: Jason from the very beginning,[32] Frodo increasingly so, starting with the Council and the Emyn Muil,[33] and finally refusing to do his duty in the Chambers of Fire.[34] Neither of the two missions aims at increasing the characters' glory: the hobbit sets off for personal reasons, i.e rescuing the Shire and finding Bilbo,[35] and Jason leaves because he wants to live in peace in his own land. He is the only Greek hero who cries at their departure (I 535) and, invocating Apollo, he only asks that the mission goes well and that everyone comes back safe and sound (I 415-416). Frodo naively admits not to know the path. In the classical epic, no hero would have accepted the task without the possibility to increase his fame and to test his valour. It is thus in the absence of such motivations that we can find the first innovative characteristic: the hero does not do what he does merely to attain glory and fame.

Instead of the wild individualism that makes Achilles retire from the fighting or Beowulf to act on his own, Apollonius and Tolkien gather a group that accompanies the hero on his mission. Jason gathers a group of heroes descended from the Gods, while Frodo ends up in a fellowship made up from members of the different races of the Free Peoples. If the works followed the narrative pat-

---

30 In *Argonautica* III 66-75 it turns out that Jason probably lost his sandal to help an old woman, actually Hera, of which he will become the favorite.
31 The traditions diverge on the motivations. Opinions differ: On the one hand we have those who believe that Pelias sends Jason on his quest hoping that he will not come back. On the other, there are those who argue that the fleece performs a double function, allowing Jason to recover the throne and to free Pelias from the curse of Frisso, who tormented him because Frisso did not have a worthy burial. Cf. Borgogno 2014, vii-xxi.
32 "But the path is not to be shunned, the toil is hard for those who venture" (I 245-246) exclaims the crowd of Iolcus as the heroes prepare themselves to sail on.
33 "It's my doom, I think, to go to that Shadow yonder, so that a way will be found." (*LotR*, TT.II.1).
34 "But I do not choose now to do what I came to do." (*LotR*, RK.II.3).
35 *LotR*, FR.I. 2.

tern of the epic, we could expect the hero to fight his way up inside the group to achieve the power, or at least to assert his primacy. However, since the leader has to be elected, Jason proclaims that the decision has to be taken by the entire group because the mission, in order to succeed, requires all members to work together (I 336-337). His advice is thus to choose *ton àriston*, the most valorous one. Everyone chooses Herakles who, astonishingly, refuses the *kŷdos*[36] and claims that the leader has to be the one who gathered them all, i.e. Jason, who immediately accepts (I 345-347). He thus becomes the *àristos*, with the duty to "be careful for everything, to take upon him our quarrels and covenants with strangers" (I 339-340).[37] There is no struggle for predominance, but we see a settlement achieved by cunning and based on seemingly modest behaviour.[38] Jason is conscious of his own limits and surrounds himself with figures who can compensate his deficiencies when needed.

Frodo, on the other side, is not the leader of the Fellowship, nor does he want to be.[39] He is "only" the Ringbearer. Ironically, in the two instances where the future course of the Fellowship hinges on his decisions, his choices prove disastrous. After the failure to cross the Caradhras, his hesitation about going or not to Moria and his desire to postpone the decision till next morning[40] allows the wolves to attack them during the night. Even worse is the result of the hour of reflection required at the foot of Amon Hen:[41] Frodo's segregation from the Fellowship attracts Boromir and starts a chain of events that cause Frodo to leave the Fellowship to carry out his duty, and lead to the death of the hero of Gondor.

Jason, whenever a decision has to be taken – for example the election of a new helmsman (II, 858-989) or in front of king Aeetes (III, 422-426)[42] – also appears

---

36 Greek word for "honor".
37 A task which Heracles would have found difficult since his strength seems to be physical rather than socio-political. For a discussion of the dichotomy between "man of skill" and "man of strength" see Clauss 1993, 30-32.
38 Most critics, not unlike Jason's companions, see him as an anti-hero, and focus on his deficiencies (in comparison to other heroes) rather than on his abilities; see Hunter 1993, 11.
39 See Honegger 2018 for a discussion of Tolkien's concept of "splintered [i.e. co-operative] heroism".
40 "I do not wish to go," he said; "but neither do I wish to refuse the advice of Gandalf. I beg that there should be no vote, until we have slept on it. Gandalf will get votes easier in the light of the morning than in this cold gloom" *LotR*, FR.II.4.
41 *LotR*, FR.II.10.
42 For a complete list of the episodes see Vian 1978.

"pale, hesitant, unable to make a choice, subject to dejection and fear" (Vian 1978, 1016). Both characters are *améchanoi*[43] but with a qualitative difference: the initial inability of Frodo to take decisions disappears[44] after he abandons the Fellowship, revealing instead a new personality, shortly glimpsed before only at Rivendell. Tolkien describes him through the eyes of Sam: now Frodo is resolute, capable of taming Gollum, cunning and has "a look in his face and a tone in his voice that he [i.e. Sam] had not known before" (*LotR*, TT.II.3). Another point of view about his change is expressed by Faramir who characterises Frodo as "corteous" (*LotR*, TT.II.4), gifted with "wit" (*LotR*, TT.II.5)[45] and worthy of his "pity and honour" (*LotR*, TT.II.5). Now Frodo can continue with the interaction; his silence is short and his words are full of reflection.

For Jason, the *amechanía*[46] can be called his main heroic characteristic[47] and, like a cloak, it hides his true personality: reflective, clever, but also humane in a way that "marks him amongst other Argonauts and makes his greatness" (Vian 1978, 1037). This is shown by his seeming discouragement during the celebration before the departure: Idmon foretold both the success of the mission and his own death (I 440-447), thus making impossible the return home of all the heroes as asked for previously in the prayer to Apollo (I 411-424). Both characters prefer dialogue over relying on physical strength and avoid, if possible, fights and useless bloodshed because, as Jason claims, "oftentimes, I ween, does speech accomplish at need what prowess could hardly carry through, smoothing the path in manner befitting" (III 188-190). The other heroes excel in deeds of arms, often relegating Jason to the last place among the names mentioned.[48] The moment he is first mentioned

---

43 Two-faced Greek adjective: the "active" sense means "without means or resources, helpless, awkward," the "passive" sense is "impracticable, unmanageable".
44 Frodo still cannot shake off his irresolution as it is evident when he refuses to destroy the Ring.
45 Faramir characterises Frodo as being wiser than Sam, who interrupted their conversation (cf. *LotR*, TT.II.5).
46 Greek word from which the adjective *améchanos* is derived and with which it shares the "active" sense.
47 Hunter connects this characteristic to the young age of Jason and sees his quest has an initiation rite to adulthood. Cf. Hunter 1993, 15-16.
48 During the battle against the Earthborn men (I 989-1002), only Heracles is mentioned by name. The others are gathered in a general "younger heroes" reference, while Jason tries to climb Mount Dindymon to oversee the lands across the Propontis. It is Pollux who wins the fight against the arrogant king Amykos (II 67-97), and in the next battle against the Bebryces, subjects to Amykos, Jason is mentioned as the last of nine heroes.

in a battle is full of tragic irony: with his infallible spear he unconsciously[49] kills Cyzicus, king of the Dolionians and friend of the Argonauts. The other two episodes where he appears engaged in battle exemplify his non-martial nature: he passes the trials of Aeetes[50] thanks to the filter of Medea and kills Apsyrtus through deceit, helped again by Apsyrtus' own sister Medea.

Frodo uses Sting once, against the Troll in Moria, and then only for his defence. Otherwise, he uses it mainly to check for the presence of orcs in the vicinity, and once to threaten Gollum in order to save Sam, yet without actually hurting him. After coming back to the Shire that is now under the power of Saruman and his lackeys, his main concern is to avoid bloodshed and killing, and he himself never uses the sword, not even when he could kill the wizard himself.[51] Finally, before leaving for Valinor, he gives it to Sam. The link between Frodo and Sting clearly shows the subversion of the conventions of the medieval epic: Tolkien separates the weapon from his bearer. Like Arthur and Sigmund, Frodo finds the weapon, but he lets Sam wield it, and his own life does not depend on the ownership of the weapon.[52] For these reasons anger and rage are replaced by new qualities unknown to the archaic epic. Even when accused by Telamon to rejoice in the loss of Heracles,[53] Jason does not show any anger (I 1290-1295). Jason is capable of forgiveness and of setting an end to the fight, even if he claims to be wounded in his soul (I 1340), and thus proves his valour by ending the quarrels. Similarly, Frodo pities Gollum: a feeling which is absent in the Shire, but that erupts as soon as he sees him, and he spares his life, even against the advice of Sam. He acts as a patient mediator and, though he suffers from the burden of the Ring and from the fatigue of his journey, his *pietas* never fails, not even during their last confrontation at the roots of Mount Doom. Even in such a situation Frodo confines himself to merely threatening Gollum.

---

49 The clash is caused by the darkness of the night. The Argonauts, who had to find shelter once again in the land of the Dolionians because of the strong storms, are attacked by Cyzicus and his army, who mistakenly thought they were enemies. Only at dawn do the Argonauts understand who they have been fighting during the night.
50 Jason, after he has yoked the bulls and has sown the teeth of the dragon in the field, fights with the earthborn warriors. Because of this episode's many connections to the rural world, some critics have interpreted it as a sort of "rural epic" (cf. Fantuzzi and Hunter 2002, 368-80).
51 Shippey 2005, 231-37.
52 In Mordor, Frodo uses an orc sword, leaving Sting to Sam and giving it to him for good before setting sail for Valinor; on the hero and his weapon cf. Flieger 2012, 147-53.
53 Heracles is left in Mysia, together with the hero Polyphemus, searching for his young friend Hylas, who had been kidnapped by a nymph (I 1187-1272).

Lastly, the hero is the one who accepts the other and his help. Jason can count on a group of five chosen heroes to face Aeetas' trials, but essential is the aid of Medea who, hit by Eros' arrows, gives[54] to the hero the magic filter with which he becomes invincible. Sam never leaves Frodo, but the Ring is destroyed (accidentally) by Gollum after Frodo's failure.[55] Medea and Gollum are thus the biggest challenges the hero has to face, symbolising what is seen as inferior[56] or inimical.[57] The two protagonists, by accepting otherness, whether willing or not, receive unexpected help in the very moment they are irremediably *améchanoi*.

Tolkien and Apollonius have thus left us a new hero, imperfect but more humane, without the aura of the divine and the self-destructive lust for death. This new hero is therefore able "to assume responsibility towards the world",[58] and his true heroic acts do not end on an individual sphere, but are always directed to a purpose that sometimes encompasses the whole world itself, because "it is the heroism of obedience and love, not of pride or wilfulness, that is the most heroic and the most moving" (*Tree* 148).

---

54 This is the first of the many actions of Medea that will allow the heroes to return home. She also advises how to easily eliminate the warriors born from the teeth of the dragon (III 1051-1060), she puts the guardian serpent of the Golden Fleece to sleep (IV 100-148), she tricks her brother Apsyrtus (IV 410-474) and, while the ship Argo returns to Iolco, she neutralizes the bronze giant of Talos (IV 1625-1688).
55 Refusing to destroy the Ring and putting it on his finger, Frodo feels the "passive" sense of *améchanos*, becoming to Sam a figure against whom nothing can be done.
56 In the Greek epic, women were not held in high esteem; Heracles, on the island of Lemnos, does not descend from the ship and apostrophizes Jason, recalling the group to duty (I 855-875); in the same way Idas rejects the idea to invocate Aphrodite instead of Ares and accuses the heroes of preferring seducing girls over fighting (III 588-572). Initially, even Jason seems sceptical towards female help (III 487-488). Apollonius gives great importance to love, which is present but not so prominent in Homer. On this theme cf. Clauss 1993, 46-74.
57 Flieger sees Gollum as a mix of two of Beowulf's enemies: Grendel and the dragon. Cf. Flieger 2012, 156-57.
58 Wu Ming 4 2010, 9 (translation mine).

Bibliography

Primary Sources

APOLLONIUS RHODIUS. *The Argonautica of Apollonius Rhodius*. Ed. George W. Mooney. Amsterdam: Hakkert, 1987.

Argonautica: Book 3. Ed. Richard Hunter. Cambridge: Cambridge University Press, 1989.

The Argonautica. Ed. Robert Cooper Seaton. London: William Heinemann, 1912.

Secondary Sources

AUDEN, Wystan Hugh. "The Quest Hero." *Tolkien and the Critics*. Eds. Neil D. Isaacs and Rose A. Zimbardo. Notre Dame, IN: University of Notre Dame Press, 1968, 40-61.

BORGOGNO, Alberto. "Introduction." *Argonautiche*. Milan: Mondandori, 2014. vii-lxxxix.

CALLIMACO. *Aitia, Giambi e altri frammenti*. Ed. Giovan Battista D'Alessio. Milan: BUR, 1996.

CARPENTER, Humphrey. *J.R.R. Tolkien. A Biography*. London: George Allen & Unwin, 1977.

CLAUSS, James J. *The Best of the Argonauts. The Redefinition of the Epic Hero in Book One of Apollonius' Argonautica*. Berkeley, Los Angeles, and Oxford: University of California Press, 1993.

FANTUZZI, Marco and Richard HUNTER. *Muse e modelli: la poesia ellenistica da Alessandro Magno ad Augusto*. Rome and Bari: Laterza, 2010.

FLIEGER, Verlyn. "Frodo and Aragorn. The Concept of the Hero." *Green Suns and Faërie. Essays on Tolkien*. Kent, OH: The Kent State University Press, 2012, 141-158.

HONEGGER, Thomas. "Splintered Heroes – Heroic Variety and its Function in *The Lord of the Rings*." *A Wilderness of Dragons: Essays in Honor of Verlyn Flieger*. Ed. John D. Rateliff. Wayzata, MI: The Gabbro Head Press, 2018, 157-175.

HUNTER, Richard. *The Argonautica of Apollonius. Literary Studies*. Cambridge: Cambridge University Press, 1993.

PEARCE, Joseph. *Tolkien: Man and Myth*. London: HarperCollins, 1999.

SHIPPEY, Tom. *The Road to Middle-earth*. London: HarperCollins, 2005.

STEPHENS, Susan. "Ptolemaic Epic." *Brill's Companion to Apollonius Rhodius*. Eds. Theodore D. Papanghelis and Antonios Rengakos. Leiden and Boston: Brill, 2008, 95-114.

VIAN, Francis. "ΙΗΣΩΝ ΑΜΗΧΑΝΕΩΝ." *Studi in onore di Anthos Ardizzoni*. Eds. Enrico Livrea and G. Aurelio Privitera. Rome: Edizioni dell'Ateneo & Bizzarri, 1978, 1025-1038.

WU MING 4. "Preface." *J.R.R. Tolkien: Il ritorno di Beorhtnoth figlio di Berohthelm*. (Italian edition of HBBS). Milan: Bompiani, 2010, 5-19.

Difendere la Terra di Mezzo. Scritti su J.R.R. Tolkien. Bologna: Odoya, 2013.

Gloria Larini

To Die for Love. Female Archetypes in Tolkien and Euripides

My essay analyses two female characters in Tolkien's works, Lúthien in *The Silmarillion*, who receives an honorary mention in *The Lord of the Rings*, and Arwen, whose story can be found in Appendix A of that same work. They will be compared to Alcestis, the eponymous female protagonist of one of Euripides' tragedy.

Many scholars believe that, apart from the biographical circumstances that associates Tolkien's wife Edith to Lúthien,[1] the story can be classified as an archetype connected to Norse legends,[2] which in turn have inspired the account in *The Silmarillion*.[3] This archetype probably derived from ancient Indo-European culture,[4] and is connected to the Hindu ceremony known as *Sati*, in which the widow voluntarily decides to burn on the pyre of her husband, as well as to the Orphic myths and doctrines which are the essential base of some stories of love and death in classical Greek and Latin texts. This mythical *fil rouge* supports the hypothesis of a probable common legendary root shared by the characters of Lúthien, Arwen,[5] and Alcestis,[6] thus linking the Norse legends to the Greek ones. In fact, some parallels are especially noteworthy. All the protagonists are beautiful women: Alcestis, for example, is defined in

---

1 It is well-known that Tolkien had the name Lúthien inscribed on the grave of his wife, thus leaving an important testimony of her connection with the character. Cf. *Letters* no. 340: "she was (and knew she was) my Lúthien [...]. I never called Edith *Lúthien* – but she was the source of the story that in time became the chief part of the *Silmarillion*. It was first conceived in a small woodland glade filled with hemlocks at Roos in Yorkshire [...]. In those days her hair was raven, her skin clear, her eyes brighter than you have seen them, and she could sing – and *dance*. But the story has gone crooked, and I am left, and *I* cannot plead before the inexorable Mandos." Unlike Lúthien, in fact, Edith died before her husband.
2 Cf. Burns 2005; Phelpstead 2011; on Norse sources, cf. Shippey 1992, 229f.
3 In these three female figures merge some archetypal *leitmotifs* from which both Euripides and Tolkien have probably drawn, even without a direct contact between the latter and the works of Euripides, although his extensive classical education is well-known.
4 Cf. Athanassakis 2001; 2002.
5 It is, in my opinion, possible to think that the invention of Arwen, an Elf older than Lúthien, although young in appearance, is related to a more advanced phase in the life of Tolkien's wife and occurred precisely at the time of the invention of this new story and character.
6 For a comparison of Lúthien, Ovid's Philomela, Alcestis and Eurydice cf. Beal 2014.

Iliad II as "the most beautiful among the daughters of Pelias";[7] they are all of royal lineage, and they all renounce their own nature, mortal or immortal, for the sake of their beloved. The element of sacrifice for love is, in fact, the main and supporting core of their stories, present also in the classic myths of Capaneus and Evadne, Phaon and Sappho,[8] Deucalion and Pyrrha, and Cephalus and Pterela, to mention only a few examples recurring in the Greek and Latin traditions.

For the composition of *Alcestis* Euripides uses the background of Greek literary and religious culture.[9] Tolkien, instead, takes inspiration from the universe of Celtic and Norse traditions, and constructs love-relationships that are impossible from the beginning because the lovers have different natures, human and non-human, and only the immortal woman can descend to a lower level renouncing her semi-divine nature in order to fulfil her love dream.[10]

To this natural diversity Tolkien adds further distinctions that are obstacles for the lovers's relationships. An element of diversity, which is not found in the myth of Alcestis, is the rank. Lúthien and Arwen are daughters of noble elven leaders (King Thingol and Lord Elrond, respectively), Beren is merely a human hero and Aragorn, although of royal lineage, is still without a throne.

A fundamental point in common, however, is the trial of courage requested by the father from the suitor. It highlights the close bond between fathers and daughters in the archetype. So Thingol, Lúthien's father, asks Beren to fetch a Silmaril, knowing very well that this means that he has to get it from Morgoth's iron crown; Elrond, Arwen's father, demands that Aragorn marries his daughter only after conquering the throne of Gondor and Arnor, and Alcestis' father, Pelias, promises her in marriage to the man who would be able to yoke two wild animals, a lion and a savage boar.[11]

---

7   Cf. Hom. *Iliad* II, 714ff.
8   Cf. Larini 2016.
9   The tragedy is inspired by a Thessalian legend: Admetus, son of Pheretes, founder of the Thessalian city of Pherae, is saved by the devotion of his wife Alcestis who chooses to die in his place. Cf. Dale 1954, who quotes Lesky 1925.
10 For the contact between Celtic and Greek *mysteria* cf. Tonelli 2015, 96, in which he recalls that Jamblicus in the *Life of Pythagoras* states that Pythagoras summed up "in a synthesis" what he had "learn[t] from the original communities Celtic and Iberian."
11 Cf. Apollodorus, I, 9, 15. The trial of courage is a *topos* successfully completed with a woman's help. In fact, Lúthien and Arwen in the first part of the story are like Medea, and Beren and Aragorn have traits that resemble Jason.

Another common element is the separation from the family. In order to help her beloved, Lúthien escapes from her father by using a rope twined from strands of her hair, another traditional fairy-tale element; Arwen, called the wise, supports and encourages Aragorn with her advice, like Medea in Apollonius' poem *Argonautica*, and Alcestis is praised as the best among wives.[12] All these women flee far from their homeland and decide to live and die with their men.[13]

The fundamental archetypal knot of renunciation and sacrifice of one's life for love is included in the Greek legend of Alcestis, but not in that of Medea.[14] This supports the hypothesis of a modification of the original myth, of which Euripides preserves only the background.[15] Also the epilogues of the stories of Lúthien and Arwen differ from that of Alcestis for various reasons. For the pain of the loss of Beren the spirit of Lúthien separates itself from the body;[16] like Orpheus she follows her lover even in death, but unlike Orpheus she is able to bring him back to life and lead him out of the Underworld by means of her magic song;[17] finally, she chooses to become a mortal and to go to Middle-earth to live with him. She renounces her life twice: first she enters a dimension of death, even though she is an Elf, then she voluntarily deprives herself of immortality to save her lover and live with him.[18]

Arwen and Alcestis, instead, renounce their lifes only once. They are protagonists of a plot with a simpler narrative core, but this difference might prove that the

---

12 Alcestis' and Medea's myths exist in many variants.
13 According to a widespread version of Medea's myth, she flees her homeland Colchis, slaughtering her family with her magic powers. However, in Euripides and other authors the love for Jason turns into hatred out of jealousy of his new marriage with Creusa, daughter of king Creon, and Medea decides to kill her own children.
14 In Euripides' version, Medea saves herself and flees victoriously on the chariot of the Sun.
15 Euripides often calls Medea "wise" (*sophé*), but in the tragedy this connotation is not positive. In fact, Medea knows many *pharmaka*, and for this reason she is dangerous. The evil nature of Medea seems to be a distortion of the archetype.
16 *Silmarillion* XIX: "But the starlight was quenched and darkness had fallen even upon Lúthien Tinúviel. Thus ended the Quest of the Silmaril. But The Lay of Leithian, Release from Bondage, does not end. For the Spirit of Beren at her bidding tarried in the halls of Mandos, unwilling to leave the world, until Lúthien came to say her last farewell upon the dim shores of the Outer Sea, whence Men that die set out never to return. But the spirit of Lúthien fell down into darkness, and at the last it fled and her body lay like a flower that is suddenly cut off and lies for a while unwithered on the grass."
17 The references to the Classics and also to Lúthien and Arwen are discussed in Brunetti 2011, 249-267, 259, in particular where the author agrees with recent criticism that Pyramus and Thisbe are the original archetype of the "contrasted love story that ends tragically".
18 Various drafts of the story are now available in *BL*, in particular 224ff., with annotations about Elves' rebirth and death. Cf. West 2003.

invention of Arwen is coherently connected to a new existential context of the author, posterior to that of Lúthien.[19]

Unlike the fate of the two elves, the consequence of Alcestis's choice is not a reunion, but the separation from her beloved despite her desire to share her love with him. Euripides creates a tragic paradox, unsolvable and contrasting with the archetype. For this reason, Alcestis' tragedy can be seen as a drama that mirrors the stories of Lúthien and Arwen.[20] Alcestis renounces happiness and living with her beloved man in order to save him; the two Elves, instead, share a similar destiny, renounce immortality, but live with their beloved men even if only for a short time.

In this comparison the temporal aspect is decisive. In Tolkien, time is limited and broken, reduced to the human dimension, to immanence, due to the contrast of the lovers' nature. On the contrary, *fulmen in cauda*, in Euripides' *Alcestis* the young mortal woman, after a total renunciation of her life and her beloved, returns on stage at the end of the tragedy when Heracles, psychopompos hero, wins her back from Thanatos so that the audience's sense of *pietas* is satisfied, and gives her to the sorrowing Admetus.[21]

Thus, we note a sort of inversion of elements in the comparison between the narrations. For Lúthien and Arwen the tragedy consists in the choice of an ineluctable end in order to realize their love. For Alcestis, instead, it is in the heroic act of drastic renunciation of her life and her husband, which, however, unexpectedly results in the prolongation of the existence of the couple. Therefore, in the epilogue of the Euripidean tragedy, Alcestis becomes the orphic image of the soul,[22] which cannot be held back by death because Eros is stronger and saves her.

---

19 The *catabasis* of Lúthien to the Underworld to save her beloved from death is replaced by the age difference and by Arwen's wisdom. This characteristic, in my opinion, reflects the passing of time for Ronald and Edith: the characters are both *alter ego* temporally dislocated in the author's imagination.
20 Tolkien himself admits some reversal of the classic traces and defines them "a kind of Orpheus-Legend in reverse, but one of Pity not of Inexorability" (*Letters* no. 153).
21 *Alcestis* is one of the few extant Greek tragedies with a happy ending. Cf. Di Benedetto 2002.
22 Beal 2014, 17.

In fact, if we look at the epilogue, Tolkien's female characters are more tragic. Unlike in Euripides' theatrical world, full of religious beliefs[23] and trust in the survival of the soul after death,[24] sacrifice for love does not result in redemption in Middle-earth. The Orphic image is part of Tolkien's narratives only in the precursors of Lúthien's story. Compared to the Greek religious thought, which often opens itself to an osmotic contact between life and death, Tolkien's mortal and immortal worlds remain totally distinct in substance, thus making Tolkien's legends end more tragically when, although after a long and happy life, the separation is total and inevitable.

The awareness of this split and the moment of the death deserves to be analysed more accurately in all three characters. In Alcestis' tragedy, the tension is placed at the beginning; in the stories of Lúthien and Arwen, instead, it is at the end, as death is procrastinated, diluted in human time. Alcestis' death is expected before her husband's, and this is heart-breaking. The awareness and the separation from the affections create a stronger *pathos* due to the impotence in front of Thanatos, the dark power who conquers even the purest and most unconditional love. Like the two Elves, Alcestis feels the approach of the fateful day in advance:

> When the day
> she felt had come, the white body
> she washed with the water brought to her
> from the river, and from her cedar arks
> took off a robe (Euripides, Alcestis, 158ff.)

Alcestis prepares herself for her death like a queen, dressed as befits her rank. However, her pain makes her break out; she embraces and kisses the bed of her wedding, cries desperately and, in the last moment, asks to be taken out into the sunlight and leaves the palace carried out in a litter[25] onto the stage.

From this moment a slow agony starts, showed by many implicit stage directions: Alcestis says she is dying in verse 322 (*all'autik[a]*), bids farewell in verse 323 (*chairontes euphrainoisthe*), but actually dies only at verse 391, when she says

---

23 The Orphic rites and *mysteria* influences in the works of Euripides are discussed in Tonelli 2015; Battezzato 2005. About Orphism in general see Anonymous 1975.
24 This supports the observations in Testi 2018, who explains that Tolkien imagines Middle-earth to be a pagan world.
25 Cf. Kott 1987, 81ff.

goodbye again to her beloved husband (*chair[e]*). The agony is prolonged also by her delivering their children into Admetus's hands, a scene well described by the poet through precise implicit stage directions.[26] Alcestis does not die alone, but is surrounded by family and her beloved, and Admetus tells her (v. 360) that if he owned the lyre of Orpheus he would go down with her to Hades in order to try and bring her back to the light again.[27]

Lúthien also is a complex character, who seems to unite in herself more traits of the archetype. At the beginning of the story, she assumes the characteristics of Heracles Psychopompos, when she manages to free the soul of her beloved in a spiritual *catabasis* caused by pain; then, she returns with him to the human world and loses her immortality by voluntary choice. She sums up within herself both the stylistic and conceptual traits of the archetype. She assumes Evadne's ways[28] when, in a long monody, Capaneus' wife sings her pain for the destiny of her man; Sappho's ways when the Greek poetess sings for Adon,[29] and becomes Orpheus when, thanks to her song – a quite conspicuous original *leitmotif* – she obtains from Mandos, in agreement with Manwë and Eru, the return to life of Beren in exchange for her immortal life.

When Aragorn lays down to wait for his death, Tolkien writes that Arwen tasted "the bitterness of the mortality that she had taken upon her",[30] and although she would still want to keep her husband alive, she knows well she cannot do so. After their final separation she withdraws away from everyone and dies alone in the silence of nature on a grey winter day:

> There at last, when the mallorn-leaves were falling, but spring had not yet come, she laid herself to rest upon Cerin Amroth; and there is her green grave, until the world is changed.[31]

---

26 For the importance of the implicit stage directions in Euripides cf. Larini 2011.
27 Euripides, *Alcestis*, vv. 360ff.: "and it would not be worthy to keep me / neither the dog of Pluto, nor Charon / who is at the oar and the souls carries / before I had not your life / led back to the light." Cf. Kott 1987, 94ff.; for the character of Alcestis in the drama cf. Kott 1987, 78ff.
28 In Euripides' *Supplices* Evadne, before throwing herself onto the pyre of her husband Capaneus, sings a monody that remembers her life with him and the decision of her death for the impossibility of living without him. About this scene and the possible links with Orphic rites and with the Indian ceremony of *Sati* cf. Larini 2016, 49f.
29 About Adon cf. Fr. 140 in Voigt 1971.
30 *LotR* App A.
31 *LotR* App A.

Like Alcestis, Arwen feels in advance that the last hour is coming, but unlike her she does not let out a lament or a cry, and the total silence of nature, accompanied by that voluntary unwinding of her body on the cold earth, is more excruciating than the long cries and acute moans of Alcestis on Euripides' stage.

Lúthien's interiority remains little investigated by the author. The story is silent about her thoughts, her emotions and moods towards her own death,[32] mentioned in the various drafts and internal variants of the myth only by means of an ordinary "faded" and a vague and delicate "vanished".[33]

It is tempting to see in Tolkien's female characters the reference to an archetype of loving fidelity linked to the Christian tradition and connected to the mystery of the indissolubility of marriage and to its sacredness.[34] However, in the stories of Lúthien and Arwen, the author does not present the image of an Eden in which the souls of the lovers can meet. Tolkien's religiosity is absorbed by the archetypes of his sources, and Middle-earth in these legends remains a pagan world without a future. Euripides, on the other hand, the "agnostic"[35] imbued with Orphic beliefs, manages to reverse the course of events in a final twist, bringing back to life the female character, although for the limited time of a human life. This becomes a Faustian moment on the Euripidean stage: the Greek tragedy ends with a happy and unexpected image of a new young bride, a veiled *eidolon*[36] that enters the royal palace holding the hand of an unbelieving but happy Admetus, thus suggesting that they are starting a new life together. So, in the theatre of Dionysus, the image of the eternity of the soul accompanied by an unconditional love is forever established.

In this comparison with Euripidean links to the archetype, the stories of Lúthien and Arwen, with their heroic deeds and their courageous choices, acquire a deeper sense, even if they cannot have positive consequences in Middle-earth.

---

32 Brunetti 2011, 249-67.
33 Cf. *BL*, especially 224 ff. For the different versions of Lúthien's death and what is written in the *Quenta Noldorinwa* cf. in particular 236, 244f, 247. Only in one of these versions does Lúthien die before Beren (cf. 254f.).
34 Heckman 2007, 583f; Richmond 2002, 13f; Kerry 2011, especially 22, 45, 154.
35 Cf. Mirto 2009, 79.
36 *Eidolon* is one of the most complex words of Greek culture. It derives from *eidos*, "aspect, form" and has different meanings: "phantom, indeterminate form, reflected image". In the Greek religion it is a spiritual entity linked to the deceased person's body, who may still appear to the senses of the living. Cf. for example Said 1990 and recently Larini 2017.

They represent the failed attempt to reconstruct the primeval eternity of Man, destroyed by Evil, through the power of a pure and absolute love. Lúthien and Arwen are extraordinary women and, at the same time, pagan metaphors of an unfinished salvation.[37]

However, it seems that Tolkien wanted to leave at least "beyond the world"[38] the possibility of the continuation of love, allowing for a salvific perspective in one of the last drafts and variations of his myth. "No one saw Beren and Lúthien leave the world and no grave marked the spot where their bodies lie": this suspended sentence reveals a faint glimmer of hope, a probable, albeit late, symptom of a more confident reflection about the reciprocal relationship between death, love, and eternity.[39]

Bibliography

ANONYMOUS. *Orfismo in Magna Grecia. Atti del Quattordicesimo Convegno di Studi sulla Magna Grecia. Taranto 6-10 Ottobre 1974*. Naples: Arte Tipografica, 1975.

ARDUINI, Roberto and Claudio TESTI (eds.). *The Broken Scythe. Death and Immortality in the Works of J.R.R. Tolkien*. Zurich & Jena: Walking Tree Publishers, 2012.

ATHANASSAKIS, Apostolos. "Shamanism and Amber in Greece: The Northern connection." *Shamanhood Symbolism and Epic*. Eds. Juha Pentikäinen, Hanna Saressalo, and Chuner Mikhailovic Taksam. Budapest: Akademiai Kiadó, 2001, 207-220.

"Proteus, the old man of the sea: Homeric Merman or Shaman?" *La mythologie et l'Odyssée. Hommage à Gabriel Germain. Actes du Colloque international de Grenoble, 20-22 Mai 1999, textes réunis par André Hurst et Françoise Létoublon*. Eds. André Hurst and Françoise Létoublon. Genève: Librairie Droz, 2002, 45-56.

BATTEZZATO, Luigi. "Le vie dell'Ade e le vie di Parmenide: filologia, filosofia e presenze femminili nelle lamine d'oro 'orfiche'." *Seminari Romani di Cultura Greca* 8.1 (2005): 67-99.

---

37 For the pagan world of Tolkien see Testi 2018; for death and immortality as a central theme of Tolkien's works, also conveyed in his stories, cf. Arduini & Testi 2012.
38 Cf. *BL* 238.
39 Cf. *BL* 255.

BEAL, Jane. "Orphic Powers in J.R.R. Tolkien's Legend of Beren and Lúthien." *Journal of Tolkien Research* 1.1, Article 1. https://scholar.valpo.edu/journaloftolkienresearch/vol1/iss1/1, (Accessed 6/10/2018), 2014.

BRUNETTI, Umberto. "La leggenda di Beren e Lúthien. Il 'classico' in Tolkien." *Studi Urbinati B*, V.81, http://ojs.uniurb.it/index.php/studi-B/article/view/202 (Accessed 6/10/2018), 2011.

BURNS, Marjorie. *Perilous Realms. Celtic and Norse in Tolkien's Middle-earth.* Toronto: University of Toronto Press, 2005.

DI BENEDETTO, Vincenzo and Enrico MEDDA. *La tragedia sulla scena. La tragedia greca come spettacolo teatrale.* Turin: Einaudi, 2002.

DROUT, Michael D.C. (ed.). *J.R.R. Tolkien Encyclopedia. Scholarship and Critical Assessment.* New York: Routledge, 2007.

EURIPIDES. *Alcestis.* Ed. Amy Marjorie Dale. Oxford: Clarendon Press, 1954.

GOUNARIDOU, Kiki. *Euripides and Alcestis. Speculation, Simulation and Stories of Love in Athenian Culture.* Lanham, New York & Boston: University Press of America, 1998.

HECKMAN, Christina. "Sacrifice." *J.R.R. Tolkien Encyclopedia. Scholarship and Critical Assessment.* Ed. Michael D.C. Drout. New York: Routledge, 2007, 583-584.

ISAACS, Neil David and Rose A. ZIMBARDO. *Tolkien. New Critical Perspectives.* Lexington, KT: University Press of Kentucky, 1981.

KERRY, Paul E. (ed.). *The Ring and the Cross. Christianity and the Writings of J.R.R. Tolkien.* Madison, WI: Fairleigh Dickinson University Press, 2011.

KOTT, Jan. *The Eating of the Gods. An Interpretation of Greek Tragedy.* Evanston, IL: Northwestern University Press, 1987.

LARINI, Gloria. "L'ontologia del personaggio di Polidoro nell'*Ecuba* di Euripide." *Lo spettro e la verità.* Eds. Gloria Larini and Franco Cardini. Padua: libreriauniversitaria.it, 2017, 115-160.

"The Archetype of the Jump from a Cliff: A Ritual Linked to Orphic and Indo-european Rites for a New Reading of Euripides." *Littera Antiqua* 11, Supplement 1012-1014 (2016): 37-59.

(ed.). *Controversie. Dispute letterarie, storiche, religiose dall'Antichità al Rinascimento.* Padova: editrice libreriauniversitaria.it, 2013.

La casa sulla scena euripidea. Didascalie implicite di annuncio e moduli linguistici, dialogici e drammaturgici per una lettura a tre dimensioni delle scene di ingresso. PhD Thesis, Florence, 2011.

LESKY, Albin. *Alkestis, der Mythos und das Drama*. Vienna and Leipzig: Hölder, Pichler and Tempsky, 1925.

MIRTO, Maria Serena (ed.). *Euripide: Ione*. Milan: BUR, 2009.

PHELPSTEAD, Carl. *Tolkien and Wales. Language, Literature and Identity*. Cardiff: University of Wales Press, 2011.

RICHMOND, Donald P. "Tolkien's Marian Vision of Middle-earth." *Mallorn, The Journal of the Tolkien Society* 40 (2002): 13-14.

SAÏD, Suzanne. "ΕΙΔΩΛΟΝ. Du simulacre à l'idole, Histoire d'un mot." *Rencontres de l'Ecole du Louvre*: *L'Idolâtrie*. Paris: La Documentation Française, 1990, 11-67.

SHIPPEY, Tom. *The Road to Middle-earth*. London: HarperCollins, 1992.

TESTI, Claudio. *Pagan Saints in Middle-earth*. Zurich & Jena: Walking Tree Publishers, 2018.

TONELLI, Angelo (ed.). *Eleusis e Orfismo. I Misteri e la tradizione iniziatica greca*. Milano: Feltrinelli, 2015.

VOIGT, Eva Marie. *Sappho et Alcaeus. Fragmenta*. Amsterdam: Polak & van Gennep, 1971.

WEST, Richard C. "Real-World Myth in a Secondary World: Mythological Aspects in the Story of Beren and Lúthien." *Tolkien the Medievalist*. Ed. Jane Chance. London: Routledge, 2003, 259-267.

Tolkien and Virgil, Ancient Lore and Literary Inspiration

"Alas for the lost lore, the annals and old poets that Virgil knew, and only used in the making of a new thing!", wrote Tolkien, and he meant it. However, he also wanted everyone to realise that the "new thing" was worth more than the "lost lore".[1] In 1936, in his lecture at the British Academy, Tolkien presented a very striking overview of Virgil's *Aeneid*, and this way he introduced one of the most relevant topics of his writing: the relationship between ancient and modern. According to Tolkien, who was a true expert of ancient literature and one of the most competent philologists of his generation, the Virgilian corpus is a unique and priceless source for Roman mythical tales, which have largely been lost, and on which Virgil drew just to write "a new thing" – a "thing" that also represents the greatest epic poem known in Latin. In this respect, the main innovation brought by Virgil lies precisely in his ability to connect the ancient mythic lore with a poetic inspiration that was at the same time original and revolutionary, and thus to connect myths to the historic present of his time. In fact, Virgil did not only glorify the history of Rome, as Ennius and Nevius had done before him, but he even provided it with a mythical past, in which the founding of the city was related to the will of Fate. To this end, he ensured to posterity the story of the Romans' ancestor Aeneas.

In the *Iliad*, Aeneas was just one of the heroes who fought in the war at Troy, destined to found a city in Asia Minor, where he would rule the Trojan survivors.[2] Virgil, by contrast, recovers the version of the myth in which Aeneas sails towards Latium and gives it divine sanction by describing the hero's arrival as ordained by the gods. So, Aeneas becomes the progenitor of the *gens Iulia* (a name derived from *Iulius*, his son), one of the most important families in Rome, to which Augustus himself belonged. And the actual founder of Rome would be

---

1 See Shippey 1992, 203.
2 See Bettini & Lentano 2013, 51-64. The first mention of Aeneas as the progenitor of the Romans can be found in Hellanicus (5th century BC).

born from this bloodline: Romulus, the fruit of the illicit affair between Rhea Silvia, a descendant of Aeneas, and the god Mars. Therefore, Virgil built for Rome not only a myth, but also a political and cultural tradition that allowed him to trace back the *gens Iulia* to divine origins, as part of Fate's design. It is evident that the poet was rethinking things from a "sacred" perspective and thus re-defined the identity of Romans. As a consequence, Augustus, the *princeps* who restored peace after many years of bloody civil war, was also given a new identity. To do so, Virgil had used the epos, the literary form through which they represented and conveyed shared values and the identity of peoples, as in the case of Homeric poems, by expertly combining old and new, and succeeded in creating one of the greatest works of mythopoiesis of the Ancient world. He had rewritten the ancient, sacred, and authoritative myths in epic form, and he had created an even bigger one.[3]

It is difficult not to recognize, in this description of the *Aeneid*, part of the literary project that Tolkien embarked upon, too: the idea of creating something new that could combine memory and fiction without, at the same time, being perceived as a lie.[4] Such a work, the cosmogony of *The Silmarillion* as well as the epic-romance development of *The Lord of the Rings*, could not but assume, as in Virgil, the form of myth:

> May I say that all this is 'mythical', and not any kind of new religion or vision. As far as I know it is merely an imaginative invention, to express, in the only way I can, some of my (dim) apprehensions of the world. (*Letters* no. 211)

Tolkien was aware of having given birth to a coherent and plausible Secondary World, which drew on reality and was linked to it in multiple ways.[5] However, since his Catholic faith prevented him from placing himself on a par with the Creator, he preferred to call his mythopoiesis "sub-creation" – a secondary creation by which he can shape the detailed and coherent world that arose from his stories:[6]

---

3 See Bettini 2015.
4 See Carpenter 2000, 99.
5 See Carpenter 2000, 194f. for a discussion of Tolkien's lecture. The terms "Primary World" and "Secondary World" are used by Tolkien to refer, respectively, to the real world in which the writer lives, and the fictional world that he creates in imitation of the former.
6 See Shippey 1992, 17-24 and Carpenter 2000, 194f.

> What really happens is that the story-maker proves a successful 'sub-creator'. He makes a Secondary World which your mind can enter. Inside it, what he relates is 'true': it accords with the laws of that world. You therefore believe it, while you are, as it were, inside. (Carpenter 2000, 245-46)

Although in different contexts, even the myth rewritten by Virgil represents a set of stories and characters which the ancients conceived as the foundations of reality and thus worth believing in. So, Tolkien is part of the tradition because of "a narrative complex that is unique and original",[7] which inherits and innovates the experience of the Norse sagas and the ancient poems. After all, antiquity was at the centre of the Professor's interests, and his philological education certainly influenced his idea of writing as a *restoration* of the lost tales, a kind of compositional invention, the outcome of which, from a literary point of view, is what Shippey calls "asterisk-reality",[8] in accordance with the philological approach of restoring texts. As well as these basic reasons, there are also some common themes, such as those of exile and travel, which are central to both the *Aeneid* and *The Lord or the Rings*.

After the fall of Troy, Aeneas becomes a refugee by the will of Fate ("fato profugus", *Aeneis* I 2), forced to find the place the gods indicate to him as the site of rebirth. This happens to be Italy, the ancient homeland of Dardanus, the progenitor of the Trojans. The journey of the homeless fugitive, therefore, is configured as the return to the land of his forefathers, a circular movement that inscribes Aeneas and Rome into the sacred shape of circle.[9]

In Tolkien, too, the journey provides the basic pattern, often followed by banishment, as is the case with the Noldor Elves in *The Silmarillion*, who were expelled from Valinor for having violated the peace (*S* Qu.IX), or with Beren (*S* Qu.XIX), Túrin Turambar (*S* Qu.XIX), or Sméagol, who fled after having murdered his cousin (*LotR*, FR.I.2). In Tolkien, as well as in Virgil, the exile often overlaps with the motif of the return. In *The Lord of the Rings*, the Elves, already exiled from the Undying Lands, are compelled to flee Middle-earth in

---

7 Respinti 2007, 22 (translated by Giampaolo Canzonieri). See also Flieger 2005, 55-85.
8 Shippey 1992, 17ff. See also Flieger 2011.
9 Cf. Virgil, *Aeneis* I 161-71. The ancient Romans considered the shape of the circle and the cyclical sequence of events as sacred symbols of safety. In this regard, see Picone 1989, 29-41.

order to escape the evil that spreads from the Dark Tower. So, they return to Valinor, their former homeland (cf. *LotR*, FR.I.3).

If, as far as the Elves are concerned, the return to the uncontaminated land of the Valar is the way by which they attempt to preserve themselves – a recovery of their "primordial state" – matters are quite different as soon as we consider the return of those who bear the burden of power. Frodo and Aragorn, the Ringbearer and the King, experience exile not by imposition but by necessity. In fact, Aragorn needs to stay hidden from the Eye of the Enemy, who believes the dynasty of Elendil is extinct, while Frodo must endure the distance from home among doubts and regrets:

> He wished bitterly that his fortune had left him in the quiet and beloved Shire. He stared down at the hateful Road, leading back westward – to his home. (*LotR*, FR.I.11)

Torment and loneliness are features of power, which Frodo, Aragorn and Aeneas are familiar with. The Virgilian hero, "troubled by great concerns", feels the weight of a task which runs counter to his will and "conceals in his heart a deep pain".[10] So, before separating from Dido by the order of Mercury, he turns to her and says:

> For, if fate allowed me to lead my life according to my wishes, and to resolve my afflictions of my own free will, first of all, I would dwell in the city of Troy, and venerate the sweet relics of my loved one, the Priam's rooftops would stand high, I would have built the new Pergamum for the vanquished by myself. [...] Not of my own volition, I'm heading to Italy. (*Aeneis* IV 340-44)

On reading these verses, it is hard not to be reminded of Aragorn's words to Éowyn:

> I do not choose paths of peril, Éowyn. Were I to go where my heart dwells, far in the North I would now be wandering in the fair valley of Rivendell. (*LotR*, RK.I.2)

Like Dido, Éowyn is a sovereign, and a woman as well. After the departure of the Rohirrim, she is entrusted with the regency and, like Dido, she falls in love with a man marked by Fate. But Aragorn cannot return her love, so the Lady of Rohan disguises herself as a rider of Rohan and joins the army, this way

---

10 Virgil, *Aeneis* I 208f.: *curisque ingentibus aeger / [...] premit altum corde dolorem.*

resembling another Virgilian character: Camilla Bellatrix, the virgin warrior, who despises marriage and was raised in the woods. Éowyn is an uncommon virgin as well, proud and indomitable,[11] but if Camilla fights openly, with her face uncovered, and falls blinded by a feminine craving for gold (*Aeneis* XI 782), Éowyn conceals her nature and manages to defeat her enemy as a woman. Unlike Camilla and Dido, who represent an obstacle to the Fate's design and are meant to die, Éowyn is saved by the king and she escapes death, because "the hands of the king are the hands of a healer" (*LotR* RK.I.8).[12]

To the *pietas* of Aeneas, who resorts constantly to sacrifices, penitential offerings and cleansing rituals, Aragorn responds with thaumaturgy, the sign of the return of the king.[13] So, for Aragorn and Aeneas, the return is part of a salvific project: the establishment of a new order able to restore peace. Both of them recover sovereignty and, with it, an essential feature of their identity. However, the fate of the Ringbearer is rather different:

> There is no real going back. Though I may come to the Shire, it will not seem the same; for I shall not be the same. (*LotR*, RK.II.7)

A new journey awaits Frodo on the last ship to Valinor, an exile that tastes like a rebirth after the descent into the "underworld" of Mordor. In fact, this consists in a figurative catabasis, which Tolkien represents through the weight of the Ring that drags Frodo down into the abyss,[14] whereas the new heroic catabasis is not for the Ringbearer: Aragorn carries it out on the Paths of the Dead, rewriting the ancient epic model.[15]

---

11 "Thus Aragorn for the first time in the full light of day beheld Éowyn, Lady of Rohan, and thought her fair, fair and cold, like a morning of pale spring that is not yet come to womanhood" (*LotR*, TT.I.6).
12 For an exam of the royal touch as the sign of the return of the priest-king, see Arduini, Barella & Bencistà 2007, 156-60. See also Monda & Simonelli (2002, 178): "Aragorn is the ancient thaumaturge king who returns to reconquer the long lost reign and reaffirm law, peace, and universal reconciliation" (translated by Giampaolo Canzonieri).
13 For a detailed analysis concerning the relationships between the healing power of Aragorn and the historical figures of the thaumaturgical kings, see Arduini, Barella & Bencistà 2007, 149ff., and Morganti 2007, 165-74. Moreover, as far as the healing power of Aragorn is concerned, see Noel 1977, 174ff., and Mathlouthi 2000, 31. About the sacred figure of the king in northern mythology, see Chiesa Isnardi 2008, 445.
14 On the issue of catabasis, between antiquity and Tolkien's corpus, the work of Liau 2003 is essential.
15 Liau 2003, 6 observes that Tolkien does not attempt to recreate the Virgilian Hades, but "to adapt this heritage to the world he imagined, to which he confers an entirely new dimension." About the role of the catabasis that turns Aragorn into a fully-fledged king, and about the relationship with the myth of Oedipus, see Arduini, Barella & Bencistà 2007, 157.

Already in Virgil, the pattern of the journey is closely linked to the descent into the Hades, accorded to Aeneas as the son of Venus and "blood of gods" (*Aeneis* VI, 125). Moreover, the topic of miraculous birth is a recurring heroic motif. Even Aragorn has an extraordinary maternal figure: Gilraen, a woman descending from the Dúnedain. She is the one from whom the long life of the king and his title of *Estel Edain*, the hope of the Dúnedain, are derived.[16] Aragorn and Aeneas, mingling with shadows and walking through a sort of underworld, perform feats that set them apart from other men. Just like the Virgilian *Avernus*, the Gate of the Dead is closed, "no living man may pass it" (*LotR*, RK.I.2). Aeneas is the chosen one, seed of the gods, but also Aragorn is no ordinary man: his lineage is that of the Númenóreans and he is the heir of Isildur, the only one who has the right to summon the Dead and to ask them to follow him.

For Aragorn, summoning the Army of the Dead is the only way. For Aeneas, descending into Hades is necessary to meet the shadow of his father Anchises, in order that he may show him the future of Rome. So, by the parenetic power of prophecy and vision, Anchises encourages Aeneas to fulfil his destiny. The character of Anchises is very close to that of Gandalf. They both play an important, exhortative, and paternal role in relation to the chosen ones. They are the ones who are able to read the signs and show the path. Both had disappeared, swallowed by a real or apparent death, and then they come back halfway through the stories, and their return represents the overcoming of the limit between life and death, between the world of the living and the afterlife. In order to show to Aeneas the souls of his descendants, Anchises gets to the high ground with him, where they can admire the long line of heroes (*Aeneis* VI 752-55). This constitutes one of the most famous passages in the poem, the last advice from Anchises to his son. Tolkien portrays a very similar scene. After Sauron's defeat, Aragorn is crowned king, but he knows that his rule as well as his life will have an end – unlike that of the Elves. Aware of the doubts that beset him, Gandalf leads the king to the top of a mountain from which, as from the high ground of Anchises, he can admire the whole kingdom. From there, as Anchises does, Gandalf shows Aragorn the future:

---

16 Cf. *LotR*, App. A.III. For the role of Aragorn as heir of Elendil and about the names of the king cf. Arduini, Barella & Bencistà 2007, 150ff.

> This is your realm, and the heart of the greater realm that shall be. [...] and it is your task to order its beginning and to preserve what may be preserved. (*LotR*, RK.II.5)

But Aragorn asks for "a sign that it will ever be otherwise" (*LotR*, RK.II.5), so Gandalf invites him to look back, and there is a White Tree growing before the king, a symbol of rebirth.[17]

> And Aragorn planted the new tree in the court by the fountain, and swiftly and gladly it began to grow; and when the month of June entered in it was laden with blossom. 'The sign has been given.' (*LotR*, RK.II.5)

The symbolism of the sacred tree also occurs in the story of Latinus, the Italic king and father of Lavinia, of whom Aeneas will become son-in-law:

> There was a laurel [*laurus*], in the middle of the palace [...] with sacred leaves, guarded with reverence for many years. It was said that father Latinus had found it, while he was building the initial bases of the fortress; then he dedicated it to Phoebus, and from it, he called the settlers "*Laurentes*". (*Aeneis* VII 59-63)

The *laurus*, consecrated to Phoebus, the god of the sun, becomes the symbol of the city. As in Tolkien, even here the king discovers it first, and he plants it in the heart of the kingdom. Going back to the mythical origins of the White Tree, we will find its progenitors in Valinor: Telperion and Laurelin. It is from these two trees that the moon and the sun were born, respectively.[18] Therefore, even in the Tolkienian mythology, the sacred trees are linked to an astral symbolism, and specifically to that concerning the sun. Furthermore, both of them play a prophetic role. If Nimloth, the White Tree, responds to the request for a sign made by Aragorn, the connection with Phoebus makes the laurel of Latinus an auspicious plant, able to portend the arrival of Aeneas.[19]

In their works, therefore, Virgil and Tolkien reinterpret reality with the means of their own culture and they revamp the truth, the former drawing it from

---

17 *LotR*, RK.II.5. The White Tree was brought to Middle-earth, with the Seven Seeing Stones, by the exiles descended from Númenor. Cf. *S*, Ak.
18 Cf. *S*, RPTA, where the tales about the Rings of Power and the Third Age come to a conclusion. Please note the assonance between the *laurus* of Phoebus and the name *Laurelin* that Tolkien has chosen for the Tree of the Sun.
19 Prophecy is another theme common to Virgil and Tolkien. It occurs frequently in the journey of Aeneas towards Latium, providing concrete signs and divine responses, and it structures the journey of the Fellowship, not only through enigmas and predictions but also through two magical objects: the palantír and the Mirror of Galadriel.

the solemnity of the myth, the latter from the belief that human imagination derives from divine inspiration and thus is able to capture one of its sparks, although in an imperfect form.[20]

However, the difference remains significant, starting with the literary form: the hexameter for Virgil, the verse of the classical epic tradition, versus the prose of the novel for Tolkien, though interspersed with songs and poems.

It would therefore be superficial to reduce the Tolkienian composition to the genre of the novel. It is rather a harmonious unity of content and style that does include poetic elements, ballads, and songs, in accordance with their known epic models. Furthermore, both works share what Tolkien himself considered a quality able to make a literary work great, no matter its form or genre, a quality which he had found in Virgil's *Aeneid*: the "impression of depth" (Shippey 1992, 203).

Virgil and Tolkien did not write works of escape or disengagement. Probably, their inclination to rethink the real derived from the experience of war: the internal conflicts that rent Rome at the time of Virgil, and World War I that Tolkien experienced first-hand.

In response to these developments, Virgil celebrated Augustus as the restorer of the peace, of an order that the war had torn, and Tolkien expressed in the only way he knew his moral vision of life and world, and suggested a way to escape death: memory.[21]

---

20 Cf. Monda & Simonelli 2002, 24.
21 Cf. *Letters* no. 211 to Rhona Beare: "But I might say that if the tale is 'about' anything (other than itself), it is not as seems widely supposed about 'power'. [...] It is mainly concerned with Death, and Immortality; and the 'escapes': serial longevity, and hoarding memory."

Bibliography

ARDUINI, Roberto, Cecilia BARELLA, and Giacomo BENCISTÀ (eds.). *Paesaggi della Terra di Mezzo. Immaginario naturale e radici culturali nell'opera di J.R.R. Tolkien*. Rome: Aracne Editrice, 2007.

BETTINI, Maurizio. "Un'identità 'troppo compiuta'. Troiani, Latini, Romani e Iulii nell'Eneide." *Materiali e Discussioni per l'analisi dei testi classici* 55. Pisa and Rome: Fabrizio Serra Editore, 2005, 77-102.

BETTINI, Maurizio and Mario LENTANO. *Il mito di Enea. Immagini e racconti dalla Grecia a oggi*. Turin: Einaudi, 2013.

CARPENTER, Humphrey. *J.R.R. Tolkien: A Biography*. New York: Houghton Mifflin, 2000.

CHIESA ISNARDI, Gianna. *I miti nordici*. Milan: Longanesi, 2008.

DE TURRIS, Gianfranco (ed.). *"Albero" di Tolkien. Come Il Signore degli Anelli ha segnato la cultura del nostro tempo*. Milan: Bompiani, 2007.

FLIEGER, Verlyn. *Interrupted Music. The Making of Tolkien's Mythology*. Kent, OH: Kent State University Press, 2005.

"Mito e verità nel *legendarium* tolkieniano." Lecture held on 25th November 2011 during the *Tolkien Seminar* in Modena, organized by Istituto Filosofico di Studi Tomistici and Associazione Romana Studi Tolkieniani. Available at http://www.jrrtolkien.it/wp-content/uploads/2012/03/Saggio_Flieger.pdf (Accessed 31/08/2018), 2011. Revision of the chapter "Points of Views: Whose Myth Is It?" in Flieger 2005.

LIAU, Nicolas. "La catabasi: J.R.R. Tolkien e la tradizione antica." Available at http://www.jrrtolkien.it/wp-content/uploads/2011/08/La_catabasi_di_Tolkien-p.pdf (Accessed 31st August 2018), 2003. Translated by Associazione Romana Studi Tolkieniani from *La catabase: Tolkien et la tradition antique*, available at link http://www.tolkiendil.com/essais/influences/catabase, (Accessed 31/08/2018).

MATHLOUTHI, Paolo. "L'idea di regalità sacra." *Minas Tirith* 9 (2000): 31-35.

MONDA, Andrea and Saverio SIMONELLI. *Tolkien. Il signore della fantasia*. Milan: Frassinelli, 2002.

MORGANTI, Adolfo. "Un giorno un Re verrà...." *"Albero" di Tolkien. Come Il Signore degli Anelli ha segnato la cultura del nostro tempo*. Ed. Gianfranco De Turris. Milan: Bompiani, 2007. 165-174.

NOEL, Ruth S. *The Mythology of Middle-earth*. Boston: Houghton Mifflin, 1977.

Picone, Giusto. "Il viaggio e il malinteso. Strutture spazio-temporali nella prima ecloga di Virgilio." *Pan* 9 (1989): 29-41.

Respinti, Marco. "Nel segno di Snorri. Le fonti letterarie di J.R.R. Tolkien." *"Albero" di Tolkien. Come Il Signore degli Anelli ha segnato la cultura del nostro tempo*. Ed. Gianfranco De Turris. Milan: Bompiani, 2007, 51-67.

Shippey, Tom. *The Road to Middle-earth. How J.R.R. Tolkien Created a New Mythology*. London: Grafton, 1992.

Virgil. *Aeneid*. In *P. Vergili Maronis: Opera*. Ed. Rogers A.B. Mynors. Oxford: Oxford University Press, 1969.

Tolkien and Authors from the Middle Ages

Valérie Morisi

Stories of Wonders and Wanderings: *The Hobbit* and *The Travels of Marco Polo*

Introduction

Considered to have been a bestseller of its time,[1] *The Travels of Marco Polo* can be seen as the travel story par excellence. Rustichello da Pisa, a writer of tales of chivalry,[2] composed it in collaboration with Marco Polo. The original was written in a hybrid form of Old French that contains numerous Italian elements.[3] Marco Polo, a merchant from Venice, and Rustichello met in 1298 when they were both in the Genoese prison. The following year the fruit of their collaboration appeared.[4] It has been supposed that the text was not finished, since the ending does not match the opening, and the narrator frequently returns to subjects that had already been dealt with in order to add further information.[5] The original title is not known and, as a consequence, it is referred to by different names. One of the most popular ones is *Il Milione* ("The Million"), derived from the nickname of the Polo family, Emilione.[6] *Il Milione* is many things at once: a romance, a merchant's handbook, an ethnographic treatise, an itinerary, and a diplomatic report.[7] So is *The Hobbit*, which follows the itinerary of Bilbo Baggins' journey, during which Bilbo will often play a diplomatic role. Furthermore, J.R.R. Tolkien's accuracy in depicting the peoples of Middle-earth can easily recall the care of the ethnographer, though a fictional one.

---

1 Cf. Lopez 1979, 61.
2 Bertolucci Pizzorusso 2008, ix.
3 Benedetto 1962, xxx.
4 Benedetto 1962, ix.
5 Benedetto 1962, xi.
6 Benedetto 1962, xi.
7 Benedetto 1962, xiv.

Tolkien and the Journey

Tolkien had already written about journeys long before *The Hobbit*, as we know from the 1967 letter that his son Christopher quotes in his discussion of the tale of Eärendel in *The Book of Lost Tales* (*BLT 2*). The poem about the mariner, which the Professor had written before or in 1914, became the starting point for the development of his larger mythology.[8] Christopher Tolkien, Tolkien's youngest son and literary executor, provides four additional poems that deal, in different ways, with the half-elven mariner, all of them preceding *The Hobbit* by far: "Éalá Éarendel Engla Beorhtast" (aka "The Last Voyage of Eärendel"),[9] "The Bidding of the Minstrel", "The Shores of Faëry or Ielfalandes Strand" (aka "The Shores of Elfland"), and "The Happy Mariners".[10]

But the journey of Eärendil leads him across the sea, and it is very different from the one undertaken by Bilbo, which is influenced in several parts by Tolkien's journey to Switzerland in 1911.[11] Noticeable parallels are to be found in connection with the attempted crossing over the Misty Mountains, especially in the fourth chapter, "Over Hill and Under Hill", and in the sixth, "Out of the Frying-Pan into the Fire". Anderson quotes a letter of Tolkien dated 1967-68, in which the author states clearly the biographical origin of the events taking place after the departure from Rivendell. The memory of his sojourn in the Swiss Alps seems to have been still very present in Tolkien's mind not only when he wrote *The Hobbit*,[12] but also when he drew his mountains.

The journey will continue to be a recurrent theme in Tolkien's works, both in poetry with *Imram*,[13] inspired by the *Navigatio Sancti Brendani*, and in prose with the extraordinary journey of Frodo and the Fellowship of the Ring in his famous masterpiece, *The Lord of the Rings*.

---

8   The date for "The Last Voyage of Eärendel" is debated: Christopher Tolkien states before 1914 (*BLT 2*, 266), but Carpenter (2016, 103), for example, claims that the poem was written in 1914 and, most recently, Garth (2003, 45) dates the origin of the poem to 24 September 1914.
9   Éarendel is the original Anglo-Saxon spelling. In the different parts of *The History of Middle-earth* this name has different spellings: Éarendel, Earendel, Eärendel, Earendil, Eärendil.
10 *BLT 2*, 267-76.
11 As Anderson points out in Anderson 2002.
12 Anderson 2002, notes nos.1 and 6 in *H* IV and VI.
13 Gulisano 2004.

Similarities Between the Two Works

I want to stress that I do not assume a direct influence for all the elements that will be discussed later. Since both works are tales of journeys in wonderful lands (as the title of my essay states), they share many elements that deserve to be examined. Also, we cannot exclude the presence of possible echoes, especially in the light of the first drafts describing Bilbo's adventures. In the initial draft of the story we find names like China, Gobi Desert, Hindu Kush.[14] The first two places, in particular, are part of Marco Polo's journey. When Gandalf and the dwarves gather in Bilbo's home to discuss a plan and to decide on the hobbit's suitability as a burglar, we read in the earliest drafts the following exchange: "Tell me what you wish me to do and I will try it – if I have to walk from here to [cancelled: Hindu Kush] the Great Desert of Gobi and fight the Wild Wire worm<s> of the Chinese" (Rateliff 2008, 9). This was later changed to: "Tell me what you want me to do, and I will try it, if I have to walk from here to the last desert in the East and fight the Wild Wireworms of the Chinese" (Rateliff 2008, 40). Every direct reference to reality disappears in the final version of the work.

It is very difficult to reach a conclusive assessment of the relationship between the two works, but it seems probable that Tolkien took at least some inspiration from the genre of the traveller's tale, so that a comparison of the two texts will yield at least some analogies, if not direct sources.

The observed resemblances concern mainly three aspects: the protagonists, the wonders (divided into wonders of nature and man-made wonders), and textual characteristics.

The Protagonists

The protagonists of the two texts show many similarities. Both come from wealthy families, both are learned, and both serve rulers. Marco Polo thus not only exhibits the remarkable knowledge of the medieval merchants,[15] but we are told that he has been studying also the languages, literature and traditions

---

14 Cf. Rateliff 2008, 17.
15 Lopez 1979, 52-73.

of the Tartars,[16] whereas Bilbo becomes one of the chroniclers of the War of the Rings and a translator of Elvish lore and literature. Marco Polo serves the "Grande Kane"[17] for twenty-seven years, whereas Bilbo joins the company of Thorin Oakenshield, King under the Mountain by birthright. In the end, they leave their masters to return home, concluding their journey.

The Travels of Marco Polo does not spend much time describing the economical situation of the Polo family, except for some information necessary to justify the journey, whereas the public office of Marco Polo is highlighted.[18] Likewise, even though Bilbo comes from a wealthy family and becomes, at the end of the journey, even richer, it is his role in the Dwarves' company that is highlighted. Bilbo himself often plays down the value of gold compared to other (simpler) delights,[19] an attitude that is explicitly commented on even by Thorin on his deathbed.[20]

At the beginning of both texts, the protagonist's fathers are mentioned, Niccolò Polo[21] and Bungo Baggins, respectively. The readers are given a short characterization of them, and *The Travels of Marco Polo* also mentions Matteo Polo, Marco's uncle, and in *The Hobbit* a passing reference to Bilbo's mother, the famous Belladonna Took.

Another resemblance, even though it does not involve directly Marco Polo, but rather his father and his uncle, can be found in the great amazement caused by the appearance of a "latino",[22] never seen before, at the court of the Great Khan. In the same way the hobbit Bilbo is a representative of a people almost unknown outside of the Shire (with the exception of the surrounding area), and this often leads to confusion – to the advantage of the company (e.g. when he meets the three Trolls[23] or in his encounter with Smaug[24]).

---

16 See Polo *Il Milione*, 19.
17 See Polo *Il Milione*, 21.
18 Bertolucci Pizzorusso 2008, xiii.
19 *H* XIII.
20 *H* XVIII.
21 Polo *Il Milione*, 5.
22 Polo *Il Milione*, 9.
23 *H* II.
24 *H* XII.

However, we must also point out some differences between the two adventurers. Thus, the two protagonists differ in age. Bilbo is more or less fifty years old when his adventure begins,[25] whereas we can infer from the text that Marco Polo is only seventeen.[26] In *The Hobbit*, Bilbo often feels homesick, whereas this aspect does not appear in *The Travels of Marco Polo*, which might be due to the text's vicinity to the genre of "Practice of Commerce". This missing element has been somehow elaborated in an imaginative way by Italo Calvino in his book *Invisible Cities*, which was inspired by *The Travels of Marco Polo*.

Wonders

The narrator of *The Travels of Marco Polo* warns us right from the start that we will meet wonders such as no one before Marco Polo has ever seen:

> Ma io voglio che·vvoi sappiate che·ppoi che Iddio fece Adam nostro primo padre insino al dì d'oggi, né cristiano né pagano, saracino o tartero, né niuno huomo di niuna generazione non vide né cercò tante maravigliose cose del mondo come fece messer Marco Polo.[27]

> It must be known, then, that from the creation of Adam to the present day, no man, whether Pagan, or Saracen, or Christian, or other, of whatever progeny or generation he may have been, ever saw or inquired into so many and such great things as Marco Polo above mentioned.[28]

In the world described by Marco Polo, nature offers countless spectacular sights, including mountains full of treasures. One mountain in particular is rich in diamonds, but extremely dangerous due to the presence of terrible and venomous snakes.[29] This description reminds the reader, of course, of the parallel in *The Hobbit*, with a dragon guarding a treasure – and the similarity increases in a later episode. In the Caragian province, the snakes show greater affinity to what we would call dragons than our "normal snakes":

> Sapiate per vero che·llì vi n'à di lunghi .x. passi, e sono grossi .x. palmi: e questi sono li magiori. Elli ànno due gambe dinanzi, presso al capo, e non ànno piede, salvo un'unghia fatta come di leone; lo ceffo à molto grande, lo naso magior

---

25 *H* I.
26 Polo *Il Milione*, 14.
27 Polo *Il Milione*, 4.
28 Polo *Travels*, 9.
29 Polo *Il Milione*, 262-63.

ch'un gran pane, la bocca tale che bene inghiottirebbe un uomo al tratto, li denti grandissimi; ed è sì ismisuratamente grande e fiera, che no è uomo né bestia che no la dotti e non n'abbia paura.[30]

Here are seen huge serpents, ten paces in length, and ten spans in the girt of the body. At the fore part, near the head, they have two short legs, having three claws like those of a lion, the face is very wide, with a nose larger than a fourpenny loaf and very glaring. The jaws are wide enough to swallow a man, the teeth are large and sharp, and their whole appearance is so formidable, that neither man, nor any kind of animal, can approach them without terror.[31]

During his journey, the Venetian notices many unusual-looking birds, even though no one can match the talking birds of *The Hobbit*; there is, however, a reference to eagles in the Polo's work which deserves particular attention in our context. We are told that the Khan hunts with eagles of extraordinary size, so that they can chase deer, foxes, roe deer and even wolves. While mentioning animals like deer, representing the most common herbivores hunted, seems understandable and merely the fact that they are hunted by eagles is exceptional, the reference to wolves appears far stranger.[32] There is a clash between these two fearsome predators also in the sixth chapter of Bilbo's adventure, where the eagles (far bigger than real ones) save the hobbit and his company from the wolves that besieged them, scattering the enemies with whirlwinds created by their wings.[33] Eagles and wolves fight against each other also in the Battle of the Five Armies.[34]

We can attempt to explain the difference between the creatures of *The Travels of Marco Polo* and those belonging to Middle-earth by using, in the broadest sense, the concepts of Tzvetan Todorov, namely the "fantastic-uncanny" and the "marvellous". The first one refers to something that seems supernatural, but for which we are given later a rational explanation,[35] as it happens in Polo's work for animals such as the griffins.[36] Todorov uses Jan Potocki's *The Manuscript Found in Saragossa* to illustrate this category, since all wondrous events find, in the end, rational explanations. The second term is not characterised by the

---

30 Polo *Il Milione*, 185.
31 Polo *Travels*, 246 (adapted).
32 Polo *Il Milione*, 141.
33 *H* VI.
34 *H* XVII.
35 Todorov 1975, 43.
36 Polo *Il Milione*, 289.

attitude towards the supernatural, but by the nature of the object in question itself. As an example, Todorov takes the fairy tale.[37] But the case of Tolkien's work is indeed more complex, since the effect of the marvelous is strengthened by Bilbo's astonishment at what he sees. Thus the Elves and Smaug are not only extraordinary for the reader, but also for Bilbo, who is part of a world from which we are excluded. We are dealing with a new level of the marvelous, with the amazement of the amazing.

The Travels of Marco Polo deviates from what was previously the norm for medieval travel literature dealing with wonderful journeys: it is no longer concerned predominantly with the monsters that the adventurer encounters, but above all with the people Polo meets. He starts noticing the man-made wonders coming from various cultural domains of the peoples he visits.[38] Starting with the description of buildings, those of the royal palaces deserve particular attention. An example is the city of Giandu, built by Kublai Khan. It contains some of his mansions, including the one made of reeds where the Khan lives during the summer months. This reed-mansion can be dismantled and rebuilt as he pleases, and is, thanks to protective spells, never hit by storms.[39] The narrator also describes the Khan's palace in Canbalu, huge and composed of many smaller palaces, near which we find the abode of his grandson, who will succeed to the throne.[40]

The same happens in *The Hobbit*, which opens with the description of Bilbo's home[41] and introduces the reader to the comforts of a hobbit-hole. Further examples for such anaologues are the description of Beorn's house,[42] as well as the subterranean halls of the Elvenking,[43] which Tolkien drew several times himself.

In *The Travels of Marco Polo* we have frequent mention of magicians and enchanters, even though no one plays such a central role as Gandalf does in *The Hobbit*. There are also individuals called "istarologi",[44] a term which in this

---

37 Todorov 1975, 53-54.
38 Classen 2012, 29-30.
39 Polo *Il Milione*, 108ff.
40 Polo *Il Milione*, 126ff.
41 *H* I.
42 *H* VII.
43 *H* VIII-IX.
44 Polo *Il Milione*, 116.

context gains particular importance, considering that in the other works set in the Middle-earth the wizards are called "the Istari".

In *The Hobbit*, as well as in *The Travels of Marco Polo* there are many languages spoken by different peoples. Even though most of these languages remain without a name, they are specifically mentioned when a locality has a tongue of its own that differs from the previous ones.

Work Features

It has been argued that Rustichello did not base *The Travels of Marco Polo* only on Marco Polo's oral report, but that Marco Polo had already made some written notes, as often done by merchant-travellers, and that these notes were also used for the composition of the text.[45] Accepting this supposition, there would be another similarity, since *The Hobbit* is said to be based on Bilbo's notes and written recollections of his travels.

A peculiar characteristic present in both texts is the narrator's direct address to the reader, with sentences that guide his attention. In *The Hobbit* these occur especially in the context of dangerous situations. In *The Travels of Marco Polo* we find apostrophic introductions and conclusions in many chapters,[46] next to reassurances of the truthfulness of the narrative.

If we follow Tolkien's argument from his "On Fairy-stories", we can consider *The Hobbit* to be a fairy story that offers its readers escapism Tolkien's meaning of the word.[47] The Middle Ages looked at stories like Polo's tale with a similar attitude.[48]

One last peculiarity shared is their translation into Latin. When *The Travels of Marco Polo* spread, they were also translated into Latin.[49] The same happened to *The Hobbit* and in 2012 Mark Walker's translation *Hobbitus Ille* was published by HarperCollins.

---

45 Bertolucci Pizzorusso 2008, xii-xiii.
46 Bertolucci Pizzorusso 2008, xiv.
47 *TOFS*, 69ff.
48 Classen 2012, 17.
49 Bertolucci Pizzorusso 2008, x.

Conclusion

Our short discussion has shown some illuminating parallels and analogues on various levels between *The Hobbit*, a fairy-tale, and one of the most famous and widespread works of medieval literature, which is linked to the historical world and part of the literary canon. Therefore it would be desirable to re-evaluate Bilbo's adventures within a larger framework than that of children's literature, according to the high opinion that C.S. Lewis had of Bilbo's adventure.[50]

Bibliography

Primary Sources

POLO, Marco. *Il Milione*. Versione toscana del Trecento. Critical edition edited by Valeria Bertolucci Pizzorusso. Milan: Adelphi, 2008.

The Travels of Marco Polo the Venetian. London: J.M. Dent and Sons; New York: E.P. Dutton, 1908.

Secondary Sources

ANDERSON, Douglas A. (ed.). *The Annotated Hobbit*. Revised and expanded edition. London: HarperCollins, 2002.

BARONI, Pietro, Caterina ISOLDI, Edoardo RIALTI, and Mattia LUPO (eds.). *Uno sguardo fino al mare*. Rimini: Il Cerchio, 2004.

BENEDETTO, Luigi F. *La tradizione manoscritta del "Milione" di Marco Polo*. Turin: Bottega d'Erasmo, 1962.

BERTOLUCCI PIZZORUSSO, Valeria. "Prefazione." In Marco Polo. *Il Milione*. Versione toscana del Trecento. Critical edition edited by Valeria Bertolucci Pizzorusso. Milan: Adelphi, 2008 vii-xxii.

CALVINO, Italo. *Le città invisibili*. Milan: Arnoldo Mondadori Editore, 2007.

CARPENTER, Humphrey. *J.R.R. Tolkien. A Biography*. London: HarperCollins, 2016.

CHANCE, Jane (ed.). *Tolkien the Medievalist*. London and New York: Routledge, 2003.

---

50 See Anderson 2002, 17-18.

CLASSEN, Albrecht. "The Epistemological Function of Monsters in the Middle Ages. From *The Voyage of Saint Brendan* to *Herzog Ernst*, Marie de France, Marco Polo and John Mandeville. What Would We Be Without Monsters in Past and Present!" *Spazi del mostruoso. Luoghi filosofici della mostruosità*. Eds. Simone Guidi and Antonio Lucci. *Lo Sguardo* 9 (2012): 13-34. http://www.losguardo.net/public/archivio/arch_09.html (Accessed 17/9/18).

FLIEGER, Verlyn. "'There Would Always Be a Fairy-Tale'. J.R.R. Tolkien and the Folklore Controversy." *Tolkien the Medievalist*. Ed. Jane Chance. London and New York: Routledge, 2003, 26-35.

GARTH, John. *Tolkien and the Great War. The Threshold of Middle-earth*. London: HarperCollins, 2003.

GUIDI, Simone and Antonio LUCCI (eds.). *Spazi del mostruoso. Luoghi filosofici della mostruosità*. (*Lo Sguardo* 9), 2012. http://www.losguardo.net/public/archivio/arch_09.html (Accessed 17/9/18).

GULISANO, Paolo. "L'Imram di Tolkien." *Uno sguardo fino al mare*. Eds. Pietro Baroni, Caterina Isoldi, Edoardo Rialti, and Mattia Lupo. Rimini: Il Cerchio, 2004, 31-40.

LOPEZ, Robert S. "The Culture of the Medieval Merchant." *Medieval and Renaissance Studies. Proceedings of the Southeastern Institute of Medieval and Renaissance Studies*. Vol. 8. Ed. Dale B.J. Randall. Durham: Duke University Press, 1979, 52-73.

RANDALL, Dale B. J. (ed.). *Medieval and Renaissance Studies. Proceedings of the Southeastern Institute of Medieval and Renaissance Studies*. Vol. 8. Durham: Duke University Press, 1979.

RATELIFF, John D. *The History of the Hobbit Part One: Mr. Baggins*. London: HarperCollins, 2008.

TODOROV, Tzvetan. *The Fantastic: A Structural Approach to a Literary Genre*. Ithaca and New York: Cornell University Press, 1975.

Claudio A. Testi

Tolkien and Aquinas

Introduction

Tolkien, on the one hand, was neither a theologian nor a metaphysical scholar. Thomas Aquinas, on the other hand, was not a writer. However, we consider the comparison of these two classic figures for the following reasons possible and necessary:

- Tolkien knew the work of Aquinas (§1).
- Tolkien's work contains matters of a philosophical nature.
- Tolkien studies often pair up the two men, without a complete overview of their similarities (§2) and differences (§3).[1]

To make this comparison, which will be done in a clear and didactic manner, it is important to consider the following:

- We will focus only on the characteristic points of Aquinas' thinking; therefore, we will avoid, for example, stating the obvious such as that both authors refer to a Creator of everything (Eru/God), this idea being a staple of every Christian thinker and not just Thomas.
- Whenever quotes from *The Silmarillion* are mentioned, one must remember that we do not have a definitive text published by Tolkien, but that the vast material of the *Legendarium* has always been an intricate crossing of different, biased point of views (elves, humans and hobbits).[2]
- Finally, one must remember that Tolkien does not develop a 'real' theology in his writings. However, in the sub-creation of his convincing Secondary

---

1 Among the first to notice the "speculative" similarities between Tolkien and the Thomistic-Aristotelic perspective was Paul Kocher (Kocher 1977). A similar stance is also taken by Franco Manni (Manni 2006). A paper explicitly dedicated to the comparison between Tolkien and Thomistic metaphysics is that of McIntosh 2009, McIntosh 2010, and McIntosh 2017. On Tolkien and Aquinas, see also: Milbank 2008; Milbank 2009; Birzer 2007; Nimmo 2001.
2 On the structure and genesis of the *Legendarium*, see: Flieger & Hostetter 2000; Kane 2009; Wittingham 2007.

World, he does include philosophical elements.³ It is our goal to highlight these features and compare them with Thomas' thinking. Moreover, we will also refer to some aspects outside the *Legendarium* (some of Tolkien's philological ideas, as well as his opinions, deduced from reading his letters), which seem particularly relevant or linked indirectly to the development of Tolkien mythology.

1 Tolkien's Knowledge of St. Thomas Aquinas

I will now sum up some arguments which show that Tolkien was aware of Aquinas' ideas.

1) I own an old edition of the *Summa Theologica*, with each volume bearing Tolkien's signature, and several Tolkien experts (Milbank, Hostetter, Flieger, Hammond & Scull, Collier) have unofficially confirmed the authenticity of the signature. Thanks to Mr Hostetter, I was able to obtain confirmation from Christopher Tolkien that this same edition of the *Summa* is mentioned in a list (written by Professor Tolkien himself) of books, which his father bought in the early 20s. Within this edition of the *Summa*, there are many notes in pencil (grey, blue and red) and also in purple ink. In the books at the English Faculty Library at Oxford, I found various notes written in the margins by Tolkien, using pencils of the same colours. A precise examination of all the annotations has not yet been completed, but we can assert that Tolkien certainly owned, and probably consulted, this important theological work.⁴

2) Father Francis Morgan, Tolkien's legal guardian, had a broad theological knowledge and, as a Catholic priest, must have received a Thomistic education, because the encyclical *Aeterni Patris* (1879) established that every priest must receive an education based on Aquinas' ideas.⁵

3) In the Birmingham Oratory, the religious teaching was relevant, as Tolkien affirms in *Letters* no. 306.

---

3 *Letters* no.153.
4 For more information about this item, see also Testi 2012b.
5 See Bru 2011 and Bru 2018we.

4) King Edward's School was founded by Cardinal Newman, who often quotes Aquinas in his writings[6] (and we should remember that Father Francis was also his Secretary).

5) Carpenter affirms that, during the Inklings meetings, a copy of the *Summa Theologica* was always within easy reach next to a copy of *Beowulf*.[7]

6) C.S. Lewis often quotes Aquinas in his writings.[8]

7) Barfield knew Aquinas' writings well, as is evident from his *Saving The Appearances*.[9] Mrs Flieger has suggested to investigate the notion of participation used by Barfield (he theorises an Original and a Final participation) and its connection with the notion used by Aquinas. I can briefly say that this notion primarily has an ontological content in Aquinas' work. This is different from Barfield's use: for him, it is only (and always) a relationship between human consciousness and the known world.

8) The Inklings also included Father Matthews, a member of the Oxford Dominicans, where Tolkien often attended mass.[10] Even today, these Dominicans are devoted to Aquinas' Teachings.[11]

9) Finally, Christopher Tolkien (in an e-mail quoted by Jonathan McIntosh) affirms that his father knew the books that were written by Jaques Maritain, who was one of the most prominent Thomists of the last century.[12]

2 Similarities

1) A first similarity is linked to the *metaphysics of being*. In the last version of the "Ainulindalë", from 1951,[13] which was subsequently included in the 1977 *Silmarillion* edition by Christopher Tolkien, it is told of how the Ainur develop the symphony initiated by Eru, who, at the end of the music, first

---

6 Cf. Newman 1982, 269, 272.
7 Carpenter 1979, chapter 3.
8 Cf. Lewis 1996, ch. II and VIII; 1973, pp. 19, 21, 110.
9 Barfield 1988, ch. XIII.
10 Carpenter 1979, 186f., West 1998.
11 See McCabe 2009.
12 McIntosh 2010, 29.
13 MuD. The account given in *The Silmarillion* is largely based on this version.

shows them the result of their symphony in the form of an image, and then creates the universe (Eä), thanks to a mysterious Flame Imperishable, which turns this image into reality.

> Ilúvatar said to them: 'Behold your Music!' And he showed to them a vision, giving to them sight where before was only hearing; and they saw a new World made visible before them, and it was globed amid the Void, and it was sustained therein, but was not of it.
>
> [Then] Ilúvatar called to them, and said: 'I know the desire of your minds that what ye have seen should verily be, not only in your thought, but even as ye yourselves are, and yet other. Therefore I say: *Eä!* Let these things Be! And I will send forth into the Void the Flame Imperishable, and it shall be at the heart of the World, and the World shall Be; and those of you that will may go down into it. And suddenly the Ainur saw afar off a light, as it were a cloud with a living heart of flame; and they knew that this was no vision only, but that Ilúvatar had made a new thing: Eä, the World that Is. (*S*, Ainulindalë)

This creation story bears a strong similarity to Thomas' key metaphysical idea, centred on the distinction between intrinsic essence and the act of being (*actus essendi*). To explain this further, we can recall that the Greeks had already discovered that each 'object' is a determined reality (this is a *man*, that is a *horse*, that is a *rose*) and they had attributed this reality to the intrinsic *essence* present in each object. The latter allows for an object to be *of a certain kind* (*man*, for example) and not of another (not a *horse*, nor a *rose*).

In light of this, Thomas further elaborates that, for something to *exist*, it is not enough to have the essence of an object (which merely tells what an object *is*), or the thought of an object (like the Ainur, who only think of the world that Eru visually shows to them), but that it also needs the *act of being*, which transforms an individual's essence into *concrete reality*. It is in this way that the *Ipsum Esse Subsistens* (namely, God: *Summa Theologica* I.q. 4 a.2) creates, having the *actus essendi* participating in everything.

The same happens to Eä: even though it has an essence after the Music ceases (as the Ainur can 'see' *what* they have created), it still needs the intervention of the Flame Imperishable to actually *exist*.[14]

---

14 McIntosh had already noticed this analogy: McIntosh 2010, 53-74; McIntosh 2009, 238; see also McIntosh 2017.

2) In both authors, Eru/God does not remove himself from his creatures 'after' creation (unlike Descartes' God, who creates the universe and then abandons it to its mechanical development), but continues to be intimately present by keeping it in existence.

> The Flame Imperishable is sent out from Eru, to dwell in the heart of the world, and the world then Is, on the same plane as the Ainur, and they can enter into it. But this is not, of course, the same as the re-entry of Eru to defeat Melkor. It refers rather to the mystery of 'authorship', by which the author, while *remaining 'outside' and independent of his work, also 'indwells' in it*, on its derivative plane, below that of his own being, as the *source and guarantee of its being*.
> (Athrabeth, Commentary, Note 11, *MR* 345, emphasis added)

> [...] a thing is said to preserve another 'per se' and directly, namely, when what is preserved depends on the preserver in such a way that it cannot exist without it. In this manner all creatures need to be preserved by God. For *the being of every creature depends on God, so that not for a moment could it subsist, but would fall into nothingness* were it not kept in being by the operation of the Divine power [...] (*S.Th* q. 104 art 1; emphasis added)

However, an important difference between Tolkien and Aquinas concerns pure spirits devoid of any matter: the Ainur/Angels. For Thomas, even angels submit to the principle that, their essence not withstanding, they require an act of being in order to exist; in the *Legendarium*, however, there is no hint of this 'mechanism' in the creation of the Ainur, in which not even the Flame Imperishable plays a part.

3) Both authors unite in asserting that the law of contradiction is the only limitation to the creative omnipotence of the sub-creator, or the Creator Himself. For Thomas, in fact:

> [...] everything that does not imply a contradiction in terms, is numbered amongst those possible things, in respect of which God is called omnipotent [...] (*S.Th.* q.25 a. 3)[15]

Tolkien states this implicitly in *On Fairy-Stories*, and explicitly in a letter:

> [...] Are there any 'bounds to a writer's job' except those imposed by his own finiteness? No bounds, but the law of contradiction, I should think [...] (*Letter* no. 153)

---

15 See Commentary on the Sentences, Lib. I d. 42 q. 2 a. 2; *Summa Theologica* I q. 7 a. 2 e I.25.3.

This principle is 'actuated' in his mythopoiesis. In the history of literature, no other writer has invested so much energy in the sub-creation of an extremely detailed world (geographically, linguistically and historically) exempt from contradictions.

4) Both Tolkien and Aquinas distinguish between *the natural and the supernatural planes*, though these are seen as being in harmony with each other.[16] This is visible in Tolkien's understanding of Fantasy, which he considers a natural attribute, in harmony with reason, but with which man can sub-create (similarly to the Creator of the primary world) Secondary Worlds.

> Fantasy is a *natural human activity*. It certainly does not destroy or even insult Reason; and it does not either blunt the appetite for, nor obscure the perception of, scientific verity.[17] On the contrary. The keener and the clearer is the reason, the better fantasy will it make. (*TOFS* 65, italics added)
>
> Fantasy remains *a human right* (*TOFS* 66, italics added)

And this activity brings us to the narrative of fairy tales; because of their inherent happy endings, they appear to be in perfect harmony with the Gospel's eucatastrophe which, in this case, is a 'tale' that is primarily real.[18]

Similarly, with Thomas, reason is considered separate from faith, which in turn can then deal with issues of natural theology (the so-called *praeambula fidei*), in harmony with Christian Revelation.[19] He therefore can maintain: "grace does not destroy nature but perfects it."[20]

5) On a logical level, we notice how in *On Fairy-Stories*, Tolkien uses analogical terminology.[21] In fact, he speaks of *creation* (a job uniquely for God) and *sub-creation* (the human activity analogical to God's own); he maintains

---

16 This theory is fully developed in Testi 2018.
17 It is not by chance that Tolkien is greatly appreciated among the scientific community, so much so that many of the names given to some new scientific discoveries are Tolkien-inspired (cf. Larsen 2007, 223-234). Henry Gee, editor of the magazine *Nature*, and a Tolkien expert, has even devoted a volume to demonstrate (not without a certain amount of humour) the scientific plausibility of a few 'fantastic' ideas of Tolkien's (for instance, the reproduction of the Ents, the fire of the dragons and so on) (Gee 2004).
18 *TOFS* 78.
19 *Summa Teologica*, I.2.2. ad 1. The idea of assumption of the firstborn, if they had not sinned, is already to be found in Augustine of Hippo (*Supra Genesi ad Litteram* 9,5,6. 10-11).
20 "Gratia non tollit naturam, sed perficit", in II Sent. d. 9 a. 8 ag 3. See.: *ibid.* ad 3; in III Sent. d. 24, q. 1, a. 3A; *S.Th.* I.62.5,co; *De Malo* q. 2 a. 11.
21 See Testi 2015 for further studies.

that *secondary* worlds exist on a different plane, but are still dependent on 'our' *primary* world; if these are well built, they will result in *real secondary worlds*, because they are derived from the *primary*, and are able to create in the reader a *secondary belief*.

In these formulations, it is noticeable how a word (creation, world, truth, belief) is primarily associated with specific subjects (God, existing universe, existing beliefs) and is secondary to others (man, extraordinary worlds, reader). These ideas are then used by Tolkien within his *Legendarium*; for example, when the role of Eru in the history of the world is used analogically to the actions of an author in a story.[22] Now, this linguistic structure is identical to the 'analogy of proportion' elaborated on by Aquinas, which occurs when a certain word (for example, 'being') is associated primarily with a subject (for example, an individual 'substance' like Socrates, that exists, *per se*), and is secondary to another (for example, an 'accident' of a singular substance, which exists only as dependant on something else). For instance, in the sentence, 'Socrates is a being', and 'the-weight-of-Socrates is a being', the word *being* has an analogical meaning (not identical, nor wholly different in each of the two occurrences). First we affirm Socrates and, secondly, his weight, which could not have occurred without Socrates existing in the first place.[23]

6) Finally, it is relevant to remember *Letters* no. 310, where Tolkien outlines a sort of 'theological demonstration' for the existence of God, crossing it with themes of morality and the ultimate meaning of life of an individual, which recalls, in parts, Thomas' fifth way of proving that God exists (*S.Th.* I. q. 2. a.3).

3 Differences

1) The most striking difference between Tolkien's *Legendarium* and Aquinas lies in the relationship between body and soul, or, to use Tolkienian terms,

---

22 See previously quoted text, and Athrabeth 322.
23 See Testi 2004, Testi 2015, for further studies.

between *fëa* and *hröa*. These are conceived, at least from an elven perspective, in a very platonic way, because:

- For the elves, it is said that the *fëa* (soul) can continue to exist even without the body. For example, when an elf has committed too much evil deeds, Mandos can keep an individual *fëa* in his Halls until the end of Arda.[24] Or when the various houseless *fëar* refuse the call of Mandos[25] and remain in Middle-earth; or perhaps the 'Lingerers', who wane by remaining in Middle-earth, which in turn causes their *fëar* to consume their bodies.[26] We are, therefore, very far from Aquinas' idea that every being is the union of body and soul. For Aquinas, the soul separated from the body cannot know of this, unless God imparts this 'knowledge',[27] and cannot even be called a 'person' (being present in a body is an essential part of this definition).[28]

- As for the return of the elves to Middle-earth (even though Tolkien abandons the idea of reincarnation in the children of the elves), it is a problem if an elf can return in a 'new' body, created by the Valar with Eru's permission – at least when looking at it from a Thomistic perspective.[29] For Thomas, in fact, the soul is the substantial form of the 'particular' body to which it belongs (so that, in the dogma of the final resurrection, people will inhabit 'their own' bodies again), and the soul cannot, therefore, be transfered to another one (whether that be a foetus or a more developed living organism).

2) However, we must note that, although Tolkien does operate within a platonic context, he does use an Aristotelic-Thomistic view when he states that the body is not the prison, but the house of the *fëa*, and therefore there will always be a permanent link between the two.[30]

---

24 *MR*, Laws, On the Rebirth and Other Dooms, 222; Converse C 132.
25 *MR* 233.
26 *MR*, Lawsb 224f.
27 *Summa Theologica* I.89.1.
28 *Commentary on the Sentences* Lib. II d. q. 3 a. 2; *Summa Theologica* I.29.1 ad 5.
29 Thomas refuses reincarnation because Man *is* the unity (*single*) of soul *and* body; therefore the soul constitutes the living principle of *that* body, and not of another (*Compendium Theologia*, I ch. 153). There have been writings by Tolkien, published recently, on this topic (Devaux 2015): even in light of these, we can still see the difference between the return of the elves in a new body and the Christian view of the final resurrection in the same body.
30 See Manni 2012.

3) The concept of how evil came into the world is also very different. In the *Legendarium*, evil enters the world at the very beginning of creation, because Eä is the 'actualisation' of the Music of the Ainur, and thus already contains Melkor's 'false note'.[31] For Aquinas, on the other hand, the world was created in perfect harmony and it only becomes corrupted afterwards, due to Original Sin.[32]

Tolkien is very much aware of this difference:

> I suppose a difference between this Myth and what may be perhaps called Christian mythology is this. In the latter the Fall of Man is subsequent to and a consequence (though not a necessary consequence) of the 'Fall of the Angels': a rebellion of created free-will at a higher level than Man; but it is not clearly held (and in many versions is not held at all) that this affected the 'World' in its nature: evil was brought in from outside, by Satan. In this Myth the rebellion of created free-will precedes creation of the World (Eä); *and Eä has in it, subcreatively introduced, evil, rebellions, discordant elements of its own nature already when the Let it Be was spoken.* (*Letters* no. 212 dated 1958, italics added)

4) Another difference to highlight is the nature of death, when understood as the separation of body and soul. For St Thomas Aquinas, "death of man is natural" (*S.Th.* II-II q. 164 a. 1 co),[33] since the body is made up of a substance consisting of opposites, and is therefore corruptible. For this reason Man was also subject to this corruption[34] inside the Earthly Paradise and indepentent of Original Sin. But God provided Adam and Eve with a soul capable of maintaining corporeity unimpaired so that, in the case of Original Justice, the severance of body and soul would have been avoided by virtue of this extrinsic-efficient cause and *not* by nature.[35] According to St Thomas, Original Sin deprived Man of this gift, so death was caused only indirectly, *per accidens*.[36]

---

31 *Letters* no. 212. See Purtill 1984, 119 and following: here, the author, with great honesty and competence, lists (and explains) the biggest differences between Tolkien and Catholic theology.
32 *Summa Teologica* I-II q. 85.
33 See also; *In Johann.* ch. 10 lect. 4; see also *S.Th.* I-II q. 85 a. 5; *De Malo* q.5 a. 5 co; *In Job* ch. 4; *Supra Epistolas ad Romanos* c. 5 lect.3.
34 *In III Sent.* d. 16 q.1 a.2 co.
35 *In III Sent.*; *S.Th* I. q. 97 a. 1; *S.Th.* I q. 102 a. 2.
36 *S.Th.* I-II. q.85 a.5.

This Thomistic thesis of the nature of death is supported by the Catholic Church, which contends:

> The Church's Magisterium, as the authentic interpreter of the affirmations of Scripture and Tradition, teaches that death entered the world on account of man's sin. Even though *man's nature is mortal* God had destined him not to die. Death was therefore contrary to the plans of God the Creator and entered the world as a consequence of sin. (*Catechism of Catholic Church* no. 1008, italics added)

Tolkien, however, at least from 1958-60, states (through the words of Andreth) that death is not the natural condition of Man: "Men are *not* by nature short-lived, but have become so through the malice of the Lord of the Darkness" (*MR* 309). If death is not natural to Man, then he must have originally been immortal by nature. "But the Elves were on their part generally ignorant of the persistent tradition among men,[37] that Men were also by nature immortal" (*MR*, Commentary 332).[38]

But the immortal nature of Man has been refuted by the Catholic Church, which explicitly condemned the following thesis:

- "The *immortality* of the first man was not a benefit of grace, but a *natural condition*"[39]
- "'regard *death no longer as a natural condition of man*, but truly as a just penalty for original guilt' since, [...] it insinuates that *death*, which in the present state has been inflicted as a just punishment for sin by the just withdrawal of immortality, *was not a natural condition of man*, as if immortality had not been a gratuitous gift, but a natural condition,"[40]

Within the theme of death, however, both Tolkien and Aquinas touch upon the original assumption that humans, if they had not sinned, would not have

---

37 In fact, in *Athrabeth*, Tolkien attributes to elven traditions (known by Finrod) the idea of death as a gift to humanity (indeed, that death is tied to human nature), something that he supported until 1958-60: I have further explained this theme in Testi 2012a.
38 The concepts expressed in *Athrabeth*, the apex of Tolkien's thought on the theme of death, will be reaffirmed, unchanged, in various successive writings, as attested to, for example, in the "Notes on Óre" of 1968 and in an interview given to the BBC that same year, where Tolkien, quoting Simone de Beauvoir, affirms that death is not inherent to human nature. Tolkien quotes the author (De Beauvoir 2001, 102): on this quotation, see Vink 2004 and 2008.
39 Denzinger n. 1978/1078, Pius V, 1566-1572, *Errors* of Michael du Bay (Baii). Condemned in the Bull "Ex omnibus afflictionibus,", Oct. 1, 1567, italics added.
40 Denzinger n. 2617/1517, Errors of the Synod of Pistoia. Condemned in the Constitution, "Auctorem fidei," Aug. 28, 1794.

known the separation of soul and body, but would have been removed from Arda (Tolkien), or to the heavens (Aquinas):

> Then basing his argument on the axiom that severance of *hröa* and *fëa* is unnatural and contrary to design, he comes (or if you like jumps) to the conclusion that the *fëa* of unfallen Man would have taken with it its *hröa* into the new mode of existence (free from Time). In other words, that 'assumption' was the natural end of each human life, though as far as we know it has been the end of the only 'unfallen' member of Mankind. (*MR*, Commentary 333)[41]

> Paradise was a fitting abode for man as regards the incorruptibility of the primitive state. Now this incorruptibility was man's, not by nature, but by a supernatural [preternatural in later theology] gift of God. Therefore that this might be attributed to God, and not to human nature, God made man outside of paradise, and afterwards placed him there to live there during the whole of his animal life; and, having attained to the spiritual life, *to be transferred thence to heaven*. (*S.Th.*, I, q. 102, art. 4: italics mine; see *De malo* q.5 a. 5 ad 9)

5) The two perspectives, although aligning in so far as historical events do not happen 'by chance', differ when it comes to the concept of Fate and/or Providence.[42] In the *Legendarium*[43]

   a) Eru fixes and can change *umbar* (fate), in which physical events happen.

   b) These events happen 'by chance, as we say in Middle-earth'.[44]

   c) The reaction of a free will (*lële*) to these events is neither fixed nor included in *umbar*;

   d) Not even Eru knows how free will would react to an event fixed in *umbar*.

The first two points are also shared by Aquinas, because it is God's providence which sustains all historical events. However, for Thomas, free will

---

41 Here Tolkien refers to the Virgin Mary (*MR* 357, note 6) since, in *Letters* no. 212, dated 1958, he states that "The Assumption of Mary, the only unfallen person, may be regarded as in some ways a simple regaining of unfallen grace and liberty."
42 On these themes, see: Shippey 2005, 222 and following this: Flieger 2009; Fornet-Ponse 2010 (in answer to Flieger's article). See Dubs 2004; Birks 2011.
43 See *FFW*, explicitly dedicated to these themes.
44 See *LotR, App. A, III*, 1163; *UT, The Quest of Erebor*.

decisions (points c and d) are still contained within Providence and are 'always' known to God.[45]

> The effect of divine providence is not only that things should happen somehow; but that they should happen either by necessity or by contingency. Therefore whatsoever divine providence ordains to happen infallibly and of necessity happens infallibly and of necessity; and that happens from contingency, which the plan of divine providence conceives to happen from contingency. (Aquinas, *Summa Theologica*, I pars q. 22 art. 4 ad 1)

Conclusion

Neither discussing Tolkien's (implicit) theological ideas nor those of St Thomas Aquinas is easy. When studying Tolkien's *Legendarium*, it is impossible not to touch on theological matters, for which Aquinas is a paramount point of reference. With this paper, I hope to have highlighted the essential similarities and differences between the two perspectives in order to clarify their relationship.

Bibliography

Primary Sources

AQUINAS, Thomas. *Commentary on the Sentences*. Bologna: Edizioni Studio Domenicano, 2001.

Summa Teologica. Bologna: Edizioni Studio Domenicano, 1985.

Opuscola Theologica. Turin: Marietti, 1954.

"Compendium Theologiae." *Opuscola Theologica*. Turin: Marietti, 1954, 9-138.

AUGUSTINE OF HIPPO. "Supra Genesi ad Litteram." *Opera Omina di S. Agostino*, vol. IX/2. Florence: La Città Nuova, 1989.

---

[45] *Summa Theologica* I q. 22 art. 2 ad 4. This does not infringe on individual freedom because God, although knowing in advance all the choices Man "will make", also knows that these will happen in a way that is completely free. To note: distinguishing the method of verification from the verified fact is not a contradiction (ibid. Ad1). See Testi 2018, 119ff. for further studies.

Secondary Sources

ARDUINI, Roberto and Claudio A. TESTI (eds.). *The Broken Scythe. Death and Immortality in the Works of J.R.R.Tolkien*. Zurich and Jena: Walking Tree Publishers, 2012. (English translation of *La Falce Spezzata*. Milan: Marietti 1820, 2009).

BARFIELD, Owen. *Saving the Appearences*. Middletown, CT: Wesleyan University Press, 1988.

BIRKS, Annie. "Augustinian and Boethian Insights in Tolkien's Shaping of Middle-earth: Predestination, Prescience and Free Will." *Hither Shore* 8 (2011): 132-147.

BIRZER, Bradley. "Aquinas." *J.R.R. Tolkien Encyclopedia. Scholarship and Critical Assessment*. Ed. Michael D.C. Drout. London: Routledge, 2007, 21-22.

BRU, José Manuel Ferrández. "'Wingless fluttering': Some Personal Connections in Tolkien's Formative Years." *Tolkien Studies* 8 (2011): 51-65.

"Unlce Curro": J.R.R. Tolkien's Spanish Connection. Edinburgh: Luna Press, 2018.

CALDECOTT, Stratford and Thomas HONEGGER (eds.). *Tolkien's The Lord of the Rings. Sources of Inspiration*. Zurich and Berne: Walking Tree Publishers, 2008.

CARPENTER, Humphrey. *The Inklings*. London: Houghton Mifflin, 1979.

CHANCE, Jane (ed.). *Tolkien and the Invention of Myth*. Lexington, KT: University Press of Kentucky, 2004.

DENZINGER, Heinrich. *Enchiridion Symbolorum*. Bologna: EDB, 1995.

DEVAUX, Michaël. *J.R.R.Tolkien. L'effiges des Elfes*. Paris: Bragellone, 2014.

DROUT, Michael (ed.). *J.R.R. Tolkien Encyclopedia. Scholarship and Critical Assessment*. London: Routledge, 2007.

DUBS, Kathleen E. "Providence, Fate and Chance: Boethian Philosophy in *The Lord of the Rings*." *Tolkien and the Invention of Myth*. Ed. Jane Chance. Lexington, KT: University Press of Kentucky, 2004, 133-144.

FLIEGER, Verlyn. "The Music and the Task: Fate and Free Will in Middle-earth." *Tolkien Studies* 6 (2009): 151-182.

Splintered Light: Logos and Language in Tolkien's World. 2nd edition. Kent, OH: The Kent State University Press, 2002.

FLIEGER, Verlyn and Carl HOSTETTER (eds.). *Tolkien's Legendarium*. London and Westport: Greenwood Press, 2000.

FORNET-PONSE, Thomas. "'Strange and Free': On Some Aspects of the Nature of Elves and Men." *Tolkien Studies* 7 (2010): 67–89.

KANE, Douglas Charles. *Arda Reconstructed*. Bethlehem, PA: Lehigh University Press, 2009.

KOCHER, Paul. *Master of Middle-earth*. New York: Ballantine, 1977.

LEWIS, Clive Staples. *The Allegory of Love*. Cambridge: Cambridge University Press, 2013.

The Problem of Pain. London: HarperOne, 1996.

MCCABE, Herbert. *On Aquinas*. New York: Continuum, 2010.

MCINTOSH, Jonathan S. *The Flame Imperishable. Tolkien, St. Thomas and the Metaphysics of Faërie*. Kettering, OH: Angelico Press, 2017. (based on McIntosh 2009).

"Ainulindalë: Tolkien, St. Thomas, and the Metaphysics of the Music." *Music in Middle-earth*. Eds. Heidi Steimel and Friedhelm Schneidewind. Zurich and Jena: Walking Tree Publishers, 2010, 53-74.

The Flame Imperishable: Tolkien St. Thomas and the Metaphysics of Faerie. Ann Arbor, MI: UMI, 2009 (PhD thesis).

MANNI, Franco. "A Eulogy of Finitude." *The Broken Scythe. Death and Immortality in the Works of J.R.R.Tolkien*. Eds. Roberto Arduini and Claudio A. Testi. Zurich and Jena: Walking Tree Publishers, 2012, 5-38.

Lettera a un amico della Terra di Mezzo. Brescia: Simonelli, 2006.

MILBANK, Alison. *Tolkien and Chesterton as Theologians*. New York: T&T Clark, 2009.

"Tolkien, Chesterton, and Thomism." *Tolkien's The Lord of the Rings. Sources of Inspiration*. Eds. Stratford Caldecott and Thomas Honegger. Zurich and Berne: Walking Tree Publishers, 2008, 187-198.

NEWMAN, John Henry. *Apologia pro vita sua*. Milan: Jaca Book, 1982.

NIMMO, Andrew. "Tolkien and Thomism, Middle-earth and the States of Nature." 2001. http://copiosa.org/Lord_Rings/lord_ring_tolkien.htm (Accessed 16/02/2014).

PURTILL, Richard L. *J.R.R. Tolkien: Myth, Morality and Religion*. San Francisco, CA: Ignatius Press, 1984.

SHIPPEY, Tom. *The Road to Middle-earth*. 3rd edition. London: HarperCollins, 2005.

STEIMEL, Heidi and Friedhelm SCHNEIDEWIND (ed.). *Music in Middle-earth*. Zurich and Jena: Walking Tree Publishers, 2010.

TESTI, Claudio A. *Pagan Saints in Middle-earth*. Zurich and Jena: Walking Tree Publishers, 2018. (English translation of Claudio A. Testi. *Santi pagani nella Terra di mezzo*. Bologna: ESD, 2014).

"Analogy, Sub-Creation and Surrealism." *Hither Shore* 12 (2015): 178-193.

"Tolkien's Legendarium as a meditatio mortis." *The Broken Scythe. Death and Immortality in the Works of J.R.R.Tolkien*. Eds. Roberto Arduini and Claudio A. Testi. Zurich and Jena: Walking Tree Publishers, 2012a, 39-68.

"Logic and Theology in Tolkien's Thanatology." *The Broken Scythe. Death and Immortality in the Works of J.R.R.Tolkien*. Eds. Roberto Arduini and Claudio A. Testi. Zurich and Jena: Walking Tree Publishers, 2012b.,175-192.

"Tolkien, Tommaso d'Aquino e l'analogia." *Divus Thomas* 2 (2004): 73-99.

VINK, Renée. "Immortality and the death of love: J.R.R. Tolkien and Simone de Beauvoir." Ed. Sarah Wells. *The Ring Goes Ever On. Proceedings of the Tolkien 2005 Conference*. Two volumes. Coventry: The Tolkien Society, 2008, 117-127.

"The Wise Woman's Gospel." *Lembas Extra* 2004. 15-40.

WEST, Richard. "Mathew, Fr. Anthony Gervase." *J.R.R. Tolkien Encyclopedia. Scholarship and Critical Assessment*. Ed. Michael D.C. Drout. London: Routledge, 2007, 411-412.

WITTINGHAM, Elizabeth. *The Evolution of Tolkien's Mythology*. Jefferson, NC: McFarland, 2007.

Elisa Sicuri

Tolkien and Malory: Writing a Mythology for England

> I am pleased to find that the preliminary opinions are so good, though I feel that comparison with Spencer, Malory, and Ariosto (not to mention super Science Fiction) are too much for my vanity!
>
> J.R.R. Tolkien, *Letters* no. 145

This is how Tolkien reacted, in a letter to Rayner Unwin, to the bold comparisons made by C.S. Lewis and Naomi Mitchison[1] in praising *The Lord of the Rings* when the first volume was published in 1954. The relationship between the Professor, Malory and, more generally, the whole Arthurian universe has always been a difficult and troublesome one, although it cannot be denied that the series of legends centred around the court of King Arthur had a considerable influence not only on "creative philology" works such as *The Fall of Arthur*, or on academic translations such as *Sir Gawain and the Green Knight*, but also on the whole of Tolkien's *Legendarium*.

It is very likely that Tolkien had come across Malory's best-known work, *Le Morte d'Arthur*,[2] if not during his school years, then almost certainly during his studies at the Faculty of English in Oxford. Furthermore, his close friend C.S. Lewis (as evidenced in his letters)[3] has also shown a keen interest in the English author on more than one occasion.[4] The Arthurian legends would profoundly influence Lewis: he was introduced to Malory by Morris and read and avidly annotated Arthurian tales throughout his life; therefore, the possibility that Tolkien might have been influenced in his readings by that should not be ruled out. However, although Tolkien's work may have been influenced, directly or

---

1 Mitchison 1954.
2 A wide and well organised collection of Arthurian tales which gathers, narrated in a unique prose, a series of tales centred around the characters of King Arthur and the Knights of the Round Table, of which the most important is the search for the Holy Grail.
3 Hooper 2003, no. 153, 94.
4 Lazo 2003, 47-48.

indirectly, by Malory's work, what the two authors had most in common were the events they experienced in their lives.

To date very little is known about Malory's life. We know that he was born into a Warwickshire family of the minor nobility, but his date of birth is uncertain although it is reasonable to believe that he was born towards the end of the Hundred Years' War and lived during the Wars of the Roses (1455-1485). This historic event, just like the First World War in Tolkien's case, profoundly influenced Malory's work. *Le Morte d'Arthur*, therefore, became a litmus test for the complex cultural transformations which defined England during this dark chaotic period of transition from the Middle Ages to the Modern Period. Unlike Tolkien's, Malory's life was far from quiet and virtuous: he was imprisoned several times for a series of "minor" offences and actually wrote *Le Morte d'Arthur* during one of his incarcerations in London. In fact, he spent his last days in prison.

During the second half of the fifteenth century the English monarchy saw the collapse of the traditional certainties which had upheld it for centuries. England in the 15th century went through the worst horrors of war, that can only be compared to the First World War, which Tolkien experienced first-hand. The crisis of the principles of dynastic rights and the gradual rise of the new minor nobility[5] inspired in Malory the need to tell an epic tale in English[6] which would contrast the crisis that the British monarchy was going through at that time with a dignified, heroic king who belonged to a distant and glorious past and who could not only speak to the old aristocracy but also to the new noble class.

---

5 Grummitt 2013, 133: "The Tudor portrait of gloom and doom (which saw 100.000 Englishmen slaughtered, the nobility decimated, and the nation impoverished) has been replaced by one in which gentry culture flourished and the domestic economy grew while fighting was limited in both duration and intensity."

6 It is important to note how, until then, the main works on the *matière de Bretagne* were mostly written in the "oïl" dialect (on the relationship between Malory and the preceding French tradition, see Darrah 1997, 4ff.). The fact that this work was written in a period of transition is demonstrated by Malory's reference to only one French source, which he scrupulously transcribed (although further studies have shown how he also used other versions of Arthurian tales written in English). This need to rely on a purely medieval *authoritative work* (or, in any case, one belonging to "another" time and place) is not alien even to Tolkien. In fact, when talking about his *Legendarium*, the Oxford Professor would often refer to himself not as its *auctor* but its mere *compilator*, who tells other people's tales or stories that, as in NCP, belong to a distant past. To take inspiration from an ancient source, whether real or invented, the presumed impersonality of the author and the shifting of the stories to a time in the distant past, all of these are stylistic expedients that both authors exploit to give more historical accuracy to their work.

The long and complicated process of rewriting, adapting and refining to which Malory and his editors (first and foremost William Caxton) subjected *Le Morte d'Arthur*, reveals a profound awareness of the changing times, a transition that could not however disregard the models of the past. The many other works influenced by Arthurian literature should not be interpreted as a nostalgic revival of medieval literature. However, for Malory the Arthurian revival was a form of defence and glorification of England (the glorious England of the ancient kings as opposed to the corrupt and degenerate country of his time). However, his intention was not to celebrate the splendours of the past just so that he could condemn the present. His aim was to open a constructive debate between past and present, so that the knights of the Round Table could represent once again[7] a model for the kings and queens involved in the bloody conflict between the houses of Lancaster and York. Although the choice to tell the Arthurian tales in a period which was culturally distant from that in which they originated may lead us to believe that this work was actually written for simple entertainment, in actual fact, it was addressed, with a strong didactic purpose, to a cultured audience. The knights of the Round Table are concrete, clearly defined characters, far from the overworked topos of the courtly hero. They are human characters, who are often faced with the same ethical and moral issues as those of the reader, in the same way as Tolkien's hobbits are not at all two-dimensional, "pre-fabricated" heroes, but share some common traits with the reader.

The search for an ancient and idealised image of one's own homeland in contrast with the horrors of war was one of the motivating factors that led Tolkien to create his own *Legendarium*, in particular all the tales that would later merge into the *Silmarillion*. A wealth of studies[8] have demonstrated that the Oxford University

---

7 In the 12th Century the Plantagenet Henry II sought to re-discover the world of King Arthur by finding the remains of the king. It fell to his son, Richard the Lion Heart, who succeeded him in 1189 on the eve of the crusade, to sanction the exhumation and removal of the remains attributed to Arthur and Guinevere to Glastonbury Abbey. The Plantagenets were great admirers of the Breton Cycle as opposed to the Carolingian Cycle favoured by the Capetians of France.
8 Among the most significant ones I would cite: Croft 2004, Garth 2003, Shippey 1995.

Professor's experiences in the trenches,[9] as well as his taking part in the Battle of the Somme, and the premature death in battle of many of his close friends, are all key elements that provide a deeper understanding of the origins,[10] and often the motivations and ethical implications, of the whole of Tolkien's work.

Moreover, we should remember that the beginning of Tolkien's mythopoesis coincided not only with the Great War but also with the end of the "Golden Century" (1813-1914) of the great collectors of myths (from the brothers Grimm to Moe and from Asbjørnsen to Lönnrot) and of the so-called British folklore studies.[11] As far as our specific subject is concerned, we can detect how Tolkien and Malory reacted in a very similar way towards historical upheavals that challenged an entire system of values. Both authors resort to "sub-creation" and to myths in order to deal with adversity and loss.[12]

We could debate forever whether it is also correct to refer to sub-creation in the case of Malory (who does not invent a Secondary World *ex novo*, but recycles well-established narratives), but in both cases we find ourselves faced with ancient themes, re-read and re-interpreted in the light of modern experiences. They did this in order to carefully define and preserve their own identity as well as that of their own nation, even (and especially) by resorting to imaginary elements. Tolkien would dedicate a small part of his writing to the Arthurian cycle before going on to create his own mythology, which would, however, be rooted in an idealised medieval era, while Malory would endeavour to combine a complex oral and written tradition in various languages with certain innovative aspects. However, although they did so in different ways, both Tolkien

---

9 Tolkien actually wrote very little about his personal experience of the trenches. However, there are many images that recall that reality and that we find for example in *The Lord of the Rings*: the putrefied faces floating just beneath the surface of the Dead Marshes; when Frodo and Sam are on Mount Doom, while everything is erupting around them, they wonder whether this is their end; Sam's shock mixed with terror when he sees an Oliphaunt for the first time, etc. (cf. Garth 2003). For other parallels between the work of Tolkien and the author's experience of war (regarding both the First and Second World Wars) see Bonechi & Manni 2005, 26-39.
10 It will suffice to cite a couple of key events: in September 1914, when the war had just begun, Tolkien began work on his "invented mythology" with his first draft of *The Voyage of Eärendel the Evening Star*; in 1916 Tolkien, after falling ill in the trenches, was repatriated, and while he was convalescing in hospital, with the tragic images of the war still fresh in his memory, he wrote *The Fall of Gondolin*.
11 Flieger 2003, 27ff.
12 Flieger 2005, 11: "The great mythologies of the world, through the stories of their gods and heroes, create order (not necessarily benevolent but accessible to human understanding) out of what would otherwise be chaos. Their stories give meaning to the overwhelming events of human existence, providing a context for good and bad fortune, for love and loss and pain and death."

and Malory, by going back to the original source, try to find a "bond" that can hold together the various pieces of a crumbling nation (as well as its cultural identity). However, as Tolkien pointed out in his letters,[13] it was the fact that England could not boast an ancient mythological tradition like the great empires of antiquity. This deficiency motivated him to create a mythology for England which would elevate it to the same level as the other important European cultures.[14] It is, however, crucial to emphasise at this point that it would be inaccurate to think that all of Tolkien's creative life was dominated by his wish to create a mythology for England throughout his career. In his letter from 1951 he was referring specifically to the creative ambitions of his younger self.[15] The older Tolkien had long abandoned this aim: after publishing *The Lord of the Rings*, his main aim would be to complete *The Silmarillion* in order to provide a context of ancient legends and tales (and therefore greater authenticity) for the stories centred around the Hobbits, as well as to refine the philosophical and cosmogonic apparatus of his Secondary World. In fact, as Flieger[16] clarifies, what Tolkien tried to do was to create a quintessentially English mythology. Furthermore, for him this was an extremely important process as a narrator of myths, because it allowed him to experiment with dif-

---

13 *Letters* no. 131: "Since I was a child I have suffered because of the poverty of my beloved country, which did not have its own tales (linked to its language and its land), at least not of the quality that I was after, and which I found (to a certain extent) in the tales of other countries. There were Greek ones, Celtic ones, Romanic ones, Germanic ones, Scandinavian ones, and Finnish ones (which influenced me hugely); but none in English, only poor material for minor folk tales. [...] But at the time (since then I have swallowed my pride) I wanted to create a collection of tales more or less connected to each other [...] which I could simply dedicate to England, my own country." In his 1936 British Academy lecture "Beowulf: The Monsters and the Critics", he also points out: "We know practically nothing about pre-Christian English mythology."
14 Tolkien was not the only English intellectual of his time to regret the lack of mythology in his country. The famous writer, E.M. Forster, in his novel *Howards End* in 1910 has his heroine, Margaret Schlegel, say the following: "Why has not England a great mythology? [...] England still waits for the supreme moment of her literature – for the great poet who shall voice her, or, better still, for the thousand little poets whose voices shall pass into our common talk" (Flieger 2005, 4). In fact, it is not entirely true that England did not have its own mythology: if you think of the story of the giant Albion, son of Neptune, from whom the island takes its name, who together with his brother Bergion (the King of Ireland and the Orkney Islands) overthrew Bardo before being brutally killed by Heracles; or of the famous foundation myth of Brutus, a descendant of Aeneas, narrated by Geoffrey of Monmouth in his *Historia Regum Britanniae* and often used in epic poems (such as Anglo-Norman *Roman de Brut* by Wace or the Middle-English *Brut* by Laȝamon) and by the royal dynasties to reinforce the prestige of one's own lineage (the name *Britannia* is indeed derived from Brutus). In such cases, however, there is a clear desire to draw on other mythologies, especially the Greek-Latin ones (the myth of Brutus faithfully recalls the myth of Aeneas and the founding of Rome) in order to add prestige to one's own origins. Therefore, I hesitate to define these stories as completely original and probably even Tolkien did not perceive them as mythology "of the highest order".
15 See note 13.
16 Flieger 2012, 237-241.

ferent settings and narrative devices as well as the techniques and the problems that arise when moving from an oral story to a written story.[17]

So, just as Tolkien created Arda, Malory wanted to bring together in a single work all the most important stories associated with the "English" hero *par excellence*: Arthur. As already pointed out above, Malory's decision to put into English material normally presented in French in previous centuries was no coincidence. This might seem almost an attempt to reclaim Arthurian literature to make it one of the founding elements of an *ante litteram* English identity. However, it is worth pointing out at this stage that, although Tolkien also worked for a long time on the Arthurian legends, he could not convince himself to accept them as genuinely English and sufficient to fill the void. This was mostly due to the fact that they had not been written in English originally,[18] and it is well known that Tolkien considered the idea of identity closely linked to language and culture.[19]

Creating a mythology for England or, in any case, being inspired by ancient legends such as those of the Arthurian cycle could be seen by Malory as a way of unifying the nation in the face of the nihilism spread by the war. And maybe it was the same for Tolkien, although in his case nationalism was often secondary to the effects that his own personal experience of the war had on him. While Malory's work could be seen as a plea to preserve English culture, Tolkien's was primarily an attempt to process his own experience of the war, perhaps seeking answers (and not merely nostalgia and escapism) in mythopoesis and in the study of ancient tales.

---

17 See Flieger 2011: "[in the *History of Middle-earth*] not only do we see Tolkien creating a mythology for England, but also experimenting with different settings, narrators and narrative devices in order to complete the transition from oral story-telling to the printed word."
18 *Letters* no. 131: "Naturally there was and is the whole Arthurian world, but despite its power it is naturalised in an imperfect way, associated with the land of Britain but not with England; and it does not replace the one I was yearning for."
19 In this case, as Flieger 2005, 4ff., reminds us, it is necessary to make a distinction between *England* and *Britain*: "It was in fact Britain, not England, that was the land of witches and fairies, diminished and degraded remnants of a Celtic mythology far older and more deeply rooted than that comparatively recent polity, England. Britain […] was a larger and older and (at the time when Tolkien and Forster were writing) a more suppressed identity than Engla-lond, the land of the English, established as a nation by successive waves of Germanic invaders from the continent who overwhelmed the earlier and more indigenous populations."

We could say that Tolkien was not only affected by his particularly traumatic experience of the Great War, but in general by the experience of war *per se*, not romanticised but internalised as a painful personal experience. His reflections could be applied to the Second World War (which he also witnessed) as well as to any other conflict with catastrophic consequences.[20] After all, it was not unusual for the politics and propaganda at the beginning of the 1900s, especially as far as dictatorships were concerned, to recall the past, in particular the Middle Ages, to re-interpret it according to what was convenient at that moment in time. Just think of the character of Saint George who kills the dragon, a widely used image in English WWI propaganda aimed at creating a patriotic fervour in young men to encourage them to enlist.[21] Even in these small details we can detect the power and persuasion that are produced by images coming from other eras, which even in modern times are still capable of inspiring strong feelings of belonging and a fascination which transcends the centuries. A fascination that both Malory and Tolkien had definitely recognised and made use of in dark chaotic times.

---

[20] Shippey himself did not see in Tolkien only a writer returning from the First World War but also a veteran of the Second World War, as he belonged to that group of intellectuals "whose subjects were war and evil [...] who wrote in non-realistic modes essentially because they felt they were writing about subjects too great and too general to tie down to particular and recognisable settings", Shippey 1995, p. 85.

[21] There were numerous posters at the time where the hero was depicted beside propagandistic phrases such as: "*Britain needs you at once*". Saint George was used as a symbol even by the powers involved in the conflict including, ironically, Germany.

Bibliography

Primary Sources

MALORY, Thomas. *Le Morte Darthur: The Winchester Manuscript*. Ed. Helen Cooper. Oxford: Oxford University Press, 2008.

Secondary Bibliography

DORSEY, Armstrong. *Gender and the Chivalric Community in Malory's Morte d'Arthur*. Gainesville, FL: The University Press of Florida, 2003.

BATT, Catherine. *Malory's Morte Darthur: Remaking Arthurian Tradition*. New York: Palgrave, 2002.

BEWER, Derek. "*The Lord of the Rings* as Romance." *J.R.R. Tolkien: Scholar and Storyteller: Essays in Memoriam*. Eds. M. Salu and R.T. Farrell. Ithaca: Cornell University Press, 1979, 249-264.

BONECHI, Simone and Franco MANNI. "La complessità dell'atteggiamento di Tolkien verso la Seconda Guerra Mondiale." *Endóre* VII:8, 2005, 26-39.

CHANCE, Jane (ed.). *Tolkien and the Invention of Myth: A Reader*. Lexington, KT: Kentucky University Press, 2004.

(ed.). *Tolkien the Medievalist*. London: Routledge, 2003.

Tolkien's Art: A Mythology for England. London: MacMillan, 1979.

and Alfred SIEWERS (eds). *Tolkien's Modern Middle Ages*. Basingstoke: MacMillan, 2005.

CROFT, Janet B. *War and the Works of J.R.R. Tolkien*. Westport, CT: Praeger, 2004.

DARRAH, John. *Paganism in Arthurian Romance*. Woodbridge: Boydell & Brewer, 1997.

FIELD, Peter J.C. *Romance and Chronicle. A Study of Malory's Prose Style*. Bloomington and London: Indiana University Press, 1971.

FLIEGER, Verlyn. *Green Suns and Faërie. Essays on J.R.R. Tolkien*. Kent, OH: Kent State University Press, 2012.

"Mito e Verità nel Legendarium tolkieniano." Conference held during the *Tolkien Seminar* in Modena, 25th November 2011, Istituto filosofico di studi Tomistici and Associazione Romana di Studi Tolkieniani: http://www.jrrtolkien. it/attivita/letteratura/saggi-e-recensioni/mito-e-verita-di-verlyn-flieger-s/ (Accessed February 15, 2019).

Interrupted Music: the Making of Tolkien's Mythology. Kent, OH: Kent State University Press, 2005.

A Question of Time: J.R.R. Tolkien's Road to Faerie. Kent, OH: Kent State University Press, 2001.

"J.R.R. Tolkien and the Matter of Britain." *Mythlore* 23:2002, 47-59.

"'There would always be a fairy-tale': J.R.R. Tolkien and the folklore controversy." *Tolkien the Medievalist*. Ed. Jane Chance. London: Routledge, 2003, 26-35.

GARTH, John. *Tolkien and the Great War: The Threshold of Middle-earth*. London: HarperCollins, 2003.

GRUMMIT, David. *A Short History of the Wars of the Roses*. London: I.B. Tauris, 2013.

HOOPER, Walter (ed.). *Letters of C.S. Lewis*. Fort Washington, PA: Harvest Books, 2003.

INGHAM, Patricia. *Sovereign Fantasies: Arthurian Romance and the Making of Britain*. Philadelphia, PA: University of Pennsylvania Press, 2001.

LAZO, Andrew. "A kind of mid-wife: J.R.R. Tolkien and C.S. Lewis – sharing influence." *Tolkien the Medievalist*. Ed. Jane Chance. London: Routledge, 2003, 36-49.

MITCHISON, Naomi. "One Ring to Bind Them." Interview in *New Statesman and Nation*, September 18, 1954.

SHIPPEY, Tom. *The Road to Middle-earth: How J.R.R. Tolkien Created a New Mythology*. London: HarperCollins, 2005.

"Tolkien as Post-War Writer." *Proceedings of the J.R.R. Centenary Conference. Keble College, Oxford, 1992. Mythlore* 80 / *Mallorn* 30. Eds. Patricia Reynolds and Glen H. GoodKnight. Milton Keynes and Altadena: The Tolkien Society and The Mythopoetic Press, 1995, 247-252.

WEST, Richard. "The Interlace Structure of the Lord of the Rings" *A Tolkien Compass*. Ed. J. Lobdell. La Salle, IL: Open Court, 1975, 77-94.

Chiara Bertoglio

Dante, Tolkien, and the Supreme Harmony

Introduction

Many are the aspects which Dante and Tolkien have in common, many more the differences between them. The former was a poet who chose to write his epic poetry in the vernacular, the latter a novelist who created new languages; the former, a medieval man who foresaw modernity, the latter a modern man who invented a fantasy "Middle Ages"; the former wrote an almost autobiographical poem, told from the subject's viewpoint, the latter wrote a *legendarium* which is the imaginary mythology of ancient people; the former theorized the role of allegory, the latter distanced himself from its use.[1] Such are a few of the many gaps separating Dante from Tolkien, but, as we will see, none of them is an unpassable abyss.

A comparison of the two has been discussed in various forms by some scholars whose works I will reference in the following pages: Hougthon (1990) has thought-provokingly interpreted the *Commedia* as a fairy-tale, applying Tolkien's theories on the *eucatastrophe* to the loss of Virgil; Seland (2006) compared Dante and Tolkien's perspectives as concerns the problem of evil; Colucci (n.d.) studied their treatment of the motif of "the journey"; Caesar (2006) compared *The Lord of the Rings* to Dante's *Inferno*; DeTardo (2007) touched on the relationship of the two authors within the systematic framework of Michael Drout's *Tolkien Encyclopedia*; Downey (2011) analyzed the influence of some of the *Commedia*'s female characters on the figure of Galadriel. References to Dante are also found in Milbank's writings, particularly in her study of Tolkien and Chesterton's theology (Milbank 2008), and in an unpublished paper presented at the 2012 Tolkien conference in Dublin (Milbank 2012).

---

1 Cf. *LotR*, Preface; however, see also DeTardo (2007, 116) and Caesar (2006, 167-68).

Other studies are also relevant to the topics I will discuss in this essay: research on music in Dante and Tolkien (which I will cite, when pertinent, in the following pages), studies on the influence of medieval philosophy and theology on Tolkien's work,[2] and about the theological vision in Tolkien's and in Dante's works.

It should be clearly stated that Tolkien's appreciation for the poetry of Dante, whom he called a "supreme poet" (*Letters* no. 294), was not free from some perplexity about the human traits of Alighieri ("Dante doesn't attract me. He's full of spite and malice. I don't care for his petty relations with petty people in petty cities"; *Letters* no. 294). Nevertheless, Tolkien himself softened this harsh judgement (which he had formulated orally during an interview of 1967), expressing his admiration for the poet's artistic value, excerpts from whose works were usually read by Tolkien and C. S. Lewis to each other. Tolkien, moreover, had been a member of the Oxford Dante Society for some time.[3]

Tolkien's interest in Dante is amply documented in his writings, both generally and in detail. Both the *Commedia* and Tolkien's narratives take place in worlds which are different from our own, and yet inextricably intertwined with it, both geographically and historically: universes partly parallel to, but also inextricably interconnected with the one we live in. Both Dante and Tolkien make use of the literary worlds they created in order to narrate the Christian history of salvation in a new and very original fashion. In Dante's case, this rewriting is explicit, whereas in Tolkien it is so implicit that it voluntarily avoids all references to religion.[4] As pointed out by Colucci,[5] both the *Commedia* and *The Lord of the Rings* are centred on the topic of the journey, both interior and exterior; topics such as the ascent of a mountain (Dante's Purgatory, Tolkien's Misty Mountains and Mount Doom), the crossing of a forest (Dante's "Selva oscura" and Mirkwood), the descent in the abysses of earth (Dante's "Inferno" and Moria), the swamp ("Malebolge" and the Dead Marshes[6]), the oases

---

2 Dubs 1981; Eden 2003; Houghton 2003; McIntosh 2010; Halsall 2015.
3 Scull and Hammond 2006, 961.
4 *Letters* no. 142: "*The Lord of the Rings* is of course a fundamentally religious and Catholic work; unconsciously so at first, but consciously in the revision. That is why I have not put in, or have cut out, practically all references to anything like 'religion', to cults or practices, in the imaginary world. For the religious element is absorbed into the story and the symbolism."
5 Colucci (n.d.).
6 Cf. Caesar 2006, 168.

("Eden" and Lothlórien), the walled cities of evil ("Dite" and Minas Morgul) and the passing of gates which determine a "before" and an "after" (the doors of Hell and Purgatory, those of Moria and the Black Gate) are central in the respective narratives. Moreover, as pointed out by Houghton (1990), both in the *Commedia* and in *The Lord of the Rings* there are mentors and leaders who play a crucial role for the protagonists: from Virgil to Beatrice and Gandalf,[7] but also Tom Bombadil, Aragorn, and Gollum, together with many others. The influence of the *Dolce stil novo* and its concept of the angelic woman is clearly discernible in some of Tolkien's characters, first of all Galadriel (followed by Arwen), in whom traits of Beatrice and Matelda are found;[8] moreover, aspects of the *cortese* literature have been observed in the figure of Gimli.[9]

As regards the villains, there are descriptions where a physical deformity mirrors the interior crookedness, where the spiritual evil provokes the brutalization of intelligent beings (see Pluto and Gollum, for example[10]), where the barbaric and vulgar – if intelligible at all – language is a sign of moral depravation (the demons and Pluto himself in Dante, the Orcs in Tolkien) and where traits of grotesque buffoonery are found (the devils' names in *Inferno* XXI.118-123 and characters such as Uglúk, Shagrat, and Gorbag.[11] In fact, the devils are fallen angels, and the Orcs are descended from Elves); moreover, Lucifer and Melkor/Morgoth are both extraordinary beings who fell into the furthermost levels of abjection, and are self-confined in the bowels of the earth.

Indeed, if we take into consideration the very *Silmarillion* in which the story of Melkor/Morgoth is told, we find important parallels between the wreckage of Dante's Ulysses and the fate of Númenor. Moreover, Milbank discusses analogies between Gríma Wormtongue and Gerion,[12] between the need for Sam to physically challenge Shelob in order to overcome the obstacle she poses, and the need for Dante and Virgil to climb on Lucifer's "body" in order to exit from Hell,[13] and between the condition foretold to Éowyn by the Witch-King and

---

7 In Downey's view, in fact, the loss of Gandalf in Moria echoes Dantesque elements (Downey 2011).
8 Caesar 2006, Downey 2011, Milbank 2012; cf. also Eden 2003, 87, as regards D. G. Rossetti.
9 Barbiano 2005, Honegger 2017.
10 Notice the use of similar phonemes in their names.
11 Cf. Caesar 2006, 168 and Milbank 2008, 75-76.
12 Milbank 2008, 71-72. For Milbank, both are connected with fraud, and are similar in their physical/spiritual traits (human face, serpentine body, and stinging tails).
13 Milbank 2008, 78-79.

that of the suicides in *Inferno* XIII.[14] Finally, the themes of exile (an existential condition for both Dante and the Elves in *The Silmarillion*, although for different reasons) and of war,[15] together with the philosophical/theological topics of free will and of the nature of evil[16] are crucial in the visions of both authors; moreover, the very concept of "comedy" found in the title of Dante's poem has many points in common with Tolkien's narrative structure.[17]

Though each of these similarities or spiritual proximities would deserve a specific discussion, in this article I decided to focus my attention on a less evident – but not less important – aspect of the Dantesque and Tolkienian epos, i.e. their respective concept of music, with special reference, in Tolkien's case to the first pages of *The Silmarillion*.

Music in the *Commedia*

The theological significance of music in the *Commedia* has been discussed principally by Schurr (1994), De Benedictis (2000) and Ciabattoni (2010). I am basing my own research on their important studies and have tried in turn to develop this topic in an article[18] to which I refer the interested reader. Dante organizes the presence of music in the *Commedia* in an entirely consistent fashion, and it becomes an instrument for transmitting deep theological truths; in brief, music is seen as a symbol of love, both as regards the mystical love (God's for human beings and theirs for God) and of the love/*agape* among human beings. Following the scheme suggested by Boethius, who divided music into the categories of *instrumentalis*, *humana* and *mundana*, Dante creates a progression of perfection in the three ultramundane realms. In Hell, we find a cacophony originating from the absence of love: souls and demons

---

14 Milbank 2008, 104.
15 Cf. Seland 2006, 2.
16 DeTardo 2007, 116.
17 As maintained by Milbank 2008, 112. Cf. also Milbank 2008, 125: "The good news is the evangelium of Tolkien's eucatastrophe, and the very excess of the story validates its status as a divine gift." Elsewhere, Milbank (2008, 112) points out that "our own desire for a reunion of the characters beyond the separations of the last chapter is to provoke in us a longing for a happy ending that does not negate but fulfils the 'natural desire for the supernatural' that both Augustine and Aquinas taught." Such a desire is very similar to the listening process of music, which is based on the dynamism between tension and relaxation and is therefore highly pertinent to our discussion of Melkor's "discordant" music.
18 Bertoglio 2016, 11-40.

are closed in their own hatred, and condemned to an existence deprived of beauty, solidarity, and empathy.[19] The only musical element which survives the infernal anguish is *rhythm*, a basic element of music, represented here by the micro- and macro-rhythms of punishments and torments. In fact, even the extreme disharmony of Hell is, for Dante, a component of universal harmony, since the punishment of evil is part of God's justice and order, which sustain the building of the universe. The *instrumentalis* element of music is represented, in Dante's *Inferno*, by the mentions of instruments, and even by the degradation of human beings (whose original vocation is to "become music", according to the full meaning of *musica humana*) who become musical instruments (as in the case of Mastro Adamo, *Inferno* XXX.49ff., whose "body" seems to be a lute but sounds like a drum).

In the *Purgatorio*, *musica humana* has an ambivalent function, similar to love itself. It is, in Ciabattoni's opinion (2010, 97ff.), mainly an instrument for the "healing" of both the soul and of society. Through the monodic, unison singing of the liturgical repertoire – known as "Gregorian" – the penitent souls learn to "intone" themselves with each other. In place of the attempts to overcome the other's voice and of the uncontrolled cries found in Hell, here we find the effort to "take the note" from one's neighbour, to intone one's voice with that of the other, to rebuild the unity of intentions, identified in the common desire for Heaven, which characterizes and unifies the purgatorial society. Moreover, monodic chant is a symbol of penance not only by virtue of the exertion it requires (to listen, to intone) but also of its liturgical function: during times of penance, it was the only musical form admitted in the Church's rites. On the other side, however, Purgatory is not free from the experience of temptation and ordeal; thus, the *femmina balba* (the "stammering woman", *Purgatorio* XIX.7ff.), with her siren-like seducing singing, is similar to the wrongly-addressed loves of human life, which reveal their corrupting and negative power in a second moment. Casella's song, instead, is "out of place" in the ante-Purgatory, in Schurr's opinion, not because there will be "no more" love songs in Purgatory, but rather because it is "not yet" the time for enjoying them. The ecstasy induced by the singer's tune is similar to the *eternità di tempo fòre* ("eternity outside time",

---

19 It may be interesting to cite Screwtape's contempt for both music and silence in *The Screwtape Letters* by C. S. Lewis. See Lewis 1961, 102-3.

Paradiso XXIX.16) enjoyed by the blessed souls in Heaven, but for which the penitent souls are not yet ready.

In Paradise, where *musica mundana* is found, Dante employs the musical symbol of polyphony (which was still a recent practice at his time) to signify the perfect balance of love and freedom, finally pacified and coincident. The individual melodic lines of polyphony obey the laws of counterpoint, embodied in the limitations posed by each part to the others; at the same time, the listener must receive an impression of total liberty and fluidity, whereby the coordination of the melodic lines is not perceived as an artifice but appears as the result of an organic and creative thought. Moreover, polyphony is a particularly efficacious symbol for the Trinitarian mystery, in which there is distinction, communion, and perfect beauty; from the "polyphony" of Trinity originates the perfect society of Heaven. The souls who have undergone the monodic purification of Purgatory and have learnt to intone with each other are now enabled to intertwine their voices freely in the polyphonic praise to the perfect beauty of God.

The Pythagorean and Platonic theme of the harmony of the spheres[20] therefore acquires an exquisitely Christian nuance, and is connected to an epistemological question: Is the ability to *improvise polyphonically* in concord the result of the perfect knowledge of each other which the blessed spirits draw from their contemplation of God?[21] Furthermore, is it their will to "accord" themselves with each other, accepting the limits that one's melody will pose to that of the other, and interpreting these limits as a gift enabling the heavenly concert to come to life, rather than as a deprivation of the individual's autonomy.

Finally, as rightly pointed out by Schurr,[22] in Dante's *Paradiso* a narrative scheme is established, in which singing and music dovetail with the *vision* and *movement* (dance) of the blessed spirits. Similar to polyphony, dance implies the coordination "for the beautiful" of free wills which renounce their individual caprice in order to achieve the happiness of society as a whole.

---

20 Cf. Godwin 1992; Spitzer 2009.
21 Cf. Aquinas, *Summa*, S.III.92
22 Schurr 1994, 47.

Music in *The Silmarillion*

In Tolkien's *legendarium* there are several examples of infernal music similar to that described by Dante, such as the violent and martial sounds of the Orcs.[23] Their counterpart is the music of water, created by Ulmo and loved by the Elves (*S* Ainul, Qu1, etc.).[24] This seems reminiscent of the enchantment felt by Dante when he heard the sound of the *ruscelletto*, the brook which, with its sweet murmur, will lead Virgil and Dante out from the infernal abyss ("a place one cannot see: it is discovered / by ear – there is a sounding stream [...]"[25] *Inferno* XXXIV.129ff.).

Yet I will focus my argument rather on the Music of the Ainur, since its principles are similar to those of music in Dante's *Paradiso*. In *Paradiso* XXIX.18, Dante describes the creation of angels as "new loves", and, for Montemaggi, this term sheds light on Dante's overall view of creation: "For Dante, the love which God is, and through which everything that is has its being, reflects itself into creation, finding new and particular expression in creatures capable of loving" (Montemaggi 2010, 63-64). Thus, Tolkien's Ainur are called to participate in the divine creativity and to "adorn" the theme proposed by Ilúvatar (*S* Ainul). As observed by Montemaggi himself, Dante states that angels do not need language in order to communicate with God and with each other. However, he chooses to represent as a language (*subsist*, *Paradiso* XXIX.15) the reflection of God's love in the angels' being. Similarly, in *Ainulindalë*, the individual Ainur know firstly only that part of Ilúvatar's mind whence each of them originated. Their first individual song, therefore, is at the same time their response to the divine call to being (i.e. their own "*subsist*") and their possibility to reveal themselves to their brethren who, contextually and consequently, grow in the knowledge of Ilúvatar himself.

At the beginning, for example, the Ainur cannot "improvise polyphonically" together, since they do not possess the knowledge of each other which is indispensable in order to foresee the shape which their brethren's melody will take; this, in turn, is necessary if they want to adapt their voices to the others,

---

23 See, e.g., in Tolkien's *H* chapter VI. Cf. Steimel 2010, 99.
24 Cf. Eden 2007, 445.
25 Italian: "Non per vista, ma per suono è noto."

in order to create a harmonious music and not a disordered cacophony. The progressive "growth" (McIntosh 2010, 58) of the Ainur[26] is therefore similar to the process of reciprocal intonation undergone by Dante's penitent souls in Purgatory, which finally produces the free polyphonic creativity of *Paradiso*. However, the process by which Dante's angels and Tolkien's Ainur know each other, and, most importantly, God, is constantly, constitutively and ontologically *in fieri*. As observed by Montemaggi, the incapacity of understanding God is an inherent feature of created beings as such, since "that which is the ground of all existence cannot itself ultimately be reduced to an object of intellectual comprehension" (Montemaggi 2010, 64).

This ontological limit is what Dante's Ulysses tries to overcome, as he believes that the knowledge of the ultimate truth is jealously kept from human beings by God, although such a truth could be grasped by them in principle. Instead, for Montemaggi, the pillars of Hercules of Dante's Ulysses are the principle of human knowledge, which cannot take place outside the relationship with God and of the dynamics of human society. Dante's *Purgatorio*, therefore, is the place where the quest for *virtute e canoscenza* ("worth [or virtue] and knowledge", *Inferno* XXVI.120) becomes the desire to "conform one's will to that which may, in love and humility, redefine it" (Montemaggi 2010, 77) – on the model of Christ, and for love, the individual conforms his will to God's. These processes are perfectly symbolized by the polyphonic singing of the angels and of the Ainur. In *The Silmarillion*, the Ainur know each other by listening to how each of them – singly and characteristically – adorns the theme of Ilúvatar. Later, they can begin to improvise polyphonically together: this happens when they acquire sufficient knowledge of each other and are willing to let their brethren's singing "limit" their own.

The Ainur's music becomes, then, Vision and Being (*S* Ainul),[27] thus reminding us of the Dantesque scheme of music/vision/movement ("so did I see the wheel that moved in glory / go round and render voice to voice with such / sweetness and such accord that they can not // be known except where joy is everlasting,"[28]

---

[26] "Yet ever as they listened they came to deeper understanding, and increased in unison and harmony". (*S* Ainul).
[27] Cf. Milbank 2008, 23-24; McIntosh 2010, 60.
[28] Italian: "Così vid'io la gloriosa rota / muoversi e render voce a voce in tempra / e in dolcezza ch'esser non pò nota // se non colà dove gioir s'insempra."

Paradiso X.145ff.). Just as Cacciaguida "sees" Dante's future in the polyphonic singing,[29] so the Ainur contemplate their own music as embodied in the Vision and Being. The dance of Dante's blessed spirits is the spatial display of a free and loving society, as polyphony is its display in time; similarly, the Ainur's Vision allows them to contemplate the wonderful and organic cooperation of their individual melodic lines to the beauty of the All simultaneously and consequentially at the same time.

In Augustinian terms, in the dance of the elements all things tend naturally to their fullness, to their "place", similar to the fire, which rises in spite of gravity, but following its own nature and its "love" (*Confessions* XIII.9).[30] For Dante, music and fire are strictly intertwined through Mars, in whose sphere he places the art of music.[31] In Tolkien, too, music and fire are connected: the Flame Imperishable (cf. *S* Ainul) is an integral part of Ilúvatar's gift to the Ainur, together with the musical theme to adorn. This theme, in Tolkien's description, seems to have the same role as the *cantus firmus* in the medieval *organum melismaticum*. The *cantus firmus* were tunes with a liturgical origin ("Gregorian"), which were sung in long note-values by the *tenor*, while one or more parts would adorn it with quicker and more elaborate "melismas", which were both strictly bound and ontologically determined by the *cantus firmus* itself.[32] Indeed, this very compositional form, the *organ melismaticum*, is cited

---

29 "Contingency / while not extending past the book in which / your world of matter has been writ, is yet / in the Eternal Vision all depicted // (but this does not imply necessity, / just as a ship that sails downstream is not / determined by the eye that watches it). // And from that Vision – *just as from an organ / the ear receives a gentle harmony* – / *what time prepares for you appears to me*." Italian: "La contingenza, che fuor del quaderno / de la vostra matera non si stende, / tutta è dipinta nel cospetto etterno; // necessità però quindi non prende / se non come dal viso in che si specchia / nave che per torrente giù discende. // Da indi, *sì come viene ad orecchia / dolce armonia da organo, mi viene / a vista il tempo che ti s'apparecchia*" (*Paradiso* XVII.37-45, my italics).

30 Augustine *Confessions* XIII.9. See Mazzotta 2014, 203.

31 "The heaven of Mars may be compared to music because [...] Mars dries things out and incinerates them because its heat is like that of fire; [...] Music attracts to itself the human spirits, which are, as it were, principally vapors of the heart." Italian: "E lo cielo di Marte si può comparare a la Musica [perché] Marte dissecca e arde le cose, perché lo suo calore è simile a quello del fuoco [...]. La Musica trae a sé li spiriti umani, che quasi sono principalmente vapori del cuore" (*Convivio* II.xiii.20-24).

32 As I maintained elsewhere, Melkor "sins" also by wanting to replace Ilúvatar's music with his own to work as the *cantus firmus* to his brethren's polyphony. Cf. Bertoglio 2018, Bertoglio 2019. See also Jensen 2010, 103.

by Dante in the *Paradiso*,³³ and can be observed also in Tolkien's representation of the Music of the Ainur.³⁴

Moreover, by using such musical symbols, the two authors can represent creation and creativity as gratuitous and almost playful beauty.³⁵ Dante describes the angels as *sustanze gioconde* ("gladdened beings" *Paradiso* XXIX.76, but *giocondo* has the same root as *gioco*, "game", and *giocare*, "to play"), thus demonstrating that, for him, play was "the activity which best revealed God's profoundest being" (Mazzotta 2014, 222). It also becomes the symbol of life in Eden (*Purgatorio* XXVIII.96) and of Paradise itself (*Paradiso* XX.117). Therefore, it symbolizes the perfect society which allows the knowledge of God through relationality.³⁶ Analogously, the Music of the Ainur is, in turn, a "play", because they see in it no other "purpose beyond its own beauty" (*S* Ainul). Indeed, the entire narration of creation seems to consciously – though implicitly – exploit the semantic ambiguity of the English verb "to play" (related to both games and music).³⁷

At the same time, this creative game of music has a further theological and metaphysical value, since it affirms – both in Dante and in Tolkien – the importance of *poiesis*, of narrativity and of language/communication in their enabling the human beings to understand and impart meaning to reality. The narrative sequence, with the order conferred to it by the author, presupposes the presence of an order in the events, which are not the fruit of a capricious casualness; similarly, the musical events are interpreted by the listener in their positioning in time, and the combination of memory and expectation creates both the pleasure and the significance of the fruition of music. Tolkien always writes of Ilúvatar that he "speaks", pronounces, "declares" his musical theme to the Ainur (in the version of the *Ainulindalë* found in the *Silmarillion* Ilúvatar never actually sings). Through language, he gives meaning to the Ainur's very being and to their being part of his thought and mind. The divine Word is the

---

33 "E come in fiamma favilla si vede, / and come in voce voce si discerne, / quand'una è ferma and altra va and riede", *Paradiso* VIII.16-18. Mandelbaum's translation, in this case, seems to miss the whole point by translating "plainsong" where an *organum melismaticum* is depicted: "And just as, in a flame, a spark is seen / and as, *in plainsong*, voice in voice is heard / one holds the note, the other comes and goes…" (my italics).
34 "A sound arose of endless interchanging melodies woven in harmony" (*S* Ainul).
35 Cf. Jones 2013, 85.
36 Montemaggi 2010, 78.
37 Cf. McIntosh 2010, 60; see also McIntosh 2012.

etymology of their singing and of all musical language, as Tolkien the linguist knew well. By suggesting that the *creatures' creativity* is a gift and a vocation they receive from their *creator*, both Dante and Tolkien affirm their faith in the order of *creation* and in the harmonious meaning of what exists. In God's mind every created thing, and even that which now seems negative, fallacious or defective, can be assumed and "woven"[38] into the divine symphony, thus giving us the hope to participate in a "Great Music"[39] which the entire choir of creation will intone in eschatological time.

Bibliography

Primary Sources

AQUINAS, St. Thomas. *The Summa Theologica*. Translated by Fathers of the English Dominican Province. New York: Benziger, 1947 (https://dhspriory.org/thomas/summa/).

AUGUSTINE. *Augustine: Confessions*. Translated by Albert C. Outler, 1955 (https://www.ling.upenn.edu/courses/hum100/augustinconf.pdf).

DANTE ALIGHIERI. *La Divina Commedia*. Translated by Allen Mandelbaum. New York: Bantam Classics, 1980-82 (https://digitaldante.columbia.edu/dante/divine-comedy/).

Opere di Dante Alighieri. Milan: Mursia, 1965.

Il Convivio (The Banquet). Translated by Richard Lansing. New York: Garland, 1990 (https://digitaldante.columbia.edu/library/the-convivio/).

LEWIS, Clive S. *The Screwtape Letters*. New York: Collier Books, 1961.

Secondary Sources

BARBIANO, Paolo. "Gimli figlio di Glóin." *Endóre* 8 (2005) (http://www.endore.it/Arretrati/8/Articoli/Gimli.pdf).

---

38 Cf. *S* Ainul: "And [the second music] essayed to drown the other music by the violence of its voice, but it seemed that its most triumphant notes were taken by the other and woven into its own solemn pattern."
39 Cf. *S* Ainul: "Never since have the Ainur made any music like to this music, though it has been said that a greater still shall be made before Ilúvatar by the choirs of the Ainur and the Children of Ilúvatar after the end of days."

BERTOGLIO, Chiara. *Through Music to Truth. Music and Theology in Dialogue with Italian Culture*. Cantalupa (TO): Effatà, 2016.

"Dissonant Harmonies: Tolkien's Musical Theodicy." *Tolkien Studies* 15 (2018): 93-114.

"Polyphony, Collective Improvisation and the Gift of Creation." *Music in Tolkien's Work and Beyond*. Eds. Julian Eilmann and Friedhelm Schneidewind. Zurich and Jena: Walking Tree Publishers, 2019 (forthcoming).

CAESAR, Judith. "Tolkien's *The Lord of the Rings* and Dante's *Inferno*." *The Explicator* 64.3 (2006): 167-170 (http://dx.doi.org/10.3200/EXPL.64.3.167-170.)

CHANCE, Jane (ed.). *Tolkien the Medievalist*. New York and London: Routledge, 2003.

CIABATTONI, Francesco. *Dante's Journey to Polyphony*. Toronto: University of Toronto Press, 2010.

COLUCCI, Beatrice. "Dante, Tolkien e il viaggio." *Eldalie* (n.d.) (http://www.eldalie.com/saggi/ DanTolk.htm).

DE BENEDICTIS, Raffaele. *Ordine e struttura musicale nella "Divina Commedia."* Fucecchio: European Press Academic Publishing, 2000.

DETARDO, Merlin. "Dante." *J.R.R. Tolkien Encylopedia: Scholarship and Critical Assessment*. Ed. Michael D.C. Drout. New York and London, Routledge, 2007. 116-117.

DOWNEY, Sarah. "Cordial Dislike: Reinventing the Celestial Ladies of *Pearl* and *Purgatorio* in Tolkien's Galadriel." *Mythlore* 29.3-4 (Spring/Summer 2011): 101-117.

DROUT, Michael D.C. (ed.). *J.R.R. Tolkien Encyclopedia: Scholarship and Critical Assessment*. New York and London, Routledge, 2007.

DUBS, Kathleen E. "Providence, Fate, and Chance: Boethian Philosophy in *The Lord of the Rings*." *Twentieth Century Literature* 27.1 (Spring 1981): 34-42.

EDEN, Bradford Lee. "The 'Music of the Spheres': Relationships between Tolkien's *The Silmarillion* and Medieval Cosmological and Religious Theory." *Tolkien the Medievalist*. Ed. Jane Chance. New York and London: Routledge, 2003, 183-193.

"Music." *J.R.R. Tolkien Encyclopedia: Scholarship and Critical Assessment*. Ed. Michael D.C. Drout. New York and London, Routledge, 2007, 444-445.

(ed.). *Middle-earth Minstrel. Essays on Music in Tolkien*. Jefferson, NC and London: McFarland, 2010.

EILMANN, Julian and Friedhelm SCHNEIDEWIND (eds.). *Music in Tolkien's Work and Beyond*. Zurich and Jena: Walking Tree Publishers, 2019 (forthcoming).

GODWIN, Joscelyn. *The Harmony of the Spheres. A Sourcebook of the Pythagorean Tradition in Music*. Rochester: Inner Traditions, 1992.

HALSALL, Michael. *A Critical Assessment of the Influence of Neoplatonism in J.R.R. Tolkien's Philosophy of Life as 'Being and Gift'*. PhD Thesis. Nottingham: University of Nottingham, 2015.

HONEGGER, Thomas. "Riders, Chivalry, and Knighthood in Tolkien." *Journal of Tolkien Research* 4.2 (2017), article 3 (http://scholar.valpo.edu/journaloftolkien-research/vol4/iss2/3).

HOUGHTON, John William. "*Commedia* as Fairy-story: Eucatastrophe in the Loss of Virgil." *Mythlore* 17.2 (Winter 1990): 29-32.

"Augustine in the Cottage of Lost Play: the *Ainulindalë* as Asterisk Cosmogony." *Tolkien the Medievalist*. Ed. Jane Chance. New York and London: Routledge, 2003, 171-182.

JENSEN, Keith W. "Dissonance in the Divine Theme: The Issue of Free Will in Tolkien's *Silmarillion*." *Middle-earth Minstrel. Essays on Music in Tolkien*. Ed. Bradford Lee Eden. Jefferson, NC and London: McFarland, 2010, 102-113.

JONES, David. *Epoch and Artist*. London: faber and faber, 2013.

MAZZOTTA, Giuseppe. *Confine quasi orizzonte. Saggi su Dante*. Rome: Edizioni Storia e Letteratura, 2014.

MCINTOSH, Jonathan. "*Ainulindalë*: Tolkien, St Thomas, and the Metaphysics of Music." *Music in Middle-earth*. Eds. Heidi Steimel and Friedhelm Schneidewind. Zurich and Jena: Walking Tree Publishers, 2010. 53-74.

"The Ainur's Music and the Trinity." Blog article, 29.10.2012 (https://jonathansmcintosh.wordpress.com/2012/10/29/the-ainurs-music-and-the-trinity/).

MILBANK, Alison. *Chesterton and Tolkien as Theologians*. London: T&T Clark, 2008.

"In a Dark Wood: Tolkien and Dante." Paper read at the School of English, Trinity College Dublin, 21-22 September 2012 (courtesy of the author).

MONTEMAGGI, Vittorio. "In Unknowability as Love. The Theology of Dante's *Commedia*." *Dante's Commedia: Theology as Poetry*. Ed. Vittorio Montemaggi and Matthew Treherne. Notre Dame, IN: University of Notre Dame Press, 2010, 60-94.

and Matthew TREHERNE (eds.). *Dante's Commedia: Theology as Poetry*. Notre Dame, IN: University of Notre Dame Press, 2010.

SCHURR, Claudia Elisabeth. *Dante e la musica. Dimensione, contenuto e finalità del messaggio musicale nella "Divina Commedia"*. Quaderni di "Esercizi, musica e spettacolo". Perugia: Università degli Studi di Perugia, 1994.

SCULL, Christina and Wayne G. HAMMOND. *The J.R.R. Tolkien Companion and Guide. Chronology*. Boston, MA: Houghton Mifflin, 2006.

SELAND, John. "Dante and Tolkien: Their Ideas about Evil." *Inklings Forever* 5 (2006), (http://www.taylor.edu/cslewis).

SPITZER, Leo. *L'armonia del mondo*. Bologna: Il Mulino, 2009.

STEIMEL, Heidi. "'Bring Out the Instruments!': Instrumental Music in Middle-earth." *Music in Middle-earth*. Eds. Heidi Steimel and Friedhelm Schneidewind. Zurich and Jena: Walking Tree Publishers, 2010, 91-106.

and Friedhelm SCHNEIDEWIND (eds.). *Music in Middle-earth*. Zurich and Jena: Walking Tree Publishers, 2010.

Tânia P. Azevedo

Gawain vs. Gauvain: Tolkien and Chrétien de Troyes

At first glance, one could think that writers like Tolkien and Troyes have little or nothing in common, but this is a case where a closer look repays the effort. They have something, or better, someone in common: a character, that unites not only their writings, but also the way in which both writers have interpreted the stories around the court of King Arthur. Gawain and Gauvain are two facets of the same hero, one that has its roots in Celtic mythology. Chrétien saw Gauvain as a valorous knight, yet one that was still one inch away from perfection. Tolkien saw Gawain as the hero England was missing to have a mythology completed. We will see how.

Chrétien de Troyes wrote his works in France during the second half of the 12th century. His five romances provide often a more light-hearted view of the so called Matter of Britain than what we see in the texts of his successors.

His five romances are, in chronological order, *Erec et Enide*, *Cligès*, *Lancelot – le Chevalier à la charrette*, *Yvain – le Chevalier au lion* and *Perceval ou le Roman du Graal*. They are living proof that Chrétien, though he did not invent the Arthurian romance genre, at least gave it a new focus by making the romantic liaison between knight and his lady into the main topic of the first four romances. He inaugurates what we know today as courtly love in the romance genre.

In these four romances, we meet Gauvain as the courtly knight, always close to Arthur, ready to fight and help those in need, and we even see him counseling Arthur.

In his last and sadly unfinished romance, *Perceval*, written towards the end of his life, Chrétien explores the Grail theme through the adventures of Perceval and Gauvain. And it is a Gauvain that differs considerably from the one we have met in the previous romances.

When the reader leaves Perceval and the focus of the text shifts towards Gauvain, we see his loyalty and word disputed by other knights like Kay, who accuses him of falsehood. Also, Gauvain is not always very successful in his adventures. However, Chrétien's work breaks off before his great duel; all we know is that he sent for Arthur so that the king could also see his fight.

Reading *Perceval* reminds us of another French text, *L'Âtre Périlleux*, also from the 12th century, where Gauvain tries to restore his name.

Gauvain's character is further degraded in the following romances: Robert de Boron, the *Vulgate Cycle* and the *Post Vulgate Cycle*, where we have the *Quête* and also the Portugese *Demanda do Santo Graal*. In these two, Gauvain even becomes a murderer. Many reasons have been discussed for this evolution of the character in continental medieval literature, but it is interesting to note that Gauvain only became 'evil' after another character had been created: Galahad, the Christian knight who will be worthy of finding the Grail.

Tolkien was perfectly aware of this evolution. But why did Gauvain/Gawain matter so much to him?

Tolkien's love for the Middle Ages is well known. It is documented not only in his vast academic work concerning medieval writings, but also in the way it has influenced his fictional works.

Middle-earth is the best example of this love for the medieval as it can be connected to sources that go as far as the ancient Norse legends. This affection is obviously intertwined with Tolkien's academic work. The most relevant work that has come through to readers, concerning medieval texts, is, undoubtedly, Tolkien's edition and translation of *Sir Gawain and the Green Knight*.

Even as a young scholar, Tolkien started working on this poem, first in an edition in Middle English with E.V. Gordon that he deemed necessary for students of Medieval Language and Literature. This was published in 1925.

But his work on the poem continued: in the W.P. Ker lecture on *Sir Gawain* that he gave in 1953, in Glasgow, he informs his audience that he has just completed his own verse translation of the poem: "Where quotation is essential, I will use a translation which I have just completed" (*MC* 74).

This translation was made "to preserve the original metre and alliteration without which translation is of little value except as a crib; and to preserve, to exhibit in an intelligible modern edition, the nobility and the courtesy of this poem, by a poet to whom 'courtesy' meant so much" (*MC* 74).

Curiously enough, we already have proof of the existence of this translation (or, at least, part of it) back in 1923, as Christina Scull and Wayne Hammond point out:

> On 15th November 1923 E.V. Gordon noted in a letter to Kenneth Sisam, who had asked for a sample translation of *Sir Gawain*, that Tolkien has prepared the requested lines of the poem (2000-2200) at some earlier time. [...] On 23rd January 1947 a copy of a translation of *Sir Gawain* by Tolkien, presumably complete, was returned to him by his friend Gwyn Jones, to whom it had been lent. (Hammond & Scull 2006, 929)

So we have at least 30 years of work on a single translation until a wider audience gets a glimpse by means of the examples used in the lecture.

Tolkien's care and love for the texts he translated and/or wrote is well known. Proof of this is the fact that many of his works have not seen the light of publication during his lifetime: one of the poignant examples is not only the translation of *Sir Gawain and the Green Knight* but the one we can now see – the prose translation of *Beowulf*.[1]

This deep interest in the old Germanic heroic legends, in medieval literature and their exquisite and complex languages, has been the main source for everything we nowadays know as 'Middle-earth'.

However, there is a reason for this, more profound than the reader can see at first glance: the author had an epic admiration for those peoples who created such heroic mythologies for their homelands. When he looked at his own country, however, there was nothing but a pale shadow in the form of the Arthurian legends – and in the almost lost Celtic elements found in them. To make matters worse, these texts have survived almost all in forms told by people who were neither from Britain proper nor who loved it, such as Robert de Boron. Tolkien was also not very fond of the Celtic imagery: "I do know Celtic things (many in

---

1 It has now been published by Christopher Tolkien, along with "Sellic Spell", a folk tale.

their original languages Irish and Welsh), and feel for them a certain distaste: largely for their fundamental unreason. They have bright colour, but are like a broken stained glass window reassembled without design" (*Letters* no. 19).

Continental medieval writers have developed the English hero differently. When reading texts as the *Quête*, one immediately sees how the heroes that descend directly from early British writings – Lancelot and Gawain – were degraded, morally and also physically. They were also replaced by a new Christian hero, Galahad, who was the only one able and worthy of finally finding the object of the most important Quest: the Holy Grail.[2] Lancelot becomes the one that betrays Arthur with his wife, Guinevere, and Gawain (Gauvain) becomes the traitor, the one that kills many of his Round Table friends and brothers.

Taking this into consideration, Tolkien has no other choice but to find an alternative tradition where the English hero has remained untouched by this degradation: the Alliterative Revival of the 14th century, where we meet the loyal Gawain.

Tolkien has dedicated many years of his life working on texts regarding this character, while developing, at the same time, the world of Middle-earth. First, he worked on the edition of the poem; then (or, perhaps simultaneously), on its translation. It is therefore undisputed that Tolkien has worked on *Sir Gawain and the Green Knight* all his life, first on the edition and then, during many years, on its translation.

Working on so many projects unfortunately delayed and stopped the completion of another work dear to Tolkien; a work that would bring to the British reader the image of the true English hero, Gawain: his unfinished alliterative poem *The Fall of Arthur*, edited and published posthumously by his son and literary executor, Christopher Tolkien.[3]

---

2   It is very interesting to speculate on the reasons why the continental medieval writers wanted to degrade Gawain. Maybe because he was closely linked to Celtic imagery, as can still be seen in texts such as *Sir Gawain and the Green Knight*. By separating Gawain from the image readers had in French romances, the Gawain-poet clearly states that there is a difference between the 'Matter of Britain' and the 'Celtic Matter'. We need to ask ourselves if Gawain should be placed in the latter group (cf. Varandas 2009, 132).
3   See also Neidorf 2017.

Christopher Tolkien is able to guess the year in which his father started working on the poem – around 1931, when 'The Lay of Leithian' and *The Legend of Sigurd and Gudrún*[4] were completed – and it was left unfinished around 1934.

However, as Christopher Tolkien puts it:

> it was driven into the shallows by the great sea-changes that were taking place in my father's conceptions at that time, arising from his work on *The Lost Road* and the publication of *The Hobbit*: the emergence of Númenor, the myth of the World Made Round and the Straight Path, and the approach of *The Lord of the Rings*. (*FA*, Foreword)

Furthermore, it should be noted that Tolkien's choice of alliterative verse[5] posed a challenge and must have proven a time-consuming task. Tolkien's alliterative poetry is characterised by parallelism, verbal variations, archaisms, and something which was typical in Old Norse and Old English poetic diction, *kennings*.[6]

The Fall of Arthur draws from a wide array of Arthurian texts, but the most significant ones that have been identified are: Geoffrey of Monmouth's *Historia Regum Britanniae*, *Le Morthe d'Arthur*, by Thomas Malory, the French poem *Mort Artu* and the English stanzaic *Morte Arthur*. Yet the main source for Tolkien's text is, undoubtedly, the alliterative *Morte Arthure*. It is only natural that Tolkien's choice would fall on this text as it is an alliterative poem of the late 14th century, and thus a near-contemporary of *Sir Gawain and the Green Knight*.

Although *The Fall of Arthur* is interrupted long before the end, we have, as Christopher Tolkien points out, around 120 pages of draft material, both prose and verse, and he guesses that the narrative would follow more or less the same line as the alliterative *Morte Arthure*.

---

[4] "He wrote two closely associated poems treating of the Völsung and Niflung (or Nibelung) legend, using modern English fitted to the Old Norse metre, amounting to more than five hundred stanzas [...]. These poems bear the titles *Völsungakviða en nýja*, the New Lay of the Völsungs, and *Guðrúnarkviða en nýja*, The New Lay of Gudrún" (*LSG*, 4).

[5] "It is not 'alliteration' because it does not depend on letters or spelling, but on sounds: it is, in fact a kind of brief rhyme: head-rhyme. The chief syllable – loudest (most stressed), highest in tone, and most significant – in each half must begin with the same consonant, or agree in beginning with a vowel (i.e. no consonant), e.g. "in **b**attle slaughtered as **b**ooks tell us" (*FA*, "Appendix: Old English Verse"). See Schwan 2017 and Sudell 2016 for detailed discussions of Tolkien's use of the alliterative metre.

[6] *Kenning* is an old Icelandic word that means 'description' and that denotes a kind of metaphor. Thus, the poet would not simply say 'the hero boarded his ship' but rather 'the hero mounted his wave-stallion'.

However, there are a few things which are new in Tolkien's narrative:

a) The poem begins *in medias res*: Arthur has already left with Gawain to fight the Saxons. This is one of the three ways, according to the manuals of rhetorics, of how to begin a narrative. Examples can be found in classical epic poetry. Tolkien thus inscribes his text into the tradition of the classical epic, and he may have intended it, more specifically, as an eulogy.

b) There is a sense of impending loss, defeat, as if the reader could guess from the beginning that the fight against fate will not lead to victory, as Christopher Tolkien points out:

> My father seems intent rather on conveying a hostile and wintry world of storms and ice, of 'ravens croaking among ruinous rocks', unpeopled save by 'phantom foes with fell voices' and wolves howling, a menacing world in which (*FA*, "The Poem in Arthurian Tradition"):

> *waiting watchful* *Fear clutched their souls,*
> *for woe they knew not,* *in a world of shadow*
>   *no word speaking* (*FA* vv. 134ff).

Moreover, this sense of vast impending danger accompanies the assertions of the poet that the declared purpose of Arthur is a matter of the gravest consequence, a great heroic gamble against fate:

> *Thus the tides of time* *to turn backward*
> *and the heathen to humble,* *his hope urged him* (*FA* vv. 5f.);

c) A very interesting detail is that no one suspects Mordred to betray Arthur,[7] even when he urges Arthur and Gawain to go to war:

> *Gawain guessed not* *guile or treason*
> *in this bold counsel* (*FA* vv. 35f.);

d) Also, Tolkien assumed that the reader knew what had happened between Lancelot and Guinevere,[8] since when we come to Canto III, Lancelot has already been banished and is in exile.

---

7 In many Arthurian texts Gawain is suspecting Mordred to be a traitor.
8 Tolkien uses two variants for spelling the queen's name: 'Guinever' and 'Guinevere'. I use 'Guinevere' throughout.

e) Also important are the glimpses we get of Guinevere's, Mordred's, and Lancelot's secret desires: Guinevere longs for Lancelot, Mordred lusts for Guinevere, and Lancelot sorely misses Arthur.⁹

In the draft pages there is a note outlining that Gawain is to die in Canto IV and his body is to be carried to Camelot in Canto V. Christopher Tolkien also found a draft of what would be Arthur's lament for the dead Gawain, which puts the narrative closer (again) to the alliterative *Morthe Arthure*.

And this is where we believe Arthur falls. His brave hero, the only uncorrupted knight he still has left, symbol of his house and his Round Table is now dead. Tolkien presents Gawain as the embodiment of chivalric virtue, so that his fall mirrors the fall of the king, of the kingdom, of true 'courtesy'. He went into the past to find the true hero, the one his homeland would be proud of, so that his memory might be remembered and his loss lamented, as Arthur does, on the final draft about the death of Gawain:¹⁰

> *now my glory is gone and my grace [...] ended.*
> *Here lies my hope and my help and my helm and my sword*
> *my heart and my hardihood and my [...] of strength*
> *my counsel and comfort*
> *[...]*
> *Ah, dread death thou dwellest too long,*
> *thou drownest my heart ere I die.*
> (*FA*, "The Unwritten Poem and Its Relation to *The Silmarillion*")

The hero Gawain is presented as true and loyal, associated with the ancient British roots and a more remote Celtic past, in opposition to Gauvain, who always falls short of the ideal.

Sadly, both fail: Gauvain fades away in time, going down in continental literature as unworthy of the Grail, and Gawain bravely fights only to see the fall of his Arthur.

It is the end of an era.

---

9   See Ruud 2016.
10 Christopher Tolkien could transcribe only part of the text due to what he calls "my father's most inscrutable hand" (*FA*, "The Unwritten Poem and Its Relation to *The Silmarillion*").

Bibliography

Chrétien de Troyes. *Arthurian Romances*. Eds. William Kibler and Carleton Carroll. London: Penguin Books, 1991a.

Romans de la Table Ronde: Erec et Enide, Cligès, Lancelot, Yvain. Paris: Gallimard Éducation, 1991b.

Hammond, Wayne G. and Christina Scull. *The J.R.R. Tolkien Companion and Guide: Reader's Guide*. London: HarperCollins, 2006.

Neidorf, Leonard. "J.R.R. Tolkien's *The Fall of Arthur*: Creation from Literary Criticism." *Tolkien Studies* 14 (2017): 91-113.

Rateliff, John D. "'That Seems to Me Fatal.' Pagan and Christian in *The Fall of Arthur*." *Tolkien Studies* 13 (2016): 45-70.

Ruud, Jay. "'Loveforsaken, from the land banished': The Complexity of Love and Honor in Tolkien's *Fall of Arthur*." *Mallorn* 56 (2015): 5-10.

Schwan, Birgit. "Searching 'for a better rhythm, or a better word or phrase': J.R.R. Tolkien's Re-Telling of the Legend of King Arthur in Alliterative Metre." *One Ring to Bind Them All. Interdisciplinary Perspectives on J.R.R. Tolkien and His Works*. Eds. Monika Kirner-Ludwig, Stephan Köser and Sebastian Streitberger. Cormarë Series 37. Zurich and Jena: Walking Tree Publishers, 2017, 111-138.

Sudell, T.S. "The Alliterative Verse of *The Fall of Arthur*." *Tolkien Studies* 13 (2016): 71-199.

Varandas, Maria Angélica "Um herói resgatado: a Importância de Gawain em *Sir Gawain and the Green Knight*." *So Long Lives This and This Gives Life to Thee. Homenagem a Maria Helena Paiva Correia*. Lisbon: Departamento de Estudos Anglísticos, F.L.U.L., 2009, 113-132.

Roberto Arduini

The Innkeeper and the Miller: Common Folks in Chaucer and Tolkien

> Even from the outside the inn looked a pleasant house to familiar eyes. [...] Barliman Butterbur was standing near the fire, talking to a couple of dwarves and one or two strange-looking men. On the benches were various folk: men of Bree, a collection of local hobbits (sitting chattering together), a few more dwarves, and other vague figures difficult to make out away in the shadows and comers. (*LotR*, FR.I.9)

In these few lines from *The Lord of the Rings*, Frodo and his companions enter the Prancing Pony Inn at Bree: a lively place full of strangers – shady figures included. Sam Gamgee, a few pages earlier, confesses: "But I won't deny I'll be glad to see this *Prancing Pony* [...]. I hope it'll be like *The Green Dragon* away back home!" The inn, that required a stopover on any long journey, is one of the great *topoi* in literature.[1] The inn features from the outset a number of iconic figures – not only the innkeeper, the adventurer, and the traveler, but thieves and murderers, too – and it is not surprising that, throughout the various inns of Middle-earth (from the *Ivy Bush* and *Green Dragon* of the Shire, to the *Prancing Pony* of Bree) visited by the reader, verbal confrontations break out between characters of drastically different worldviews: between the Gaffer and Sandyman; Sam Gamgee and Ted Sandyman; and finally Barliman Butterbur and the Shire hobbits.

Six hundred years before *The Lord of the Rings*, English literature had already visited a famous inn, *The Tabard Inn* of Southwark, then a suburb of London.[2] There Geoffrey Chaucer assembled a group of pilgrims departing for Canterbury, a destination that rivaled other popular places of pilgrimages such as Compostela, Rome, and Jerusalem.[3] This is the beginning of the *Canterbury Tales*: the cast of characters does not include wizards, Dwarves or Elves, but it does in any

---

1 Peyer 2009.
2 The Tabard Inn in Southwark was the traditional starting point for pilgrims to Canterbury. The inn was rebuilt after the fire of 1676 and then it assumed the new name of "The Talbot". In 1875, despite many protests, it was closed and demolished.
3 Boitani 1991, 44-46.

case contain a varied sampling of the society of the time. There are adventurers, clerics, warriors and thieves. There is high society (abbots and nuns, knights and squires), and common folks (the cook and the miller) too. Then there is also the innkeeper – and even the author himself, represented within his own work. It can be read in The Prologue: "Great fun our host provided, [...] / A large man he was, with piercing eyes, / As fine a burgher as in Cheapside lies; / Bold in his speech, and wise, and fairly taught, / And as to manhood, lacking there was not" (Chaucer, *CT* vv. 747-57).[4] Here we might begin to see the faint resemblance to Barliman Butterbur ...

An Ungenerous Letter

A remark from Tolkien in his letters may prove a useful starting point to consider the common ground between Chaucer and Tolkien, and the areas in which the former may have influenced the latter. As a professor of English language and literature, it is only natural that Tolkien engaged with Chaucer: he first read him at the age of ten,[5] taught several academic courses on Chaucer, quoted him in several letters, published essays on him, and even edited some of his works. On at least one occasion Tolkien found himself playing Chaucer in a theatrical performance. In the letter regarding this performance, Tolkien shares a candid opinion of the medieval poet:

> Privately, as one student of Chaucer to another, I might perhaps say that these lines seem to me to allude to the erroneous imagination that Chaucer was the first English poet, and that before and except for him all was dumb and barbaric. That is of course not true, [...]. In [England's] long 1200 years of literary tradition Chaucer stands rather in the middle than the beginning. I also do not feel him springlike but autumnal (even if of the early autumn) and not kinglike but middle-class. (*Letters* no. 32)

These notions are repeated in the preface to the essay that Tolkien edited on *Sir Gawain and the Green Knight* (1953) and in his *Valedictory Address* (1959). They therefore suggest a well-established and unchanging opinion over the years. Tolkien's view of Chaucer in the letter can be broken down into three points:

---

4 All references to Chaucer's *The Canterbury Tales* (henceforth abbreviated as *CT*) are to *The Riverside Chaucer*.
5 Carpenter 1977, 36; Garth 2003, 15.

1) He is not the first English poet and before him all is not mute and barbaric.
2) He falls in the middle of 1200 years of English literary tradition, at the beginning of an autumnal phase.
3) He is more middle-class than kinglike.

This first point in Tolkien's assessment of the *Canterbury Tales* author is naturally linked to the fact that the professor taught and studied the literature of Old English (Anglo-Saxon), whose most famous work is *Beowulf*. Old English evolved from its earlier Germanic language roots after the Norman conquest into Middle English, much influenced by French and Latin, so that the new 'Middle' English differed considerably from the mostly Germanic Old English. Tolkien saw the evolution of English literature as a single continuum, while by convention the literature of Old English has been held separate from later works.

The professor also considered Chaucer to be an autumnal poet, because for Tolkien the highest points of English literature had already passed; Chaucer was positioned somewhere toward the end of Tolkien's teaching curriculum. This second point, however, requires some more extensive consideration. In the period in which Chaucer lived, England was linguistically divided into five different dialects,[6] but Latin reigned in the courts of law and French was spoken by courtiers and the wealthy classes. Tolkien considered the dialect of the West Midlands[7] as the heir to Old English. It was this vernacular variety of Middle English that produced at that time the works of the so-called "*Pearl* poet" who inspired the *Alliterative revival*, a return to a poetic style based on alliteration and not on rhyme.[8] This movement disappeared due to the rise of the variety that Chaucer helped to spread,[9] the south-eastern dialect, which was backed by London's economic supremacy.[10] Tolkien was an expert on the northern and western languages of England, "a region

---

6   Pezzini 1981, 102.
7   The idea of continuity between Old and Middle English was also expressed by R.W. Chambers in 1932 in *On the Continuity of English Prose*. Cf. Drout 2007, 122-128. See also Shippey 1995, 214f.
8   Pezzini 1981, 112. See also Pearsall 1981 and Pearsall 1982. Tolkien took on the alliterative verse on many occasions: *LB*, *LSG* and *HBBS*. The *Lay of the Children of Húrin*, published in the *LB*, includes as many as three thousand verses. But the best-known examples are naturally the poems in *The Lord of the Rings*, in which most of the alliterative verses are associated with Rohan, which in Tolkien's conception, is directly related to the Anglo-Saxons. See also Fisher 2010, 11-20. Shippey has compiled a list that includes ten poems, five fragments and more than sixty verses (see Shippey 2013, 11f.).
9   The dialect of London was rather silent in the fourteenth century, yet it imposed itself on others. Pearsall writes that "Chaucer's poetry, by its size and quality, is the main proof of this change, its fundamental product and perhaps also the main protagonist." See Pearsall 1977, 197.
10 McCrum, MacNeil, & Cran, 80f.

of great interest" as he writes in the Preface to Walter Haigh's *A New Glossary of the Dialect of the Huddersfield District*.[11] All the works written in the dialect of the West Midlands were the subject of several of his studies:[12] the professor came to hypothesize the existence of a school of manuscript production in that dialect in the early thirteenth century[13] and, among other things, he unfortunately missed a chance to write a grammar and a literary history of this dialect, as Shippey has noted.[14] *Sir Gawain* was the subject of long study by Tolkien, including its moral issues and the engagement with them, which put into play the values and codes of chivalric society.[15] Chaucer, on the other hand, introduced rhyme and dealt with much more profane subjects. For this reason, Tolkien, although he esteemed him, called him "middle-class" (*Letters* no. 32).

A Medieval Innovator

When Chaucer was born in ca. 1340, for the last 250 years the language of English literature had been primarily French (in reality it was the Anglo-Norman dialect brought by William the Conqueror which had slowly evolved). It is the language found in the *chansons de geste* and the Matter of Britain. By the time the poet died in 1400, Middle English was spoken at court and used in the writing of literary works. It would take another century for these changes to become permanently established, but it was Chaucer who initiated this cultural revolution. Of course, other elements also played a decisive role (including the Hundred Years War between England and France and the Black Death, the

---

11 Drout 2007, 120. See also Shippey 1989.
12 The professor made a careful study of the three fundamental works of the so-called Alliterative Revival in *SGPO* published posthumously only in 1975. Tolkien published an introductory essay on the alliterative verse in Ancient English: see "Preface". For further information, see Phelpstead 2013, 47-56; Tolkien also widely writes about this matter in *Letters* no. 238.
13 Tolkien made this hypothesis in the essay "Acrene Wisse and Hali Meidhad", and "it was accepted as positive", as noted in Shippey 1989, 21. See also Drout 2007, 121. Subsequent studies have also identified some possible monasteries as the centres of production.
14 Shippey reported this opinion during the *Tolkien Seminar* of January 12, 2013 in Modena: "Tolkien never seems to have contemplated writing an academic monograph on the medieval literature of his land, the West Midlands. No one has ever written a monograph, and recent investigations of medieval English literature (all written by scholars from London and Oxford, if you ask me) sometimes come to deny that there is such literature. Tolkien could and should have written such a work, but he did not."
15 Tolkien's acquaintance with the *Sir Gawain* poet lasted fifty years: see Arduini 2009, 149 and also Shippey 2005, Chance 1986 and Chance 2001.

bubonic plague, which between 1349 and 1350 reduced the population from four to two million).[16]

French culture thus permeated the English courts and society in those years.[17] Chaucer was one of the first writers to write directly in English, ever since his first work, *The Book of the Duchess* in 1370.[18] Chaucer was a man of letters, an attentive scholar of the English, French, Italian, and Latin cultural traditions, respectively, of his period: he knew Ovid, the *Romance of the Rose*, Dante, and Boccaccio, and constantly sought new forms of expression, strange fantasy worlds, and new experiences within this immensely rich tradition. These authors were the main models that the author took for his English poetics: the stories, the frame, and the rhyme are indebted to Boccaccio.[19] Chaucer knew the splendor of the court, as well as the accounting offices and the poor districts of London; he had a vast experience of life. His poetry, like that of Shakespeare, ranges from sordid to refined. His works were a novelty for England and above all for a language like Middle English. He is thus rightly believed to be the initiator of English literature. Tolkien's opinion was based more on his own particular considerations rather than on the intrinsic value of Chaucer's work and his influence on later literature.

Deep Knowledge

The Oxford Professor, however, also saw a model in the medieval poet. In particular, Tolkien is indebted to Chaucer for the structure of certain works, the style, the idioms, some characters, and the social environment in which they move. Tolkien studied and was inspired by Chaucer ever since George Brewerton, his teacher at King Edward's School, introduced him to the medieval master in the original Middle English.[20] John Bowers, William H. Green,

---

16 Barisone 1986, v.
17 Pezzini 1981, 113ff.
18 The most complete account of Chaucer's life and career can be found in Brewer 2000 and *The Riverside Chaucer*, xi-xxii.
19 Earlier critics argued that the idea of a "frame" containing a series of stories was inspired by Boccaccio's *Decameron*. While recognizing in *The Canterbury Tales* the evident influence of some of Boccaccio's minor works, contemporary critics are rather doubtful about the possibility that the English poet knew the masterpiece of the Italian storyteller. For the influence of Boccaccio and other Italian poets, see Boitani 1977, Boitani 1983 and Ruggiers 1979,160-84.
20 Carpenter 1977, 36.

and especially Jane Chance have explored Chaucerian links to some episodes of Tolkien's major works.[21] Jane Chance, in particular, has investigated the influence of Chaucer on *Farmer Giles of Ham* and *The Hobbit*. For Tolkien's first novel, Chance draws a parallel between the Chaucer figure and the narrator of *The Hobbit*, going so far as to criticize the latter's presence and making a list of negative characteristics: "The narrator, like a tale-telling pilgrim, must be regarded as one additional character. The arrogant, unimaginative, and very 'adult' narrator assumes this story about little Hobbits must be relegated to an audience of little creatures – children. The narrator's pride, patronizing attitude, and literalism betray his 'coldness'" (Chance 2001, 55).[22] The first debts to Chaucer, however, date back to the period during which Tolkien was still trying to create a mythology for England, between 1915 and 1930,[23] in which all his texts of fiction were closely related to the history of Great Britain, or rather, they were designed to fill the gaps caused by the lost or never recorded legends and myths of the British Middle Ages. The concept of a Fairy Realm occurs twice in the *Canterbury Tales* and while *elvishness* is a feature most often attributed to men in *The Lord of the Rings*, Chaucer also assigns it to himself.[24] Tolkien tries to explain the presence of two apparently contradictory versions of Faerie in the native tradition of the fairy tale. *The Canterbury Tales* mention them both. In "The Merchant's Tale", Pluto and Proserpine are presented as the king and queen of the kingdom of the dead. The connection between the hereafter and the Fairy Kingdom dates back to a long tradition that includes King Arthur's Avalon, the Welsh Annwn, or the Irish land of eternal youth, Tir-na-Nog. "The Wife of Bath's Tale", by contrast, recalls the days of King Arthur, when the whole of Britain was "full of fairies" and the queen of the Elves danced in many pastures while now "no man can see the Elves",[25] thus referring to the tradition of a land of fairies that once showed itself openly in our mortal world, but has long since vanished from sight.

---

21 Bowers has pointed out the parallels between the dances of Baccadoro and Tom Bombadil and the numerous dances in *The Canterbury Tales*: see Bowers 2011, 27. Green (1995, 58), then, compares the episode of Rivendell in *The Hobbit* to *The Pardoner's Tale*.
22 See also Chance 2001, 71 and 125-33.
23 Cf. Garth 2003, 87.
24 Cf. Shippey 2005, 67ff.
25 Boitani 1991, 863f.

In *The Book of Lost Tales I*, the stories are introduced by a frame in which the protagonist Eriol is the first man to find the Straight Road and reach the land of the Elves, Tol Eressëa, which had existed in isolation from the human race for millennia. Eriol comes upon the Cottage of Lost Play, an oasis of peace, rest, and imaginative sustenance. The Elves host him for many months, telling each other their stories about the early Middle Ages; it follows the same pattern as the *Canterbury Tales*.[26] Scholars have noted numerous other influences by Chaucer on Tolkien's work, such as "Kortirion among the trees",[27] "The Hoard",[28] and "The Lay of Aotrou and Itroun".[29]

A Matter of Style

In the *Canterbury Tales*, the pilgrims represent all the 'classes' (or 'estates') of fourteenth century England. After the nobles (including the Knight, the young Squire, his son, and their Yeoman-Archer) come the representatives of the clergy (the Prioress, the Nun, the three Nun's Priests, the Monk, and the Friar), then those of the bourgeoisie (the Merchant, the Clerk, the Man of Law, the Franklin, the five citizens belonging to the same confraternity with their Cook, the Shipman, the Physician, and the Wife of Bath), who are followed by two humble and virtuous people (the Parson and the Farmer, his brother) and finally we have a group, in which the poet ironically includes himself, composed of plebeians and villains (the Miller, the Manciple, the Reeve, the Summoner, and the Pardoner).[30]

These characters, static at first, soon come to life: they speak and act, revealing their interests, their attitudes, their antagonism. A word is enough, a real or imagined allusion, to stir them up: some lash out violently, others ignore any provocation or go completely silent. It is established that the Knight will be first to speak, but soon the coarse voices of the Miller, the Reeve, and the Cook have the upper hand and the decorum of the initial process is irretrievably broken. This

---

26 Allan Turner suggests that the structure of the *BLT* may have been inspired by Chaucer, but also by William Morris, also an admirer and imitator of the medieval poet with his *The Earthly Paradise*: see Turner 2013, 210f. *The Earthly Paradise*: vedi Turner 2013, 210f.
27 Cf. Garth 2003, 107f.
28 Shippey 2004, 282.
29 Likhacheva 1993.
30 Boitani 1991, 208-220.

three-dimensionality is reached because Chaucer adapts the language to the needs and the personalities of very different characters, welcoming with realism and sympathy for all the faces and the strangeness of life, the sublime virtues, and hypocrisies.[31] At the same time, he does not exclude the solemn intensity of a structure constituted by the stages of the pilgrimage, punctuated along the entire route by information on the distance, the towns offering food and rest, and the flow of day and night. The same happens in *The Lord of the Rings*, a novel in which one can also follow the phases of the moon and the passing of the seasons. The medieval poet manages to bring his characters to life by varying their style very much. On the one hand, he assigns to intellectuals and nobles a high style, in tune with the most elevated rhetorical arts, full of abstract and imaginative terms, of schemes and formulas divorced from tangible experience.[32] To the common people, on the other hand, he gives a discourse in which material accuracy prevails, a bare and concrete terminology of sensible, intuitive, and vivid images. The two styles are not always separated, indeed their combinations are almost indefinite: just as imaginative tales do need a touch of realism, so too does a realistic story depend on a precise rhetorical structure.[33]

Tolkien elaborated on the poet's style in his essay, "Chaucer as a Philologist: The Reeve's Tale",[34] which discusses the poet's use of the northern dialect to characterize the manner of speaking of the two clerks in *The Reeve's Tale*. Tolkien suggested that Chaucer had intentionally placed a regional dialect in the mouths of these characters to achieve a comic and satirical effect, a fact which scholars had previously dismissed as due to orthographic inconsistency.[35]

Like Chaucer, Tolkien uses linguistic variations at regional, cultural, and psychological levels to great effect in his narratives. In *The Lord of the Rings,* he clearly distinguishes between the upper-class talk of the Tooks, the Bagginses and the Brandibucks from the rural and more 'working-class' dialect of the Cotton and Gamgee families.[36] The language of the Elves is harmonious and musical, while

---

31 Bloomfield 1986, 179-94, Windeatt 1986, 195-212 and Brewer 1986, 227-42.
32 Tolkien greatly admired Chaucer's "high style": see *Letters* no. 182.
33 Windeatt 1986 and Brewer 1986.
34 The essay on *The Reeve's Tale* was published in *Transactions of the Philological Society* (1934) and was republished in 2008 in *Tolkien Studies* 5. Horobin (2001) gives a critical assessment of Tolkien's argument.
35 *The Riverside Chaucer*, 850, n. 4022.
36 See Johannesson (2004) for a discussion of the dialect(s) of the Shire.

their style is formal and archaic, even when expressed in the Common Tongue. The language of the Orcs is guttural and harsh, and their style is slang. Strider is simpler and more direct than the lofty register of Aragorn: a particularly successful touch, given that they are the same person, and linguistic change signals his progress from Wanderer to King. Sam Gamgee, with his use of aphorisms, his funny imprecations (like "Noodles!" or "You're now't but a ninnyhammer" *LotR, TT*.IV.1), his father the Gaffer and, above all, Gollum/Smeagol are also valid examples of Tolkien's use of idiomatic expressions, dialect, and peculiar speech patterns in order to more fully develop his characters.

Tavern Characters

Offspring of the Ancient Roman *tabernae*, the inns of the Middle Ages were – day and night – an important social space for those who frequented them. In every medieval city, the inns welcomed travelers just inside the walls. By the year 1000, Paris already counted more than four thousand inns.[37] After a day of work, artisans, peasants, and workers spent time in the inns – with the risk of getting drunk and suffering the reproaches of their wives once they returned home. For young people, the tavern was an equally attractive destination. The inns also represented a certain amount of social risk and their activity was therefore often regulated.[38] Specific rules were laid down to limit wine consumption and regulate gaming, especially playing at dice, which was another activity very common at the inns. The linking of drinking wine and playing games was inevitable, yet it could be very dangerous, especially when bets were involved. The innkeepers were required to scrupulously follow the rules imposed by the authorities, but they still had many privileges: in addition to the retail sale of wine and food, it was also possible to sell entire casks, a sign of the growing economic significance of such a trade.[39]

This reality is reflected in the sources and literature of the time. It is no coincidence that an inn and its host also appear in Langland's *Piers Plowman*, a contemporary of Chaucer. The second vision of the poem depicts an inn,

---

37 Verdon 2002.
38 Peyer 2009, above all Part II, chap. IV 87-124.
39 Ermini Pani, Somma & Stasolla 2014, 101.

albeit one of the lowest order: the scene aims to present daily life in an English tavern with all its baseness and varied humanity.[40] A frequent visitor to the inns was François Villon, a French poet, thief, and murderer, who was just a little older than Chaucer. Villon might even have died in a fight or in some squalid tavern.[41] At any rate, his poems about hangmen and murderers, cursed poets, street singers, and highway men are tragic and irreverent. In his most significant work, *The Testament*, he does not fail to show his gratitude to the inns, where he spent much of his time.[42]

It may be surprising to note that the inn is not only a meeting place for men. Women also frequented inns, as can be seen in the well-known *Carmina Burana*,[43] which comprises poetic texts of the eleventh and twelfth centuries. In its songs and poems we see the same panoramic view of society as given by the cast of *The Canterbury Tales*. In the latter, even the Prioress drank, but making sure that "Her upper lip was always wiped so clean / That on her cup no speck or spot was seen" (*CT*, 'Prologue' vv. 133-34). And the Summoner "when a deal of wine he'd taken in, / Then would he utter no word except Latin" (*CT*, 'Prologue' vv. 637-38), while Robin the Miller got into a drunken argument with the innkeeper Harry Bayley, who acts as host and guide to the company of pilgrims. The exchange is heated: "Wait, Robin, my dear brother, Some better man shall tell us first another: Submit and let us work on profitably", he says. "Now by God's soul", cried he, "that will not I!", replies the miller (*CT*, 'Miller's Prologue' vv. 3129-33). For her part, the Wife of Bath candidly confesses that "Well could I dance to tune of harp, nor fail / To sing as well as any nightingale / When I had drunk a good draught of sweet wine" (*CT*, 'Wife of Bath's Prologue' vv. 457-59). In turn, the Manciple, before starting his story, is forced to appease the exuberance of the drunk and annoying cook by offering him a drink (*CT*, 'Manciple's Prologue' vv. 88-89). Every evening the situation is tense, and a fight is never far from breaking out. Nevertheless, the host comes to praise the wine as nature's peace-keeper: "I see well it is necessary, / Where'er we go, good drink with us we carry; / For that will turn rancour and all unease / To accord and love, and many a wrong appease. 'O Bacchus,

---

40 Boitani 1991, 99-122.
41 Bonner 1960, xxiii.
42 Villon 1971, "Ballata e orazione", vv. 1249-65, 189.
43 Rossi 1989, canto 196, stanza 5-6, 207.

thou, all blessed be thy name / Who canst so turn stern earnest into game!'" (*CT*, 'Manciple's Prologue' vv. 95-100).

Having defined the environment and the company that frequents it, we can now concentrate on the inn's proprietor. Here very interesting links to Tolkien's works emerge. The host cited by Chaucer, Harry Bayley, was a real person who represented the suburb of Southwark from 1376 to 1378.[44] From the beginning ist is him who controls the course of the narration, inviting one or the other of the pilgrims to come forward. In some moments, however, other voices assert themselves, like those of the Wife of Bath, the Second Nun, and the Canon's Yeoman. Other times, he does not hesitate to interrupt a story or to silence a pilgrim, as happens with the parodic ballad of Sir Thopas, narrated by the Chaucer character.[45]

This brings us back to Tolkien: in *The Lord of the Rings*, according to Carpenter (1977, 192), "the heart of the book is to be found in the inns and gardens of The Shire, Tolkien's representation of all that he loved best about England." In fact, the portrait of the Chaucerian host has much in common with the short, fat, and ruddy innkeeper of the *Prancing Pony*, Barliman Butterbur. His generous and instinctive character is mired by a poor memory; he forgets to send Gandalf's letter to Frodo, leaving Frodo in the dark about Gandalf's plans and thereby delaying (nearly disastrously) his departure from the Shire. Butterbur remembers the letter only when Frodo himself reaches Bree and stays at the Pony. But the innkeeper also reveals surprising qualities. After Frodo inadvertently slips on the Ring, disappearing in front of everyone, Butterbur warns him: "if you're going to do any more tumbling, or conjuring, or whatever it was, you'd best warn folk beforehand – and warn *me*" (*LotR*, *FR*.I.9). Later, he generously offers to help the four hobbits, even when he learns that their assailants come from Mordor. "Well, you do want looking after and no mistake" (*LotR*, *FR*.I.10). After the Nazgûl chase away all the horses and ponies from the inn, the innkeeper buys a pony for the Hobbits out of his own pocket. Later he informs Gandalf that Frodo and the others have left with Strider. Butterbur, despite his clumsy

---

44 Popham 1928, 43.
45 Chaucer, *CT*, 'Sir Thopas' vv. 919-25.

appearance, proves himself to be surprisingly capable: "he can see through a brick wall in time," (*LotR, FR*.II.1) as Gandalf observes.

The figure of the host is not the only shared element between the two authors. As noted, one of Chaucer's pilgrims is a Miller, involved in many of the discussions in the *Canterbury Tales*. The clash between the Miller and the Reeve closely resembles that between Sandyman and the Gaffer in *The Lord of the Rings*. In medieval society, the miller had a prominent position in the villages because everyone had to bring their grain to him to have it ground into flour. Millers sometimes abused their power in skimming more than their fair share of grain. This is precisely what happens in *The Reeve's Tale*, in which a miller is punished for his crimes, told directly in reaction to *The Miller's Tale* that preceded it. The same hostility appears in the Ivy Bush Inn on the Bywater Road in *The Lord of the Rings*. The Gaffer, who does not have much sympathy for Sandyman, the miller of Hobbiton, replies to the insinuations made about the death of Frodo's parents as follows: "You shouldn't listen to all you hear, Sandyman." Tensions rise further when Sandyman questions the Baggins' fortune, until the Gaffer snaps: "'And you can say *what you* like, about what you know no more of than you do of boating, Mr. Sandyman,' retorted the Gaffer, disliking the miller even more than usual. 'If that's being queer, then we could do with a bit more queerness in these parts. There's some not far away that wouldn't offer a pint of beer to a friend, if they lived in a hole with golden walls.'" (*LotR, FR*.I.vi). The clash will later be repeated – in another inn, the *Green Dragon* – between the sons of these two characters: Sam Gamgee and Ted Sandyman. Tolkien thus upholds the hostility toward the miller figure. Even the mill itself comes to a bad end: sold to Sharkey (Saruman) upon his arrival, it is replaced by a new-fangled, mechanized mill, where Ted works during the occupation of the Shire.

In conclusion then: while Tolkien considered Chaucer "not kinglike but middle-class," he nonetheless admired him to the point of imitating his style and borrowing from his characters. The impact of the great medieval poet shows most clearly in Tolkien's scenes of common life in the inns and in the figures of the innkeeper and the miller.

Bibliography

Primary Sources

CHAUCER, Geoffrey. *The Canterbury Tales.* Eds. Robert Boenig and Andrew Taylor. Peterborough: Broadview Press, 2008.

The Riverside Chaucer. Third edition. Eds. Larry Benson, Robert Pratt, and F.N. Robinson. Oxford: Oxford University Press, 2008.

I racconti di Canterbury. Eds. Ermanno Barisone and Harold Bloom. Milan: Oscar Mondadori, 1986.

VILLON, François. *Opere.* Eds. Attilio Carminati and Emma Stojkovich Mazzariol. Milan: Mondadori, 1971.

Secondary Sources

ARDUINI, Roberto. "'We meten so selden by stok other ston': *Sir Gawain and the Green Knight* and J.R.R. Tolkien." *Studi anglo-norreni in onore di John S. McKinnell.* Ed. Maria Elena Ruggerini. Cagliari: CUEC editrice, 2009, 149-170.

BARISONE, Ermanno. "Introduzione alla vita e le opere di Geoffrey Chaucer." *I racconti di Canterbury.* Eds. Ermanno Barisone and Harold Bloom. Milan: Oscar Mondadori, 1986, v-xv.

BLOOMFIELD, Morton. "Chaucerian Realism." *Chaucer Companion.* Eds. Piero Boitani and Jill Mann. Cambridge: Cambridge University Press, 1986, 179-194.

BOITANI, Piero. *La letteratura del Medioevo inglese.* Rome: Nuova Italia Scientifica, 1991. (Republished by Carocci Editrice in 2001).

Chaucer and the Italian Trecento. Cambridge: Cambridge University Press, 1983.

Chaucer and Boccaccio. Oxford: Society for the Study of Mediaeval Languages and Literature, 1977.

BOITANI, Piero and Jill MANN (eds.). *Chaucer Companion.* Cambridge: Cambridge University Press, 1986.

BONNER, Anthony. "Introduction." *The Complete Works of François Villon.* New York: Bantam, 1960, i-xxvi.

BOWERS, John M. "Tolkien's Goldberry and The Maid of the Moor." *Tolkien Studies* 8 (2011): 23-36.

Brewer, Derek. *Chaucer and His World*. Revised edition. London: Eyre Methuen, 2000.

"Chaucer's Poetic Style." *Chaucer Companion*. Ed. Piero Boitani and Jill Mann. Cambridge: Cambridge University Press, 1986, 227-242.

Carpenter, Humphrey. *J.R.R. Tolkien: A Biography*. New York: Houghton Mifflin Harcourt, 2014.

Chance, Jane. "Tolkien and His Sources." *Approaches to Teaching "Sir Gawain and the Green Knight"*. Eds. Jane Chance and Miriam Miller. Revised edition. New York: Modern Language Association of America, 1991, 151-155.

Tolkien's Art. A Mythology for England. Revised edition. First edition 1979. Lexington, KT: University Press of Kentucky, 2001.

Chance, Jane and Miriam Miller (eds.). *Approaches to Teaching "Sir Gawain and the Green Knight"*. Revised edition. New York: Modern Language Association of America, 1991.

Diemer, Peter and Dorothee. "Die Carmina Burana." *Carmina Burana. Text und Übersetzung*. Ed. Benedikt Vollmann. Frankfurt am Main: Deutscher Klassiker Verlag, 1987, 1289-1298.

Drout, Michael D.C. "J.R.R. Tolkien's Medieval Scholarship and its Significance." *Tolkien Studies* 4 (2007): 113-176.

Eden, Bradford Lee (ed.). *Middle-earth Minstrel. Essays on Music in Tolkien*. Jefferson, NC and London: McFarland Publishers, 2010.

Eilmann, Julian and Allan Turner (eds.). *Tolkien's Poetry*. Cormarë Series 28. Zurich and Jena: Walking Tree Publishers, 2013.

Ermini Pani, Letizia, Maria Carla Somma, and Francesca Romana Stasolla (eds.). *Forma e vita di una città medievale. Form and life of a medieval city. Leopoli – Cencelle*. Spoleto: Fondazione Centro Italiano di Studi sull'Alto Medioevo, 2014.

Fisher, Jason. "Horns of Dawn: The Tradition of Alliterative Verse in Rohan." *Middle-earth Minstrel. Essays on Music in Tolkien*. Ed. Bradford Lee Eden. Jefferson, NC and London: McFarland Publishers, 2010, 7-25.

Garth, John. *Tolkien and the Great War: The Threshold of Middle-earth*. New York: Houghton Mifflin Harcourt, 2003.

Green, William H. *The Hobbit: A Journey Into Maturity*. New York: Twayne Publishers, 1995.

Helms, Philip W. (ed.). *Peace and Conflict Studies in Tolkien's Middle-earth*. Highland, MI: American Tolkien Society, 1993.

HOROBIN, Simon C.P. "J.R.R. Tolkien as a Philologist: A Reconsideration of the Northernisms in Chaucer's Reeve's Tale." *English Studies* 82.2 (2001): 97-105.

JOHANNESSON, Nils-Lennart. "The Speech of the Individual and of the Community in *The Lord of the Rings*." *News from the Shire and Beyond – Studies on Tolkien*. Eds. Peter Buchs and Thomas Honegger. Cormarë Series 1. Second edition. First edition 1997. Zurich and Berne: Walking Tree Publishers, 2004, 13-57.

LAWTON, David (ed.). *Middle English Alliterative Poetry and Its Literary Background*. Suffolk: St. Edmundsbury Press, 1982.

LEVY, Bernard S. and Paul E. SZARMACH (eds.). *The Alliterative Tradition in the Fourteenth Century*. Kent, OH: Kent State University Press, 1981.

LIKHACHEVA, Svetlana. "The Rash Promise and Breach of Marital Troth in *The Franklin's Tale* by Chaucer and *The Lay of Aotrou and Itroun* by Tolkien: An Alternative Ending." http://www.nto-ttt.ru/sl/aotrou.shtml (Accessed 08/11/2018), 1993.

MCCRUM, Robert, Robert MACNEIL, and William CRAN. *La storia delle lingue inglesi*. Bologna: Zanichelli, 1992.

PEARSALL, Derek. "The Alliterative Revival: Origins and Social Backgrounds." *Middle English Alliterative Poetry and Its Literary Background*. Ed. David Lawton. Suffolk: St. Edmundsbury Press, 1982, 34-53.

"The Origins of the Alliterative Revival." *The Alliterative Tradition in the Fourteenth Century*. Eds. Bernard S. Levy and Paul E. Szarmach. Kent OH: Kent State University Press, 1981, 1-24.

Old English and Middle English Poetry. London: Routledge & Kegan Paul, 1977.

PEYER, Hans Conrad. *Viaggiare nel Medioevo: dall'ospitalità alla locanda*. Laterza Editore, 2009.

PEZZINI, Domenico. *Storia della lingua inglese. Dalle origini alla fine del Quattrocento*. Vol. 1. Brescia: editrice La Scuola, 1981.

PHELPSTEAD, Carl. "For W.H.A." – Tolkien's Poem in Praise of Auden." *Tolkien's Poetry*. Eds. Julian Eilmann and Allan Turner. Cormarë Series 28. Zurich and Jena: Walking Tree Publishers, 2013, 45-58.

POPHAM, Henry Ewart. *The Taverns of London Topographically Arranged*. London: Cecil Palmer Publisher, 1928.

REYNOLDS, Patricia and Glen H. GOODKNIGHT (eds.). *Proceedings of the J.R.R. Tolkien Centenary Conference*. Milton Keynes: Tolkien Society, 1995.

ROSSI, Piervittorio (ed.). *Carmina Burana*. Milan: Bompiani, 1989.

RUGGIERS, Paul G. "The Italian Influence on Chaucer." *Companion to Chaucer Studies*. Ed. Beryl Rowland. London: Oxford University Press, 1979, 160-184.

SHIPPEY, Tom. "Tolkien's Development as a Writer of Alliterative Poetry in Modern English." *Tolkien's Poetry*. Eds. Julian Eilmann and Allan Turner. Cormarë Series 28. Zurich and Jena: Walking Tree Publishers, 2013, 11-28.

The Road to Middle-earth. Third edition. HarperCollins, 2005.

J.R.R. Tolkien Author of the Century. New York: Houghton Mifflin Harcourt, 2000.

"Tolkien and the Gawain-Poet." *Proceedings of the J.R.R. Tolkien Centenary Conference*. Eds. Patricia Reynolds and Glen H. Goodknight. Milton Keynes: Tolkien Society, 1995, 213-219.

"Tolkien's Academic Reputation Today." *Amon Hen* 100 (1989): 18-22.

TURNER, Allan. "Early Influences on Tolkien's Poetry." *Tolkien's Poetry*. Eds. Julian Eilmann and Allan Turner. Cormarë Series 28. Zurich and Jena: Walking Tree Publishers, 2013, 205-221.

VERDON, Jean. *Night In The Middle Ages*. Notre Dame, IN: University of Notre Dame Press, 2002.

WINDEATT, Barry. "Literary Structures in Chaucer." *Chaucer Companion*. Eds. Piero Boitani and Jill Mann. Cambridge: Cambridge University Press, 1986, 195-212.

Tolkien and Authors from the Modern Period

Amelia A. Rutledge

Tolkien and Sir Walter Scott: Critiques of the Chivalric/Heroic Imaginary

In his essay "Ofermod", J.R.R. Tolkien's critique of Beorhtnoth's decision to allow passage to the invaders in *The Battle of Maldon* corresponds closely to Sir Walter Scott's critique of chivalry in "An Essay on Chivalry" and to Scott's unfavorable view of Richard the Lionheart's recklessness in *Ivanhoe*. Tolkien states that "this element of pride, in the form of the desire for honour and glory, in life and after death, tends to grow, to become a chief motive, driving a man beyond the bleak heroic necessity to excess – to chivalry" (HBBS, "Ofermod" 144) and maintains this critical stance toward those who place a personal ideal above responsible leadership, e.g. Túrin, Fëanor, or – briefly – Éomer. Both authors' critiques of recklessness also extend to those whose fanaticism blinds them to all humane considerations; both flaws are grounded in self-blinding wilfulness. Using examples from Tolkien's *The Lord of the Rings* and *Narn I Chîn Húrin / The Children of Húrin*, as well as Scott's *Ivanhoe* and *The Tale of Old Mortality*, which has more varied examples than *Waverley*,[1] I will discuss not specific references to Scott by Tolkien, but indicate parallels in *mentalité* in both authors' works. Brian Rosebury asserts that one finds not specific references to another writer in Tolkien's work, but echoes of other writers that "are for the most part implicit, evanescent, absorbed into a self-sufficient text" (Rosebury 2003, 151-52). Just as Scott does not confine his critique to "chivalry", extending it to include the fanatical obduracy of Lucas Beaumanoir, John Balfour of Burley or John Grahame of Claverhouse, so does Tolkien go beyond glory-seeking leaders to a critique of the self-focused rashness of a Túrin, and especially to obduracy that extends across the whole *legendarium* and can be seen in characters such as Morgoth, Sauron, and Fëanor.

---

1 See Turner 2019 for a discussion of parallels and shared elements in *The Lord of the Rings* and *Waverley*.

John Hunter states that, unlike most historical novels, *The Lord of the Rings* combines both the traditions of fantasy and historical fiction, producing "passages with a sophisticated sense of historical change and loss that is characteristic of the *Waverley* novels at their most direct" (Hunter 2005, 70), observing that Tolkien's fantasy works within the medievalizing tradition both of Scott and of James Macpherson; he wrote a self-conscious historical novel about Middle-earth.[2] Although Scott was more honest about his embellishing of historical details, he had the same desire "to preserve the last fragmentary remnants of a lost culture that animated Macpherson" (Hunter 2005, 67). Hunter also claims that *The Lord of the Rings* lacks what in *Ivanhoe* is "an ironic and critical distance from the excesses of medieval culture not just because of generic differences, but also because the later novel lies outside the Lukácsian model of the hist. novel" (Hunter 2005, 69). This is not the case, since Tolkien's self-contained secondary world uses for Frodo the same pattern Lukács described of the "middling" hero caught up in world-changing affairs (cf. Lukács 1983, 34-35). Although a critique of "chivalry" is the obvious point of contact between the two authors, Scott's strongly negative depictions of fanaticism and its attendant obduracy are also evident in the two novels, and while not as explicit as Scott's, Tolkien's critical stance is evident in his depictions of Boromir, Denethor, Fëanor, Túrin, and of Saruman's vengeful behavior as "Sharkey" in the Shire.

Tolkien distinguishes between the heroic behavior of a subordinate (Beorhtnoth's men) and of a commander who must avoid personal glory-seeking when he is responsible for others. Scott makes a similar point regarding dedication to religious and political ideals – the Scottish Covenant (Burley) versus the established church (Claverhouse) in *The Tale of Old Mortality*: Burley, Claverhouse, or the preacher Ephraim MacBriar all sacrifice lives – even their own, in the case of MacBriar – for their cause and callously deploy murderous force. Whereas Scott uses the doubts of a focal character to assess the values operative in his novels, Tolkien creates an ironic view of deeds and consequences to illustrate the tensions inherent in heroic necessities. To conceptualize the mechanisms of chivalry and fanaticism, it is useful to consider the construct "cultural imaginary" as a lens through which to view the common ground between Scott and Tolkien. Graham Dawson, in *Soldier Heroes: British Adventure, Empire*

---

2 See also Fimi 2017.

and the Imagining of Masculinity (1994) speaks of "cultural imaginaries [...] networks of interlinking discursive themes, images, motifs, and narrative forms available within a culture [...] articulating its psychic and social dimensions" (Dawson 1994, 48). The concept need not apply only to historicized gender constructs, since the cultural imaginaries of heroic action or religious purity, as benchmarks for identity-formation, operate for both authors, often devolving into romanticized enthusiasm or brutal fanaticism. For both authors, the best kind of heroism appears not in the hegemonic imaginaries designated by their societies, although this is possible, but in what Lukács would call a "mediocre, average" figure such as Frodo Baggins or Henry Morton – or "from below", as a Samwise Gamgee or a Cuddie Headrigg, their respective servants.

Ivanhoe and "Essay on Chivalry" (1818) both disparage chivalric excess – "harebrained" ("Essay on Chivalry" 16) is one term of opprobrium – and he describes Richard the Lionheart's chivalry as "brilliant but useless" (*Ivanhoe* 365). The power of a cultural imaginary is illustrated by Wilfred's vigorous defense of chivalry and glory to Rebecca (*Ivanhoe* 249) as he lies bedridden from tournament injuries, while at the same time a real battle rages outside Torquilstone. In *The Tale of Old Mortality*, "chivalry" serves as a minor element, e.g. Morton's love-rivalry with Evandale for Edith Bellenden. Claverhouse, whose imaginary is that of the nobleman or "gentleman soldier," recommends Froissart's praise of chivalry (*OM* 382) to Morton as cultural indoctrination, but uses that author's disregard for commoners to rationalize his own callous deeds.

Scott's other concern in *Ivanhoe* and in *The Tale of Old Mortality* is his consistently negative view of fanaticism. One example is the Templar Grand Master, Lucas Beaumanoir, described as "an ascetic bigot" (*Ivanhoe* 304). In a self-praising speech, he describes himself as constantly seeking to eradicate heterodoxy (*Ivanhoe* 305). The victim of his zeal is the Jewish woman, Rebecca, the object of Templar Brian de Bois-Guilbert's parody of knightly infatuation. Beaumanoir and Bois-Guilbert – foils to Scott's gentler ironic treatment of Wilfred – are a *précis* of Scott's critiques of fanaticism and chivalry. The Covenanters in *The Tale of Old Mortality* are fighting for their religious freedom, but Scott is unsparing in his depiction of their ruthless striving after doctrinal purity. The same preacher, Ephraim MacBriar, who later refuses to recant even under torture by the Scottish Privy Council (*OM* 394), uses Scripture to authorize

Morton's execution (*OM* 369-75). Burley is described as lacking in moderation – whether for religion or for power (*OM* 261) – and his "stern fanaticism" (*OM* 98) disguises his desire to become a leader among the Covenanters. In a scene that combines both motifs, Claverhouse – exploiting the eagerness for battle of the Cornet Richard Grahame, his nephew and heir – coldly sends the inexperienced youth as herald (*OM* 216). Almost predictably, Burley kills young Grahame for exceeding his herald's warrant. Francis R. Hart observes that both Claverhouse and Burley are fanatics, and that it is no surprise that they end as allies, betraying their failed causes for the Highlanders' uprising at the end of the novel (Hart 1966, 70). For these leaders, fervor is a thin disguise for the will to power.

As noted above, unlike Scott, who makes explicit assertions about his characters' inclinations, Tolkien places his characters in situations that demonstrate their motivations. In addition to his explicit condemnation of reckless "chivalry" that puts others at risk, it is behavior in war that is treated both critically and ironically. For example, Éomer, falsely believing that his sister Éowyn had died in battle, begins a wild charge against Sauron's troops: "his fury had betrayed him" (*LotR*, RK.V.6); shortly after, the need to be a leader returns him to sanity just before Aragorn's fleet arrives to turn the battle. The similarities between Scott and Tolkien regarding "knightly/warrior imprudence" are best demonstrated, however, by a consideration of all of the *legendarium*, not just *The Lord of the Rings*.

As noted above, Tolkien, like Scott, depicts the negative effects of the fanatical will to domination. The latter is not only a trait of his powerful antagonists – Morgoth, Sauron, or Saruman – but also of Eldar such as Fëanor and the humans, Túrin and Denethor. In the essay "Myths Transformed", Tolkien describes Morgoth's delusion: "that he could destroy other beings and rid Arda of them completely. Hence his endeavour always to break wills and subordinate them to or absorb them into his own will and being" (*MR* 396). Sauron's flaw was that he loved order and disliked confusion and waste; in this, Tolkien compares him to Saruman. Sauron's love of intellect and order was corrupted into imposing the only "acceptable" order – his own. The same might be said of Denethor: in his final madness, he proclaims his willingness to destroy himself and his son rather than accept the ending of the Stewards' rule over Gondor.

In his final speech after he mocks Gandalf's counsel of hope and before he begins his self-immolation, he proclaims: "I would have things as they were in all the days of my life [...] But if doom denies this to me, then I will have *naught*" (*LotR*, RK.V.7). Prior to this moment, he has accused Gandalf of not only having designs on Gondor, but also of wanting "to stand behind every throne, north, south or west" and of planting Peregrin Took as a spy "within [his] very chamber" (*LotR*, RK.V.7). His fixation on maintaining the old order of the Stewards' rule combined with his guilt over his reckless command to Faramir and combined with his misreading of the vision of Aragorn's commandeered fleet in the *palantir* impels him to his suicidal act. Tolkien's mimetic harshness here contrasts with the gentler, albeit grudging acceptance Cedric gives to Ivanhoe – and to a changing order – at their reconciliation (*Ivanhoe* 376). Further, what Clare Simmons calls a "limited assimilation" of Saxons and Normans (Simmons 1990, 84) is signified by the presence of ranking Normans at the nuptials of Wilfred and Rowena (*Ivanhoe* 398); similarly, there is the Faramir/Eowyn marriage that unites Gondor and Rohan, and Aragorn and Arwen reunite the two strains of human/elf lineage, although not without Arwen's sacrifice of the lifespan of the Eldar.

Fëanor moves from grief at his father's murder by Melkor, whom he renames Morgoth, to an absolute focus on regaining the Silmarils. After despoiling the Teleri of their ships and leading his followers and many of his allies into exile in spite of Mandos's warning, Fëanor's oath becomes the sole motivation for his deeds, and he seeks the Silmarils with fanatical zeal. It is this abdication of moral concerns that relegates him to Mandos indefinitely. In an encounter with fanatical wilfulness, Scott's Ivanhoe, forgetting his own defense of knightly striving for glory, remonstrates with Richard, to no avail: "Wilfred [knew] how vain it was to contend with the wild spirit of chivalry which so often impelled his master upon dangers which he might easily have avoided, or rather, which it was unpardonable in him to have sought out" (*Ivanhoe*, 364). This is precisely Tolkien's criticism both of Beorhtnoth and of the elderly Beowulf: with others' lives at stake, the commander or king is not in the same moral position as the knight-errant – Wilfred or the young Beowulf. Similarly, Túrin, who resembles in his haplessness very much his model, Kullervo (Flieger 2012, 185) and, in his self-righteousness, Gisli

Súrsson of *The Saga of Gisli the Outlaw*. Túrin becomes ever more obstinate about getting submission to his will, e.g. overruling advice to destroy the bridge into Nargothrond. When he advocates a more aggressive defense of Nargothrond, "[deeds] which neither Morgoth nor Manwë can unwrite" (*CH* 161) his words echo the "chivalric" flaw discussed in "Ofermod". He is countered by Gwindor: "You think of yourself and your own glory"(*CH* 162) – words Wilfred of Ivanhoe is not allowed to say to his king.

There are doubtless other examples of the kinds of resonances between the works of Tolkien and Scott. Apart from sharing a medievalizing approach to narratives, the two most striking correspondences remain the critiques of empty chivalric deeds in the context of responsibility and an awareness of the destructive effects, both physical and moral, of unchecked fanaticism. In E.L. Risden's words, a source need not be explicitly visible in a text, but it is always there "peripherally" (Risden 2011, 21). Both Scott and Tolkien depict the wilfulness that characters conceal under a "greater cause," be it orthodoxy, or a cultural imaginary that "requires" heroic action as part of self-actualization. The distance between a Burley and a Richard, or a Túrin, is not that great. Tolkien is not overshadowed by Scott, but neither is the older writer untraceable in Tolkien's works.

Bibliography

Dawson, Graham. *Soldier Heroes: British Adventure, Empire and the Imagining of Masculinity*. New York and Abingdon: Routledge, 1994.

Fimi, Dimitra. "The Past as an Imaginary World: The Case of Medievalism." *Revisiting Imaginary Worlds: A Subcreation Studies Anthology*. Ed. Mark J. P. Wolf. New York and Abingdon: Routledge, 2017, 46-65.

Flieger, Verlyn. *Green Suns and Faërie: Essays on Tolkien*. Kent, OH: Kent State University Press, 2012.

Hart, Francis Russell. *Scott's Novels; The Plotting of Historic Survival*. Charlottesville, VA: University Press of Virginia, 1966.

Hunter, John. "The Reanimation of Antiquity and the Resistance to History: Macpherson – Scott – Tolkien." *Tolkien's Modern Middle Ages*. Eds. Jane Chance and Alfred K. Siewers. New York: Palgrave Macmillan, 2005, 61-75.

Lukács, György. *The Historical Novel*. Lincoln, NE: University of Nebraska Press, 1983.

Risden, E. L. "Source Criticism: Background and Applications." *Tolkien and the Study of His Sources: Critical Essays*. Ed. Jason Fisher. Jefferson, NC: McFarland, 2011, 17-28.

Rosebury, Brian. *Tolkien: A Cultural Phenomenon*. 2nd ed. New York: Palgrave Macmillan, 2003.

Scott, Walter. "An Essay on Chivalry." First published in the *Supplement to the Encyclopedia Britannica*, 1818, 3-126. Accessed at https://analepsis.files.wordpress.com/2013/08/wscottessaychivalry.pdf.

Ivanhoe. Ed. Graham Tulloch. London and New York: Penguin Books, 2000.

Old Mortality. Ed. Angus Calder. Harmondsworth: Penguin Books, 1975.

Simmons, Clare A. *Reversing the Conquest: History and Myth in Nineteenth-Century British Literature*. New Brunswick, NJ: Rutgers University Press, 1990.

Turner, Allan. "One Pair of Eyes: Focalisation and Worldbuilding." *Sub-creating Arda: World-building in J.R.R. Tolkien's Work, its Precursors and its Legacies*. Eds. Dimitra Fimi and Thomas Honegger. Cormarë Series 40. Zurich and Jena: Walking Tree Publishers, 2019, 17-29.

Luisa Paglieri

Tolkien and Shakespeare: Debtor Against His Will

Introductory Observations

Tolkien, as everybody knows, claimed not to like Shakespeare, even to hate him (*Letters* no. 163). Moreover, it can be said that Tolkien did not like drama as a genre. Drama, according to him, was "naturally hostile to Fantasy" (*TOFS* 61) and was a medium unsuitable for talking about Faerie, since it is very difficult to stage fantasy worlds convincingly. However, Tolkien knew Shakespeare's works very well: Shakespeare's influence on the Professor exists and is not superficial.

Sometimes Tolkien makes use of Shakespearean elements deliberately, in other cases the influence is not exactly intentional but must be credited to Tolkien's educational background as someone who had attended an English grammar school. According to Mario Praz, Shakespeare is the interpretive key to the entire English literature. All post-Renaissance English writers are influenced by him to some extent. Shakespeare is a part of their cultural heritage or they anticipate him in topics and motifs.[1] This is also true for Tolkien's works, where the reader can notice some influences which are explicit, while others, more indirect, are due to the shared background mentioned.

Among the explicit influences it is necessary to take a closer look at the ones derived from *Macbeth*, *King Lear* and probably *The Tempest*. As for the others, it is appropriate to speak of common themes or comparable elements in content and on the level of style. Of course, the deeper one digs, the more shared motifs one finds. However, Shakespeare is the more varied writer and makes use of a great variety of subjects and settings, while Tolkien remains more faithful to his world: his books and his favourite themes are interconnected.

---

1 Praz 1964, 190.

Tolkien's sources, however, are astonishingly varied, ranging from the biblical tradition to the classic poems, from northern and Celtic mythology to the Arthurian and Charlemagne cycles, to popular ballads, to tales and children's poetry.[2] Sometimes Tolkien seems to draw his inspiration from Shakespeare, but then he changes the perspective and deals with the same subject in a different way.

Also, both writers rarely invent, but prefer to adapt sources and pre-existing elements, re-interpreting them in new and sometimes unusual ways, so that the reader never gets the impression of encountering a mere repetition of already existing motifs.

Shakespeare's Great Tragedies and Tolkien

Macbeth is one of Shakespeare's works whose influence on Tolkien is manifest and palpable.

The motif of the Battle of the Trees is well rooted in Celtic traditions (it also appears in the *Mabinogion*) and a trace of the same myth can be found in Livius (the battle in the Silva Litana). Of course, Tolkien's use of this myth is very different from Shakespeare's. In his book trees can really walk.

Another element from *Macbeth* taken up by Tolkien is the motif of the prophecy that, following a long literary tradition, hides a trap. Macbeth cannot be killed by someone born of a woman and, true enough, he will be killed by Macduff, who was delivered by means of a Caesarean section. By analogy, the Lord of the Nazgûl cannot be killed by a man and it is therefore a woman who, together with a hobbit, kills him.[3]

Some features of Macbeth's can be found paralleled in Denethor's tragic pride, which leads him to suicide. Neither of the two is willing to survive a defeat and both are unwilling to repent. In this sense, both are far from the Christian ethos and we cannot exclude, given Tolkien's interest for the Goths, that Denethor owes something to Ermanaric, who committed suicide after being defeated by

---

2 See Fisher 2011 and Day 1994.
3 Shippey 2005, 205ff.

the Huns. And the reader could find an echo of Macbeth the usurper even in the figure of Boromir.[4] Like Macbeth, Boromir refuses the king's authority and wants to replace him. But the man from Gondor is clearly a man with many positive aspects while the Scottish lord lacks most of them.

Thorin, too, is somehow similar to the ambitious Macbeth but in Thorin's case the problem is not so much a desire to usurp the throne, but rather greed. The fall of the great, of the powerful, defeated by their own passions or by a fatal weakness, is very typical of Elizabethan drama[5] and is, in general, more prominent in drama than fiction. Another element that the play and *The Lord of the Rings* have in common is the role of the king as a healer. The English king Edward the Confessor has healing powers while in Macbeth's kingdom, illegally governed by an usurper, alarming events happen that indicate the disruption of the natural order.[6] *Macbeth* is the only Shakespearean tragedy where Anglo-Saxon (i.e. pre-Norman Conquest) characters are present or referred to, and some scenes take place in London during the reign of Edward the Confessor, i.e. before the Norman conquest in 1066.

Some people have pointed out the parallels between Galadriel with her "prophecies" and the three witches in *Macbeth,* in this case seen as fatal Norns and not as degraded hags. This connection seems to me tenuous and without a direct link.[7] However, Galadriel's terrible, formidable side has many literary precedents in form of pagan goddesses, faerie queens, and even the Virgin Mary who is referred to in the Catholic tradition as "terrible as an army". Galadriel is also called "sorceress" like the goddess Freya in Old Norse literature. Another analogy can be noticed between Malcolm and Aragorn, who are both ideal sovereigns.

The elements that *The Lord of the Rings* and *Macbeth* have in common are numerous and we can also find parallels in style and vocabulary, such as alliteration and a language rich in archaisms.[8]

---

4 Croft 2007b, 221.
5 See, for example, *Othello, The Jew of Malta* by Marlowe, etc.
6 Croft 2007b, 219.
7 Croft 2007b, 219.
8 Shippey 2005, 123.

Denethor's character, in particular, reminds the reader of another Shakespearean play, *King Lear*. Denethor's partiality for one of his sons is paralleled in King Lear's preference of some daughters, and also of another character, Gloucester, who prefers the brilliant and treacherous son Edmund to the detriment of the modest and faithful Edgar. In fact, in the subplot of *King Lear* the same motif is repeated. This motif of an unworthy son or daughter being preferred to a more virtuous sibling is very common in fairy tales and in epic poems and plays an important role in English literature (cf. *As You Like It*).[9] The gloomy atmosphere of *King Lear*, the old king's hopeless wanderings, the feeling of an ineluctable fate, the undeserved suffering of the good and the setting of the play in an archaic and barbarous world are rather reminiscent of Tolkien's *The Children of Hurin*. In *The Lord of the Rings*, Théoden, who dismisses the faithful nephew Eomer and listens to the flattering Wormtongue, is similar to Lear who banishes the honest Kent, and Tolkien's epic seems also to echo *King Lear* in some of the expressions used. Thus Shakespeare characterises the attitude of Lear's daughters towards their father as: "There is a great abatement of kindness" (*King Lear* I.iv), which is paralleled in Gandalf's observation: "The courtesy of your hall is somewhat lessened of late, Théoden son of Thengel" (*LotR*, TT.VI). However, the ending in Tolkien's book is less dramatic: Tolkien had a "tender heart"[10] and a Victorian-Edwardian cast of mind and did not participate in the harsh sensationalism of the Elizabethan writers.

Two Key Themes: Elements of Magic and Nature

The supernatural is a crucial element in Shakespeare's plays, even, according to some critics, one of his key features. Ghosts, fairies, and premonitions are numerous in the bard's works. The two writers handle this element in a very different way but the playwright's influence on Tolkien is undeniable.

Gandalf owes something to Prospero and it has been suggested to compare Gollum to Caliban (an outcast like him) or to Othello, victim of an obsession. (We can add that Gollum, with his monologues, is the most theatrical caracter

---

9 See Porrex and Ferrex in *Gorboduc*, the poem *The Tale of Gamelyn* (14th century), and *Arcadia* by Philip Sidney.
10 Shippey 2005, 363.

in *The Lord of the Rings*). The character of Prospero shows several ambiguous aspects: some critics have commented on his ambiguity, his manipulating attitude and his control over the spirits and the island, elements that make Prospero similar to Saruman.[11] In *The Tempest* there is a hint of a myth concerning trees: in fact Ariel had been imprisoned in a tree by the witch Sycorax (the myth of the dangerous tree appears also in *The Lord of the Rings*, in the episode of Old Man Willow). Ariel, defined as an "airy spirit", is somehow similar to the Elves who are connected, according to Tolkien, to light, and contrast with the dark chthonian element.

As for the presence of fairies in Shakespeare's works, they are to be found mostly (but not exclusively) in two plays: *The Tempest* (where we find Ariel and other spirits such as Juno, Ceres, Iris, and some nymphs) and *A Midsummer Night's Dream*. Hints about the fairy world can also be found in *Romeo and Juliet* (the famous description of Queen Mab'), *The Merry Wives of Windsor*, and *Henry IV*. It is widely known that Tolkien did not approve of the reductive and sometimes ridiculing portrait of fairy people found in Shakespeare. This reductive view, afterwards adopted also by the Victorian writers, concerns also their physical appearance: they are very small, lacking in majesty and dignity.[12]

Shakespeare uses many different words to refer to the fairy creatures: *spirits*, *faeries*, *elves*, and even *shadows*. Puck says "we fairies" and "we shadows" and calls Oberon (besides "fairy lord", "captain of our fairy band", and other names) "king of shadows". Puck is a complex character. His true name is Robin Goodfellow and Oberon calls him so. "Puck" was originally no proper noun but a common noun meant a particular type of fairy, not always benign, sometimes with malignant and dangerous features.[13] Men call this fairy "hobgoblin", as the fairy that speaks in the first act tells us. Puck is essentially a sprite: he calls the human beings "mortals", so apparently he is not subject to death. While

---

11 Riga 2007, 196f.
12 See *Letters* no.151. However, early in his career as a writer, Tolkien shared a similar outlook. In the poem *Goblin Feet* there are tiny fairies and in *The Hobbit* the Elves of Rivendell are funny and light-hearted.
13 See Ryan 2009. The name Puck derives from the Anglo-Saxon noun *puca* or *pucca* which means spirit and is related to the words *puki* (Norwegian), *puke* (Swedish), *puge* (Danish), *puks* (Low German), *pwca* or *bwca* (Welsh). These terms could derive from the Indo-European root *bog* (supernatural being). Besides, in the English language, both medieval and modern, there is a certain terminological confusion between the terms *elf* and *fairy*.

Shakespeare follows the popular conception of the Little People (largely indebted to the Celtic tradition that ascribed a whimsical disposition to these supernatural beings, who were often very small), Tolkien primarily taps into to the Old Norse tradition that described elves as powerful and majestic beings, deities indeed, although less powerful than the great Aesir like Odin and Thor. A proper cult was dedicated to elves, which included often the offering of sacrifices. Instead, in Shakespeare's plays, the members of the little People have some supernatural powers but they use them for limited purposes (nasty tricks, manipulating the emotions in love relationships, to abduct children) while Tolkien's Elves perform deeds that influence the destiny of Arda.

Tolkien, following Snorri's tradition, ascribes beauty and positive features to elves, but in folk tradition they are often wicked or at least untrustworthy.[14]

Yet Shakespeare and Tolkien share another theme: the theme of nature in general and of the forest in particular. Forests accompany Tolkien's readers as "green spaces" almost continuously. In the same way the setting in the woods is very frequent in Shakespeare's plays. The critic Northrop Fry coined the term "Green World" to refer to this specific type of setting: the Green World is the friendly world of the woods, a world with female connotations, which stands in contrast to the city, i.e. the world dominated by the male element.

In the play *As You Like It* the forest of Arden offers shelter and functions as a sanctuary and an alternative world. It is also the kingdom of animals and, above all, it is a real and active "character", able to influence people.[15] The villains, after entering the forest, change for the better and are purified, and even the virtuous characters become spiritually richer. There is an evident parallel to Lothlórien which, according to Aragorn, transforms people who venture in there.[16] The forest is a place of initiation, and both writers make use of this fundamental symbol. In *As You Like It* it is said that even rivers and stones can talk and have a language. Tolkien, and also Saint Bernard, would certainly

---

14 In many popular ballads they kidnap or kill human beings (see the famous popular ballad about the Elven King's Daughter). In some medieval texts like *Sir Orfeo* Faerie is a dangerous place.
15 Animals are the free citizens of this wild kingdom, "the native burghers of this desert city" (II.1). Furthermore, the concept of the forest-as-character, as visible in Touchstone's statement "let the forest judge" (III.2), reminds of C.S. Lewis's *The Chronicles of Narnia* where the forest is seen as an agent, too.
16 *LotR*, FR.II.VI. In *The Tempest*, too, Nature is allied with the powers of Good (Praz 1967, 155).

agree.[17] In the same play we also find a comparison between the corrupted life of the court and the farmers' and woodmen's honest and simple life. Yet Shakespeare's depiction of the rural world goes beyond idealism found in many of the pastoral works of the Renaissance. Shakespeare knew the rural world very well, he had experienced it first hand. As a consequence, his forest is not an ideal Arcadia and it is telling that the shepherdess Audrey's language is rustic and "ungrammmatical" and lacks the elegant eloquence of many characters found in pastoral literature.

The predilection for the rural setting and its small communities is clearly shared by Tolkien.[18] We should also remember that Shakespeare and Tolkien are fellow countrymen: Shakespeare's roots are in Warwickshire, not very far from Sarehole where Tolkien spent formative years of his childhood. Thus, the two writers share the same visual images and landscape impressions.

Power, Kings, Commoners

Both writers focus on the theme of power. In Shakespeare, the theme of legitimacy and usurpation has a prominent place. Tolkien, by contrast, is more straightforward, and his models are less conflictual: the royal blood and the king's charisma preserve their aura, while Shakespeare is a Renaissance man, who brings Machiavelli's theories into the discussion.

Kingship is, for both writers, more than a simple form of how a nation can be goverened since it partakes in the divine authority of God's rule – even if this is more problematic in Shakespeare. In Shakespeare's historical plays there are references to the sacrality of the person of the king. The deepest and most complex discussion of this theme can be found in *Richard II,* where the sovereign is compared to Jesus and his dethronization to the Passion.

The theme of the maturation of the heir to become worthy of the throne can be seen in both Aragorn and Hal (i.e. Henry V). Tolkien, however, approaches the topic differently because Aragorn must not repudiate his past.

---

17 *As You Like It* (act II, scene 1, 1-18).
18 Catà 2012, 329.

The motif of the king in disguise, so frequent in fiction, is present in the play *Measure for Measure* as well as in *The Lord of the Rings*. In other Shakespearean plays a new, worthier king succeeds an usurper or tyrant (Malcolm, Albany, Fortinbras), so that also in Shakesperare's plays the motif of "the return of the king" after a chaotic period is a constant motif.

With the creation of the hobbits, Tolkien pays his tribute to the popular English ideal of the rural idyll. The same thing can be said for Shakespeare, who describes his servants, farmers, commoners, bourgeois in a similar way. The peasants of *As You Like It,* the "mechanics" of *A Midsummer Night's Dream,* the wives of Windsor, like the hobbits, owe much to the English countryman or the small landowner as he is described in English literature from Chaucer to Fielding and to Agatha Christie. It is always the same rural background, a world sometimes narrow, but on the whole pleasant.

The Warrior Princess, the Bandit, and other Shared Themes

With the character of Eowyn, Tolkien makes use of the old theme of the warrior woman, not unfamiliar also to Shakespeare.[19] Only wicked women or women who egg others on to do evil deeds are lacking. Characters comparable to Lady Macbeth, Goneril, Regan, or Dionyza (the villainess in Pericles) are missing in *The Lord of the Rings* .

In Tolkien there are plenty of powerful female characters such as Melian or Galadriel. Both are the queens of the wood, like Titania, and all three are reminiscent of the great Goddess to whom Goldberry, too, is linked. Arwen, by contrast, could be seen as representing another mythical character, the supernatural wife of a human king (who strengthens his royalty), a character absent in Shakespeare.

In *The Merchant of Venice* the co-protagonist Portia disguises herself as a man in order to be accepted in a male dominated world. The camouflage is a very

---

19 See Queen Margaret in *Henry VI* and the Countess of Salisbury in *Edward III*. The latter is a play once considered apocryphal but now ascribed mostly to Shakespeare (Melchiori 1994). For the character of the warrior woman, see Chiesa Isnardi 1991, 303f.

common theatrical device, often used by Shakespeare.[20] We have the examples of Portia, Viola, Julia, and Rosalind. Their disguises are similar to Eowyn's because they allow a woman to act freely in a patriarchal society. The resourceful Portia was very loved by Victorian women and by suffragists.[21] Since Portia's part is a very long one, a quarter of the whole play, she could be considered one of, if not *the* main protagonist of the play.

Furthermore, we often have the following situation in Shakespeare: a man (or woman) who, unappreciated or the victim of persecution, retires into a forest and sometimes becomes a bandit or an outcast. This is the case with Valentine in *The Two Gentlemen of Verona*, Orlando, the Duke, and Rosalind in disguise in *As You Like It*. This theme, recurring in many epics, from the *Ramayana* to the Charlemagne cycle, is also traceable in Tolkien's works – see Turin, Beren, and even Aragorn.[22]

Other elements common to both writers are the role ascribed to a ring (as in the *The Merchant of Venice* and in *The Two Gentlemen*), the unintentional murder of a friend or relative (a very ancient topos, mostly epic, to be found in *Henry VI* and in *The Children of Húrin*), the intelligent disobedience that acts against an irrational or morally misguided order for a higher good (Eomer, Faramir, Hama, Kent, and the provost in *Measure for Measure*), the visions concerning the kings of the past or future (*Richard II*, *Macbeth*, and also *LotR*, CA.I.VIII), and the presence of supernatural entities, not only elves and fairies, but also spirits, deities, etc.

Shakespeare's and Tolkien's works show a mixture of different temporal dimensions and elements belonging to different cultures. Gondor, similar to a Renaissance city, is contemporary with the barbaric Rohirrim and also with the Hobbits, characters typical of a certain rural society in the nineteenth century. Shakespeare, in the same way, mixes different civilizations and eras as a matter of course.

---

20 This device has the additional advantage of allowing male actors to play these roles without having to disguise themselves as females since Elizabethan theatre companies had no female actors.
21 Montanino 2012, 33.
22 Flieger 2003, 99.

The Quest for and the Love of the Word

One of the so-called "romances", *Perycles, Prince of Tyre* is a very peculiar theatrical experiment that transposes a narrative work, a medieval romance derived from a Hellenistic tale, onto the stage. This play, interpreted by many critics as the description of an initiation journey,[23] narrates Perycles' adventures and is structured as a real quest. The subject matter, the vicissitudes of a couple, is derived from the classics and appears again in many chivalric poems. Tolkien certainly was influenced by these sources.

Perycles has been neglected by critics as a work that shows similarities to and shares a sensitivity with *The Lord of the Rings* and *The Hobbit*, even though there are several common themes. Thus the character of Cerimon, a healer who shows many parallels to a demigod, echoes Aragorn and also Gandalf. The latter, after his initiation experience and "re-birth", looks more than half divine. Then there is the presence of evil. In *Perycles* we have incest as the original sin, the archetypal form of evil, and the starting point of the action. Furthermore, there are trials that the characters must face, including solving riddles, the presence of supernatural events, and finally the "return of the king" with Perycles recovering his kingdom. Besides, the play is rich in archaisms, a feature that brings it close to the chivalric world and to Tolkien.

However, the type of the maiden who is virtuous and subject to trials, like Marina or Imogen, is missing in Tolkien's fiction. With the exception of Eowyn, Tolkien's female caracters are rather static, and there is neither a Cinderella nor a Donkey Skin, there is neither evolution nor initiation by trial.

The comedy *The Two Gentlemen of Verona*, however, is a real chivalric romance transposed onto the stage, and also here we find some parallels to *The Lord of the Rings*.

The two writers have another common feature: a deep love and veneration for language.

The magical, metaphysical, creative role of words in Tolkien's works is well known, as well as his philological expertise and deep knowledge of language

---

23 Daiches 1972, 298

and languages.[24] Shakespeare's areas of expertise are different, yet he is generally praised for his amazingly creative talent for handling words as well as for the breadth and richness of his vocabulary.

The Bard and the Professor worship the word, and know its evocative power and its musicality: Shakespeare's songs are "music" even without the accompaniment.

Finally, we could mention the fact that both Tolkien and Shakespeare are heirs of the bardic traditon of dramatized poetry: to this heritage English drama owes much. Even Tolkien, who read aloud his texts to his friends, and who, following the same tradition, used to dramatize his readings.[25]

Bibliography

Primary Sources

SHAKESPEARE, William. *King Lear*. Ed. R. Wilson, London: Macmillan, 1986.

King Richard II. London and New York: Methuen, 1982.

King Henry IV.1. London: Methuen, 1978.

A Midsummer Night's Dream. London: Cambridge University Press, 1971.

The Two Gentlemen of Verona. Harmondsworth: Penguin, 1968.

The Complete Works of William Shakespeare. shakespeare.mit.edu, 1964 (accessed August 2018).

Secondary Sources

CARPENTER, Humphrey. *J.R.R. Tolkien: A Biography*. Boston: Houghton Mifflin, 2000.

CATÀ, Cesare. *Filosofia del fantastico*. Rimini: Il Cerchio, 2012.

CHANCE, Jane (ed.). *Tolkien the Medievalist*. London and New York: Routledge, 2003.

CHIESA ISNARDI, Gianna. *I miti nordici*. Milan: CDE, 1991.

---

24 Flieger 2002, 33ff.
25 Carpenter 2000 (part four, chapter III).

CROFT, Janet Brennan (ed.). *Tolkien and Shakespeare: Essays on Shared Themes and Languages*. Jefferson, NC: McFarland, 2007.

"'Bid the Tree Unfix His Earthbound Root': Motifs from *Macbeth* in J.R.R. Tolkien's *The Lord of the Rings*." *Tolkien and Shakespeare: Essays on Shared Themes and Languages*. Ed. Janet Brennan Croft. Jefferson, NC: McFarland, 2007, 215-228.

DAICHES, David. *A Critical History of English Literature*. 4 volumes. London: Secker & Warburg, 1972.

DAY, David. *Tolkien's Ring*. London: HarperCollins, 1994.

FISHER, Jason (ed.). *Tolkien and the Study of his Sources*. Jefferson, NC: McFarland, 2011.

FLIEGER, Verlyn. "Tolkien's Wild Men: From Medieval to Modern." *Tolkien the Medievalist*. Ed. Jane Chance. London and New York: Routledge, 2003, 95-104.

Splintered Light. Kent, OH: Kent State University Press, 2002.

MELCHIORI, Giorgio. *Shakespeare, genesi e struttura delle opere*. Bari: Laterza, 1994.

MONTANINO, Francesca. "Shylock è un gentleman! *The Merchant of Venice*, Henry Irving e l'Inghilterra vittoriana." *Proceedings of the "Shakespeare and his Contemporaries" Graduate Conference*. Ed. Mark Roberts. Florence: British Institute of Florence, 2012, 196-214.

PRAZ, Mario. *Storia della letteratura inglese*. Florence: Sansoni, 1967.

"Introduzione a Shakespeare." *Tutte le opere*. Florence: Sansoni, 1964, ix-xxi.

RIGA, Frank P. "Merlin, Prospero, Saruman, and Gandalf: Corrosive Uses of Power in Shakespeare and Tolkien." *Tolkien and Shakespeare: Essays on Shared Themes and Languages*. Ed. Janet Brennan Croft. Jefferson, NC: McFarland, 2007, 196-214.

ROBERTS, Mark (ed.). *Proceedings of the "Shakespeare and his Contemporaries" Graduate Conference*. Florence: British Institute of Florence, 2012.

RYAN, J.S. "Before Puck – the Púkel-men and *puca*." *Tolkien's View. Windows into his World*. Zurich and Jena: Walking Tree Publishers, 2009, 223-233.

SHIPPEY, Tom. *J.R.R. Tolkien: la via per la Terra di Mezzo*. Genua and Milan: Marietti, 2005.

Sara Gianotto

Tolkien and Alfieri. Fëanor and the Characters of Alfierian Tragedy.[1]

'Fair shall the end be,' he cried, 'though long and hard shall be the road! Say farewell to bondage! But say farewell also to ease! Say farewell to the weak! Say farewell to your treasures! More still shall we make. Journey light: but bring with you your swords! (Fëanor in *The Silmarillion*, chapter IX)

Squillan più forte / le trombe? Ivi si vada: a me il mio brando / basta solo. Tu scostati, mi lascia; / obbedisci. Là corro: ivi si alberga morte / ch'io cerco.[2] (Saul in *Saul* V.3)

Introduction

John Ronald Reuel Tolkien and Vittorio Alfieri[3]: one an English professor who lived the majority of his life in 20th century Oxford, the other an Italian intellectual, who lived during the second half of the 18th century, traveling both in Italy and in Europe. The first a middle class Catholic, the other an anticlerical noble; different were also their favoured forms of expression, from Tolkien's prose (sometimes even written in verse), to Alfieri's carefully structured tragedies and rhymes.

But even through these enormous differences, it is possible to establish a dialogue between these two authors: Alfieri based his entire artistic production on the tragic nature of his characters, even turning himself into one of those characters in his *Vita*; Tolkien made use of tragic characters on very few but terribly important occasions, most notably Fëanor, the Elf, who will be the

---

1 Translated from Italian by Andrea Rispoli.
2 The trumpet sound / louder and louder? Thither let me go: / For me my sword alone will be sufficient. / Thou, quit me, go: obey. I thither run: / There, where the death I seek for has home.
3 Vittorio Alfieri was born in Asti in 1749 and died in Florence in 1803; during his life he traveled far and wide. As he states himself in his autobiography, his spirit was restless, and always needed new inspirations and new ways to assert his values, freedom being the first amongst these. What we are dealing with is a writer who criticised the ever present and dominant discourse of Enlightenment of the time, and got ever closer to the ideals of Romanticism, soon to become the predominant literary movement. His production was fruitful, in fact he wrote 21 tragedies, several political prose pieces, some comedies, some poetry (for example the *Rime*) and his autobiography, the *Vita*.

subject of this paper. The goal of our investigation of Fëanor and the Alfierian tragic characters is to discover how these two authors, seemingly so far away from each other, are still able to communicate through the use of archetypes which represent fundamentals of human nature.

Tragedy

The literary genre of tragedy has its roots in Ancient Greece, during the 6th century BC; Aristotle defines it in his *Poetics* as follows:

> Tragedy, then, is an imitation of an action that is serious, complete, and of a certain magnitude; in language embellished with each kind of artistic ornament, the several kinds being found in separate parts of the play; in the form of action, not of narrative; through pity and fear effecting the proper purgation of these emotions. (*Poetics*, 1149b 24-28)

Tragedy is thus the genre that puts on stage the drama of the human being, uncovering the passions of the human soul. It is concerned with universal themes, such as freedom, death, heroism, down to the vilest of deeds, all in order to evoke a catharsis in the audience. In fact, members of the audience may empathically identify with the impulses that generate such actions, and in doing so are able to condemn those evil deeds; the final *nemesis* is in fact the punishment for those misdeeds, which evokes sensations such as compassion and terror, therefore allowing the foresaid catharsis and making the audience aware of their emotions.

The goal of this essay is to understand whether Tolkien also made use of such stylistic features in his work, despite the fact that it is not a proper tragedy.

For Alfieri, tragic poetry was the natural way of expressing himself;[4] composing poetry, putting on stage tragic characters, and following his political views and his freedom were one and the same. Given his personality and his convictions, it could not have been otherwise; he himself wrote, in his answer to Calzabigi: "Ciò che mi mosse a scrivere da prima, fu la noia, e il tedio d'ogni cosa, misto a bollor di gioventù, desiderio di gloria e necessità di occuparmi in qualche

---

4 Binni (2015, 52) wrote that "it is possible to understand how the very foundations of the poet Alfieri were terribly dramatic, how his choice to produce tragedies was his only answer to his tragic calling, his need to express himself through contrast, conflict and action-reaction."

maniera, che più fosse confacente alla mia inclinazione."[5] In his tragedies, most of his protagonists are lofty and elevated. They are moved by the raging flames of their passion for freedom, pursuing it even to the death, as can be seen in the figures of Saul, Mirra, Antigone, and others. As can be expected, Tolkien seems, at least on the surface, to move far away from all these ideals. First of all, he mostly writes prose and never wrote for theatre. For him, writing was an instinct born from his love of languages and for the history those languages carried. Even so, amongst all of his characters, two of them seem to share many of the characteristics we find in Alfierian heroes. Both of them are to be found in *The Silmarillion*: the Elf, Fëanor, and the Man, Túrin Turambar. There would be much to write on both of these characters, but for limitations of space, we will focus on Fëanor.

The Structure of the Story – Fëanor as a Tragic Character

Let us then take a closer look at the character of Fëanor and analyse his story in order to discover how both his actions and his very being can be classified as tragic according to Alfieri's models.

Fëanor was born in Aman, in the Year of the Trees 1169,[6] as the son of Finwë, High King of the Noldor, and Míriel Serinde, also of the Noldor race. What we are dealing with is, then, a noble character, of royal lineage. His life was filled with great deeds. Most notable of all was without a doubt the creation of the Silmarils, the most beautiful gems ever to exist, which contained in their essence the light of the Two Trees of Valinor. These were, however, stolen by Melkor, the fallen Vala, and it was because of this that Fëanor swore a terrible oath to take back the gems whatever it takes. This oath was imposed on his sons and all those who decided to follow him. Fëanor's attempt to fulfil his oath led to terrible deeds and, in the end, caused his death.

We can already see how the structure of the story is similar to that of a tragedy, which Alfieri also used. It is not possible to summarize all of Alfieri's tragedies,

---

5 "What brought me to write was, first, boredom, and the tedium of all things, together with the fires of youth, the desire for fame and the necessity of occupying myself, in a way that was fitting of my talent." "Risposta dell'Alfieri al Calzabigi", in Alfieri 1978.
6 AAm1, *MR* 101.

but we can identify some recurring elements in his storytelling and structure, and will therefore look at just some of his most important works. First of all, Alfieri stated that a proper tragedy needed to be

> a five-act tragedy, with each act filled only with the subject so far as possible, the whole play spoken only by characters involved in the action, not by confidantes or lookers-on. It has to be a tragedy with a single plot-line, moving as swiftly as possible while allowing for the passion which is always present to a greater or lesser extent. Furthermore, it has to be as simple as the custom of art allows, dark and fierce as far as nature permits, and as ardent as I could make it.[7]

Therefore, a tragedy needs to be focused on and centred around the character. In the story of Fëanor, we can see how there is one theme, the creation of the Silmarils, and how many more stories unravel following this event. Artistotle, in his *Poetics*, points out several fundamental elements, such as vicissitudes (a situation's sudden change to its opposite), which corresponds to Fëanor's rejection of the idea of giving up the Silmarils.[8] His oath of vengeance, on the other hand, is a catastrophe: it occurs as a consequence to a previous action and it brings about pain and suffering, both for Fëanor and for his kind. Lastly, we can see a moment of recognition, which allows a progress from ignorance to knowledge, even if it is negatively connotated. This development occurs when Fëanor realizes that Melkor's true intentions were to steal the Silmarils rather than to help Fëanor free himself of the Valar's influence and so-called "imprisonment". These three elements are prominently present in Alfieri's work. We can see them in Virginia's death in the tragedy that bears her name, or in how, with clever deceit, a dying Eteocle is able to kill his brother in the *Polinice*; or also in the voluntary death of Antigone. These are all key moments placed at the end of each tragedy, all of which cause terrible suffering. In Fëanor's case, the catastrophe is not placed at the end of his story. His death was just a consequence of his oath, and it was not the worst event. Let me just mention two of the many terrible events that dominated Fëanor's rebellion. There is first the Kinslaying at Alqualondë, or the crossing of the Helcaraxë. We can

---

7 Alfieri, "Risposta dell'Alfieri al Calzabigi", in Alfieri 1978. The original reads: "di cinque atti pieni, per quanto il soggetto dà, del solo soggetto; dialogizzata dei soli personaggi attori, e non consultori o spettatori; la tragedia di un solo filo ordita; rapida per quanto si può servendo alle passioni, che tutte più o meno vogliono pur dilungarsi, semplice per quanto uso d'arte il comporti, tetra e feroce, per quanto natura il soffra, calda quanto era in me."

8 In fact, we would expect Fëanor to answer positively to the Valar's request, so that the Trees could be saved and the light could be restored. However, this does not happen and the tragedy begins.

draw a direct comparison by comparing Fëanor's refusal to the choice made by Antigone, who preferred death to the marriage with Emone. As for the moment of recognition, we can see it paralleled in the one between Antigone and Argia, even though, in this case, it is a positive one.[9]

According to what we observed, we can see how there are several similarities between the narrative structures of these stories. It is possible to see Fëanor as a tragic character similar to those in Alfieri's tragedies. We shall now discuss the recurring *topoi*, and the ways in which these characters can make both audiences and readers ponder on the nature of the human soul.

Creative Power and Moral Freedom

What is the motivation for these characters, both in Tolkien and in Alfieri, to act how they do? They are all moved by an inner flame, an unquenchable energy that compels them to act, even if it is for different reasons.

Fëanor is a Noldor Elf and represents both the beautiful and terrible potential of his kind. Verlyn Flieger (2002, 99-100) writes: "The Noldor embody the highest level of humanity's achievement and potential. Of all the Three Kindreds, they make the most material contributions to art and science." In *The Silmarillion* we can read about the Noldor:

> great became their knowledge and their skill; yet even greater was their thirst for more knowledge, and in many things they soon surpassed their teachers. They were changeful in speech, for they had great love of words, and sought ever to find names more fit for all things they knew or imagined. (*S*, Qu.5)

It was a loremaster of the Noldor, Rúmil, who created the first alphabet to write down language; later, Fëanor perfected it in form of the Tengwar, known and used by almost everyone in Middle-earth. It is therefore not by chance that the Noldor have been attached to Aulë more than to any other Valar. This can be seen as a sign that the enormous potential of mankind can be used to achieve excellence or end up in the abyss of the worst excesses. Like Aulë, they were gifted with great creative *vis*, but unlike him they were not able to let go of

---

9 All these elements come back later during the aforementioned story of Túrin Turambar.

their creations or submit to a greater authority.[10] Tolkien, being the philologist that he was, expresses all this in the root of the word "Noldor". He writes in the appendix of *The Silmarillion* that *ngol*, meaning "wise, wisdom", is the root of the word Noldor. He then specifies that "wise", in this case, is used to designate one who possesses knowledge, but not necessarily astuteness of judgement.

Fëanor possesses all of these characteristics in greater measure than any other, and he can be seen as a perfect representation of the Noldor type.[11] In *The Silmarillion*, his birth is described as follows: "In that time was born in Eldamar, in the house of the King in Tirion upon the crown of Tuna, the eldest of the sons of Finwë, and the most beloved. Curufinwë was his name, but by his mother he was called Fëanor, spirit of fire" (*S*, Qu.6). Fëanor is in fact the name given to him by his mother, a practice amongst the Elves which could imply prophetic elements, revealing the essence of a child's character.[12] The name given to him by his father, Curufinwë, is the union of the name Finwë with the word *curu*, meaning "skill". These same concepts are repeated several times: "Fëanor was the mightiest in skill of word and of hand, more learned than his brothers; his spirit burned as a flame" (*S*, Qu.5) and again

> Fëanor grew swiftly, as if a secret fire were kindled within him. He was tall, and fair of face, and masterful, his eyes piercingly bright and his hair raven-dark; in the pursuit of all his purposes eager and steadfast. Few ever changed his course by counsel, none by force. He became of all the Noldor, then or after, the most subtle in mind and the most skilled in hand. (*S*, Qu.5)

Fëanor, then, is ruled by a passion for knowledge and creating things. Originally, this is a fully legitimate desire,[13] yet it makes him ignore the boundaries of what is "right", so that this passion becomes perverted and leads him into madness and addiction.

Alfierian characters are equally passionate, but their hearts beat for the protection of moral freedom. Antigone prefers dying to submitting to the blackmailing of the tyrant Creonte; Mirra tries with all her might to resist the inane passions of her father Ciniro, choosing to die as well; Saul fights against himself, in a

---

10 See Flieger 2002, 100ff.
11 Shippey (2005, 281-88) stresses that Fëanor is a pure Noldor, and that his characteristics and his behaviour is in agreement with the ideals found in the Old Norse heroic tradition.
12 *MR* 216-17, *Peoples* 339-40.
13 Shippey 2001, 237-42.

conflicted struggle between his thirst for power, the love of his children, and his royal duties. It is in such situations that Alfieri's characters are elevated above the average moral framework, and when put face to face with death, they find the strength to rise above the petty and mundane world. This inner struggle evokes in the audience both sympathy and admiration.[14] Furthermore, Alfieri's characters can be put into different categories.[15] We have the lovers, like Carlo or Emone, the protectors of freedom, like Timoleone or Bruto, the strong women, like Antigone or Virginia, and the tyrants, such as Creonte or Filippo. Each of these characters has something that drives them, be it love, which can also be filial or parental, the pursuit of justice, or a negatively connoted thirst for power. They are all, however, attributable to the pursuit of freedom and are therefore an affirmation of life, a pivotal characteristic of human nature. Fëanor fits this mould perfectly. He, too, wants to affirm his being through his creations, his freedom to create without having to submit.

The Moment of Choice and Solitude

One of the central parts of Fëanor's story, which we find in many of Alfieri's characters, is the crucial moment when the protagonist needs to prove himself. This moment arrives in the aftermath of Melkor and Ungoliant's attack on the Trees. The only hope the Valar have of saving them is by healing them through the light enclosed within the Silmarils. Manwë therefore asks Fëanor to give them up, so that Yavanna might undo Melkor's evil deed. However, this is no easy choice for Fëanor, as he makes explicit:

> For the less even as for the greater there is some deed that he may accomplish but once only; and in that deed his heart shall rest. It may be that I can unlock my jewels, but never again shall I make their like; and if I must break them, I shall break my heart, and I shall be slain. (*S*, Qu.9)

At the end of his speech, he decides against giving them up. The deed is done, the point of no return has been crossed, and nothing shall be like it was before. From here onwards a chain of events will unfold, each more nefarious than the one before. Fëanor was not able to give up his attachment to his creation, and

---

14 See Fubini 1967.
15 As he himself states in his *Parere sulle Tragedie*.

love has turned into blind craving. As becomes clear, to renounce them would have been the right choice for the greater good, even if it had not been easy.[16] Yet even before this events, Tolkien has given us clues as to the path that Fëanor would take. Thus we can distinguish clear hints at Fëanor's growing obsession with his work when he threatens his brother Fingolfin, or when he decides to hide the Silmarils from everyone's sight. Yet it would have been possible to make the right choice until the moment of his rejection, which triggered a sequence of ever more terrible acts, such as the oath or the kinslaying.

We can see a similar pattern in Saul, because he is a tyrant and therefore already on the path to his downfall. He is, already at the beginning of the tragedy, a tormented character, stuck in a conflict between kingship and parenthood.[17] Saul is a fallen king, he has already lost his legitimacy for the clerical caste, and David is already anointed to succeed him. But being king is part of his own being, and he cannot abandon it. Furthermore, he himself is aware of his growing senility. The realisation that he is not fully his old self anymore destroys him. In him, we see the conflict between dreams of grandeur and the limits imposed by being a human. Also, we must not forget the important role that the looming presence of God plays. We come to a crucial moment when Saul, overwhelmed by his rage, tries to kill David: "Who, who boasts thus? Is there another sword in the camp / next to mine, which I unsheathe? He's a blasphemer, let him perish, / Who dares defy it."[18] Afterwards, this rage increases to the point of Saul killing the priest Achimelech: "Quick, let him be dragg'd hence to punishment; / To agonizing and protracted death."[19] All the efforts of his children to bring him back to sanity are for naught, and in the last act Saul sinks into a delirium. Another characteristic which brings together Saul and Fëanor is their solitude and isolation. They find sanctuary within themselves, refusing help from their loved ones, and we could make an interesting comparison here between Saul's sweet daughter Micol, and the wise Nerdanel, wife to Fëanor.[20] We see a similar trope in Filippo as well: a

---

16 See Flieger 2002, 110ff.
17 See De Benedetto & Perdichizzi 2014.
18 *Saul*, act III, scene IV. Original: "Chi, chi si vanta? Havvi altra spada in campo / Che questa mia, ch'io snudo? Empio è, si uccida / Pera, chi la sprezzò."
19 *Saul*, act IV, scene IV. Original: "Or via, si tragga / a morte tosto; a cruda morte e lunga."
20 Nerdanel distances herself from him when he begins to develop his resentment towards the Valar. She will later make one last desperate (and in the end futile) attempt to stop him from departing from Aman after the oath (see *Peoples* 353-68).

tormented tyrant, who isolates himself from everyone and begins to see enemies everywhere, until this makes him commit murder and, in so doing, causes both his son and wife to kill themselves.

Fate and Free Will

We have seen why the characters act, and how they usually find themselves on the wrong side of the *sublime*. The question arises therefore: do they really have a choice, or are they condemned by fate? For Tolkien, the discussion of Fate and Free Will has been going on for some time, and is far from concluded.[21] First of all, we know that fates differ from race to race. Men are free to determine their destiny for themselves, an integral part of the Gift of Iluvatar.[22] It is different for the Elves, since they are linked much more intimately to Arda and to its fate. As said, the argument is far from resolved. For our purpose, we will concentrate on the moment of Fëanor's refusal to give the Silmarils to Yavanna. At that moment, the jewels had already been stolen, even though no one yet knows about the theft, and we read in *The Silmarillion*: "The Silmarils had passed away, and all one it may seem whether Fëanor had said yea or nay to Yavanna; yet had he said yea at the first, before the tidings came from Formenos, it may be that his after deeds would have been other than they were" (S, Qu.9). Flieger draws our attention to this passage and argues that this is in complete constrast to the idea that the Music, already sung, controls the fate of the Elves. She then goes on that this shows that what is laid down by the Music is the general fate of the Silmarils, and not Fëanor's specific individual actions. This way, she concludes, Tolkien wants to show that Free Will applies to a protagonist's control over his or her actions, but does not extend to a control of outside events. An Elf cannot change Fate, but he or she can change his or her own decisions and therefore influence future actions and events.[23]

Fate has always been a fundamental element in tragedies from their very origin. Thus in ancient Greek tragedies, such as Oedipus, even the Gods cannot escape from the clutches of fate. For Alfieri, fate presents itself mostly in his

---

21 Tolkien himself dedicated FFW to this very theme. This same question is also at the heart of the debate between Flieger (2009) and Fornet-Ponse (2010).
22 See *S*, Qu.2. Shortly after we get to know that their deeds will be to the glory of Eru, too.
23 See Flieger 2009.

works set in an ancient Greek framework. Matters become interesting when we start drawing comparisons between him and Tolkien. Alfieri's protagonists often find themselves trapped in having to make a choice in a situation that is beyond their control. Mirra, for example, falls tragically in love with her father, just like Carlo, son of Filippo, falls in love with Isabella, his father's wife, or how Saul inevitably finds himself deteriorating at the end of his life. There is something greater that controls the protagonists' destinies, but the greatness of Alfieri's heroes, be they good or evil, is found in their reactions to these situations. They try not to allow it to dominate their lives but, given their status as champions of moral freedom, oppose it with all their might. Their free will is always prominently displayed. Thus Saul causes his own demise through his own actions. In many cases, the only way for these characters to control their destiny is death. This death, however, is always seen as a brave choice in the name of freedom, and never as surrender. Antigone, threatened by Creonte's blackmailing, finds in death the most extreme representation of freedom, as does Mirra who, instead of succumbing to her inane passion, decides to regain her dignity by stabbing herself. Again, Saul makes for a great example: he, in the end, chooses death to atone for and end his heinous acts and terrible decision, as a solution to his conflicts and to regain his stability and sense of self.

Fëanor instead dies as the consequence of a rash and foolish decision in battle. He is killed by Gothmog, the Lord of Balrogs, because, following his anger, he allowed himself to become separated from his men. His death brings no redemption, but appears to be a punishment for his *ofermod*. His last inconsiderate act ends thus tragically, and for him there will be no coming back[24] since his body immediately dissolves, burned by the intense heat of his own *fëa*. It is interesting to note how Tolkien describes this death in a matter-of-fact tone in just a few sentences, as if to underline the absence of heroism.

Conclusion

We can see that the initial thesis of this essay has been confirmed: even the British writer was able to put to good use the stylistic features of tragedy, mak-

---

24 The fate of the Elves beyond the death of their body was a subject on which Tolkien often changed his mind (see Converse, Reincarnation).

ing Fëanor a fully-fledged tragic character. Considering the comparisons that have been made throughout the essay, while keeping in mind the great differences between the two authors, it can be stated that the Elf would fit in well amongst the characters of Alfieri's work. Moved by a great love for his creations, he isolates himself and causes his own downfall. In doing so he appears as a tyrant, comparable to Filippo and Saul. The comparison with Saul is particularly accurate, since both characters are torn. Furthermore, both characters follow their own destiny without giving any thought to the "conseguenze collettive".[25] Saul finds back to himself in death; Fëanor, by contrast, does not and leaves behind a catastrophic oath. We get a similar message from both authors: however desperate the situation might be, and despite the constant oppression of fate, there is always a choice, and it is up to us to take it. If we do not choose, we leave nothing behind but the void.

Bibliography

Primary Sources

ALFIERI, Vittorio. *Vita*. Ed. G. Cattaneo. Milan: Garzanti, 2014.

Tragedie. Ed. Bruno Maier. Milan: Garzanti, 1989.

Parere sulle tragedie e altre prose critiche. Ed. M. Pagliai. Asti: Casa d'Alfieri, 1978.

The Tragedies of Vittorio Alfieri: Complete, including his Posthumous Works. Ed. E.A. Bowring; based on C. Lloyd's translation, 1815. Posthumous tragedies translated by E.A. Bowring. London: George Bell and Sons, 1876.

Secondary Sources

ARISTOTLE. *Poetics*. Oxford: Oxford University Press, 2013.

BINI, Walter. *Alfieri. Scritti 1969-1994*. Florence: Il Ponte Editore, 2015.

CAMERINO, Alfonso. *Alfieri e il linguaggio della tragedia. Verso, stile, tòpoi*. Naples: Liguori, 1999.

---

25 "Collective consequences", becoming part of what Wu Ming 4 describes as "imperfect heroes" (see Wu Ming 2010).

DEBENEDETTI, Giacomo. *Vocazione tragica di Vittorio Alfieri*. Rome: Editori Riuniti, 1977.

DI BENEDETTO, Arnaldo and Vincenza PERDICHIZZI. *Alfieri*. Rome: Salerno Editrice, 2014.

FLIEGER, Verlyn. "The Music and the Task: Fate and Free Will in Middle-earth." *Tolkien Studies* 6 (2009): 151-181.

Splintered Light. Kent, OH: The Kent State University Press, 2002.

FORNET-PONSE, Thomas. "'Strange and free' – On Some Aspects of the Nature of Elves and Men." *Tolkien Studies* 7 (2010): 67-89.

FUBINI, Mario. *Ritratto dell'Alfieri e altri studi alfieriani*. Florence: La Nuova Italia, 1967.

RAIMONDI, Ezio. *Le pietre del sogno. Il moderno dopo il sublime*. Bologna: Il Mulino, 1985.

SHIPPEY, Tom. *J.R.R. Tolkien. Author of the Century*. London: HarperCollins, 2003.

The Road to Middle-earth. London: HarperCollins, 2005.

WU MING 4. *L'Eroe Imperfetto*. Milan: Bompiani, 2010.

Cecilia Barella

Tolkien and Grahame

Twentieth Century Classics

In 2012, when the Olympic Games took place in Great Britain, the British Library staged a most valuable exhibition titled *Writing Britain. Wasteland to Wonderlands*.

It showed the link between the greatest British writers during the centuries and the British landscape, and displayed original manuscripts, illustrations, and maps. Different sections of the exhibition represented the different environments of the English landscape: the moor, the river, the countryside, the city, and the factory as well.[1]

During an important international event such as the Olympic Games, the British Library exhibition was intended to celebrate the essence of Britishness, recalling how the literature of this country, so well known all over the world, is closely connected to the landscape from which it originates. Indeed, the landscape is often not just background but one of the main protagonists in the works of some of Britain's foremost writers and poets. *Writing Britain* included Kenneth Grahame (1859-1932) and J.R.R. Tolkien (1892-1973).[2]

Although it takes time for a book to become a classic, there are exceptions such as *The Wind in the Willows* (1908) and *The Hobbit* (1937).

In his review of *The Hobbit* in the *Times Literary Supplement* (*TLS*, October 2, 1937), C.S. Lewis (2002, 81) wrote: "Prediction is dangerous: but *The Hobbit*

---

1 See Hardyment 2012.
2 The exhibition included *The Wind in the Willows* (1908) by Kenneth Grahame in section "6.Waterlands, 6c Rivers of Light" (with Charles Dickens, George Eliot, Charles Kingsley, E.M. Forster, and Gerard Manley Hopkins among others); *The Hobbit* (1937) by Tolkien was in section "1. Rural Dreams, 1d Eco-writing" with Oliver Goldsmith, Kazuo Ishiguro, Evelyn Waugh, and *Watership Down* (1972) by Richard Adams, who is the author (alongside Grahame and Tolkien) that best represents Englishness in the twentieth century, see Watkins 1992.

may well prove a classic." In the same review, Lewis mentioned Gahame's masterpiece, too.

In addition to Kenneth Grahame's great value for British literature in general, he has the double merit for Tolkien scholars of being one of the few writers the professor explicitly speaks of with esteem, and of being one of his sources of inspiration.

Tolkien knew *The Wind in the Willows* very well. He mentioned it in 1939 in his essay "On Fairy-Stories" and also in some of his letters. Thus in 1943, writing to his son Christopher (*Letters* no. 51) he compared a colleague of his to Mister Toad. In 1944 he wrote to Christopher again on the same subject:

> I hear that there is just coming out *First Whispers of the Wind in the Willows*; and the reviews seem favourable. It is published by Kenneth Grahame's widow, but it is not, I gather, notes for the book, but stories (about Toad and Mole etc.) that he wrote in letters to his son. I must get hold of a copy, if poss. (*Letters* no. 77)

Animal Tales and More

There is a distinction between fairy tale and fable: the fairy tale is an unlikely story that implies magical elements, while in the Greek-Latin tradition, the fable is a moral short story whose characters are talking animals.

The Wind in the Willows is halfway between an animal story and children literature. In fact, Grahame's novel has many characteristics of the fable: it is an animal story, its protagonists (the Water Rat, the Mole, the Toad, the Badger) have very prominent character traits, which recall the species they belong to but at the same time they also recall human types. Finally, it is a novel divided into chapters, but in fact tells episodes in themselves that have the structure and completeness of the fable – while ensuring the reoccurrence of familiar characters.

Tolkien himself considers *The Wind in the Willows* an animal story,[3] and Alex Lewis analyzes in detail the relationship between the creation of the Hobbits and the influence that animal stories may have had on Tolkien, badgers in

---

3 "I would also include *The Wind in the Willows* in Beast-fable" (*TOFS* 36, fn. 2).

particular, even from a linguistic point of view. He also quotes the philologist and Tolkien scholar Tom Shippey, and underlines how some surnames and toponyms of the Shire come from the ancient Welsh for badger: *broch*. He argues that translators have often been misled in the interpretation of the word because in many English toponyms *brock* is the variant of stream (Lewis & Currie 2002, 74-75). The same concept is synthesized by Hammond and Scull in their *Reader's Guide to The Lord of the Rings*:

> *Brock* is an old word (in OE) for the badger (*Dachs*) still widely current in country-speech up to the end of the nineteenth century and appearing in literature, and hence in good dictionaries, including bilinguals [...] It occurs in numerous place-names, from which surnames are derived, such as Brockbanks. Brockhouse is of course feigned to be a hobbit-name, because the "brock" builds complicated and well-ordered underground dwellings or "setts". (Hammond & Scull 2005, 754)

Beyond names, the resemblance between the Hobbits and the Badger (and the Mole, the other character of the novel that digs dens) is precisely in their personality: love for the home, a comfortable home with food and a study room, love for security and tranquility.

In Grahame, the underground world never has a negative connotation. The Badger says: "There's no security, or peace and tranquillity, except underground" (Grahame 2009, 98). Not so in Tolkien: places like Moria and Shelob's lair are very dangerous. C.S. Lewis (2002, 31) writes about the Badger:

> Consider Mr Badger in *The Wind in the Willows* – that extraordinary amalgam of high rank, coarse manners, grufness, shyness, and goodness. The child who has once met Mr Badger has ever afterwards, in its bones, a knowledge of humanity and of English social history which it could not get in any other way.

In some respects, the heir of the Badger is Tom Bombadil, who is wise and learned, almost outside of time because, as Badger says: "People come, they stay for a while, they flourish, they build, and they go. It is their way. But we remain. There were badgers here, I've been told, long before that same city ever came to be. And now there are badgers here again" (Grahame 2009, 99).

Toad is the protagonist of many adventures of the novel, but the point of view of the whole story is that of the Mole. This is similar to the Hobbit point of view of *The Hobbit* and *The Lord of the Rings*. The Hobbits, too, are a shy and furtive people.

The similarity between the opening scene of *The Wind in the Willows* and *The Hobbit* is remarkable: both novels start in the den / house of the protagonists. In 1908 Mr Mole does spring-cleaning:

> The Mole had been working very hard all the morning, spring-cleaning his little home. First with brooms, then with dusters; then on ladders and steps and chairs, with a brush and a pail of whitewash; till he had dust in his throat and eyes, and splashes of whitewash all over his black fur, and an aching back and weary arms. Spring was moving in the air above and in the earth below and around him, penetrating even his dark and lowly little house with its spirit of divine discontent and longing. It was small wonder, then, that he suddenly flung down his brush on the floor, said, "Bother!" and "O blow!" and also "Hang spring-cleaning!" and bolted out of the house without even waiting to put on his coat. (Grahame 2009, 1)

The following excerpt is the opening of *The Hobbit* so often mentioned and analyzed by biographers and scholars of the Oxford professor because it introduces the readers to the whole Middle Earth:

> In a hole in the ground there lived a hobbit. Not a nasty, dirty, wet hole, filled with the ends of worms and an oozy smell, nor yet a dry, bare, sandy hole with nothing in it to sit down on or to eat: it was a hobbit-hole, and that means comfort. (*H* 3)

A long description of the Baggins home and family follows, then Tolkien returns to the Spring scene:

> By some curious chance one morning long ago in the quiet of the world, when there was less noise and more green, and the Hobbits were still numerous and prosperous, and Bilbo Baggins was standing at his door after breakfast smoking an enormous long wooden pipe [...]. (*H* 5)

But there is another scene from Grahame's novel that Tolkien picks up, both in *The Hobbit* and in *The Lord of the Rings*,[4] making it almost a quotation and a tribute to his predecessor: the crossing of the Wild Wood. In *The Wind in the Willows* it reads as follows:

> He penetrated to where the light was less, and trees crouched nearer and nearer, and holes made ugly mouths at him on either side. Everything was very still

---

4 Cf. *The Hobbit*, chapter 8 "Flies and Spiders" and *The Lord of the Rings*, FR.I.6.

now. The dusk advanced on him steadily, rapidly, gathering in behind and before; and the light seemed to be draining away like flood-water. Then the faces began. It was over his shoulder, and indistinctly, that he first thought he saw a face, a little, evil, wedge-shaped face, looking out at him from a hole. When he turned and confronted it, the thing had vanished. (Grahame 2009, 64)

In *The Hobbit* when Bilbo and the dwarves enter Mirkwood, Tolkien uses almost the same words to describe the scene (the trees at the sides of the path and the eyes in the dark) and Bilbo feelings, as well as when the hobbits, in *The Lord of the Rings*, cross the Old Forest on the border of the Shire.

Stories for Children and More

Whether *The Wind in the Willows* is a story of animals or not, or whether it is written for children or not, are questions that have been discussed for a long time and that have not been answered conclusively.[5]

In his essay "On Three Ways of Writing for Children", C.S. Lewis said that the best literature for children (he was dealing with fantastic literature in particular) is the one that arises from the inspiration of the author regardless of the audience it is written for. This is why both adults and children can love good books. In a sense, he nullified the literary categories and the readers categories as well, a position also shared by Tolkien. Among other examples, Lewis mentioned *The Wind in the Willows* and *The Hobbit*.

The Wind in the Willows was based on a series of bedtime stories and letters Grahame wrote to his son Alastair (he was born in 1900). As his books *The Golden Age* (1895) and *Dream Days* (1898) had been very successful both in Great Britain and in the USA, his publishers asked him for more books. Grahame wrote down his bedtime stories in 1907, and *The Wind in the Willows* surpassed all expectations: "Rather than being a book written for adults about the lives of children like his previous works [...] [it] was a book written for children that parodied the lives of adults" (Gauger 2009, xxxv).

---

5 See Hunt 2010.

The first English publisher, Methuen, announced it as a "satire", an "allegory of life" (Hunt 2010, vii). The prestigious *TLS* reviewed it on October 22, 1908 on the same page where it reviewed *A Room with a View* by E.M. Forster.

According to C.S. Lewis, Tolkien's *Hobbit* also began as a bedtime story for the author's children – like Grahame's book.[6] Unlike *The Lord of the Rings*, *The Hobbit* is a children's book, perhaps even more than *The Wind in the Willows*. Years later, Tolkien would regret this aspect of the book – perhaps with too severe an attitude. On November 22, 1961 he wrote in a letter:

> I have only once made the mistake of trying to do it, to my lasting regret, and (I am glad to say) with the disapproval of intelligent children: in the earlier part of *The Hobbit*. [...] *The Lord of the Rings* [...] was not written 'for children', or for any kind of person in particular, but for itself. [...] Children are not a class or kind, they are a heterogeneous collection of immature persons, varying, as persons do, in their reach, and in their ability to extend it when stimulated. As soon as you limit your vocabulary to what you suppose to be within their reach, you in fact simply cut off the gifted ones from the chance of extending it. (*Letters* no. 234)

Lastly, nostalgia is a theme that is present in the works of both writers.[7] Here we mention briefly only a few essential traits.

"The Piper at the Gates of Dawn" is one of the chapters of *The Wind in the Willows* that most interested critics, although it is often omitted from both the English editions and the translations.

It is a short chapter, in the middle of the novel, that interrupts the adventure of Toad and tells about Mole and Rat looking for the puppy of their friend the Otter, by boat. They are attracted to the music of a pipe and land on an island in the middle of the river and find the little otter lulled by the piper, Pan, who looks like a faun (a faun like the future Mr. Tumnus in the *Chronicles of Narnia* by C.S. Lewis). Rat and Mole are in ecstasy, they feel happiness, peace, and fear at the same time. This chapter constitutes one of Grahame's highest literary achievements, and is a one-of-a-kind chapter to be found in a children's book. Pan telepathically communicates with Rat but also leaves the gift of oblivion against too painful a longing.

---

6 "[...] Lewis Carroll, Kenneth Grahame, and Tolkien. The printed story grows out of a story told to a particular child with the living voice" (Lewis 2002, 31).
7 See Morgan 2011.

Among Tolkien characters, Sam Gamgee, a hobbit, often expresses nostalgia; but this feeling is embodied in the people of the Elves above all. For Tolkien as for Grahame, nostalgia represents the yearning, the very perception of transcendence.

> It may happen that we perceive this sensation while we cannot precisely define what we are regretting. It may happen when we gaze at a beautiful landscape and the eye doesn't find obstacles. Then, perhaps, is simply born within us the nostalgia of the Infinite which is placed – how to say? – "genetically" within us by the Infinite One who has created us in his image. Within us, at times, there is the awareness of being as foreigners on this earth: it is urged by a voice that sometimes whispers, sometimes shouts to our heart that we are made for something immense that definitely transcends the narrow and sometimes suffocating bounds in which we live. This same inner voice is somehow reassuring, it also makes us aware that one day we can finally return to our true home. (Spirito 2003, 86)

Many Adventures and many Returns

Grahame's novel seems to be composed of two stories, which at times are parallel and sometimes intertwine, especially in the end: the adventures of Toad, and the rural life of Rat, Mole and Badger that takes place between the river and the forest.

Today it is just in the pages dealing with the three animals that critics identify the essence of Grahame's work, those in which he has poured his vision of life (at least, life as it "should" be).

However, the adventures of Toad are those that have most captured the attention, imagination, and complicity of children, starting with Alastair, the son of the writer. It is no coincidence that the plays (e.g. by A.A. Milne in 1929) and movies (e.g. by Disney in 1949) were based on Mr. Toad's adventures.

Grahame was able to put in the same book the yearning for adventure and homely security, love for one's own little world. This is true of the English people but also, in a more universal sense, of childhood, and here lies one of the reasons for the success of the book over a century.

Tolkien's plot is more complex but contains the same dualism. He invents the indolent race of the hobbits, placing them in a fertile countryside of Middle-earth and then "pushes" some of them out of their cosy homes.

Moreover, in *The Lord of the Rings*, Tolkien also adopts a chronological but non-linear narrative structure: when the Fellowship of the Ring divides, we follow the adventure of Men and Elves on one side, and on the other the adventures of the Hobbits, which are in turn divided into different paths.

Grahame, Tolkien, and Richard Adams (they are all linked in some way to Oxford), represent the authors of what Tony Watkins (1995, 166) calls "country-bred fantasy", stories that represent love for the earth, nature, pre-industrial English countryside, with almost philosophical accents, and therefore with a high educational value. Unlike American fantasy, these stories deal with homecoming adventures.

In *The Wind in the Willows*, the theme of the return occupies the last three chapters: 10, 11, and 12. The novel does not end with the return of Toad but with the reconquest of Toad Hall, that had fallen into the hands of ferrets, weasels and stoats; just as *The Lord of the Rings* does not end with the return of the hobbits from the war but with their reconquest of the Shire.

The hobbits are able to reconquer the Shire thanks to the experience and maturity they have acquired in the long adventure of a year across the border. In fact, their heroic gestures were not made to seek glory but when it seemed that it was the only right thing to do, like Merry's fight on the Pelennor fields by Eowyn's side.

Similarly, Rat and Mole, who have had adventurous aspirations during the past year, reconquer Toad Hall in spite of the bully braggart friend Toad, who also participates together with the wise Badger who plans the reconquest. In the name of Toad Hall, as well as of the Shire, love for home and love for adventure can eventually find a common ground and be reconciled.

Conclusion

In the comparison between Grahame and Tolkien, *The Wind in the Willows* is usually associated with *The Hobbit*, but there are many similarities with *The Lord of the Rings* too. Moreover, the influence that Grahame's novel had on Tolkien, and in particular the synthesis of their two masterpieces indirectly led to the birth of a new literary genre in the last thirty years of the twentieth century: the *animal fantasy*, or *animal epic*.

The forerunner of the genre can be identified in Richard Adams's masterpiece *Watership Down* (1972). It is basically a long journey between life and death, but there are other aspects of Adams's novel that remind us of Tolkien: an invented language, a detailed geography (therefore maps), stories inside the main story (a sort of mythology of rabbits), and poems embedded in the narrative.

Adams had no intention to create a literary genre, like Tolkien had no intention to give birth to the modern fantasy, but very respectable heirs followed *Watership Down*, such as *The Cold Moons* (1987) by Aeron Clement (on badgers) and *Duncton Wood* (1980) by William Horwood (on moles). Moreover, Horwood wrote four books (*Tales of the Willows*, 1993-1999) that are a sequel to *The Wind in The Willows* and were appreciated by Grahame fans and by critics.

In his 1975 essay "Some Ingredients of *Watership Down*", Richard Adams proceeds from the previously cited essay by C.S. Lewis and in turn recommends *The Wind in the Willows* and *The Hobbit* as books for readers of all ages, and adds *Animal Farm*, Dickens and some others. He continues that they are, above all, books that have "taken account of the nature of the world in a responsible manner. No aspect of real life has been wrongly suppressed or untruthfully left out in a way damaging to the book's integrity" (Adams 1975, 163) – qualities that Adams has not found in *The Lord of the Rings*.

Grahame's thought about imagination and adventure is perhaps best expressed in the last few lines of chapter 11, when the Mole, who is mild and a good listener

> drew his arm through Toad's [...] [and] made him tell him all his adventures from beginning to end, which Toad was only too willing to do [...] Indeed, much that he related belonged more properly to the category of what-might-have-

happened-had-I-only-thought-of-it-in-time-instead-of-ten-minutes-afterwards. Those are always the best and the raciest adventures; and why should they not be truly ours, as much as the somewhat inadequate things that really come off? (Grahame 2009, 283)

This passage sounds like a legitimate justification for adventure in general when it is located in one's imagination, and for the escapist narrative of Grahame as a writer in particular. He had already been very successful and was a member of intellectual circles also frequented by Yeats and Wilde, among others. However, to earn a living he had to work as a bank employee, and he had a family life that was far from happy.

The same concept sounds familiar to Tolkien readers too, who know the poetics of escapism theorized in his essay "On Fairy-Stories":

> The world outside has not become less real because the prisoner cannot see it. In using escape in this way the critics have chosen the wrong word, and, what is more, they are confusing, not always by sincere error, the Escape of the Prisoner with the Flight of the Deserter. (*TOFS* 69)

Grahame portrays the little world on the river bank, almost invisible to the eyes of tall and hasty men such as we are, just as the world of the Shire is small and concealed for the great peoples of Middle-earth.

Bibliography

Primary Sources

GRAHAME, Kenneth. *The Annotated Wind in the Willows*. Ed. Annie Gauger. New York: Norton, 2009.

The Wind in the Willows. Ed. Peter Hunt. Oxford: Oxford University Press, 2010.

Secondary Sources

ADAMS, Richard. "Some Ingredients of *Watership Down*." *Thorny Paradise. Writers on Writing for Children*. Ed. Edward Blishen. London: Kestrel Books, 1975, 163-173.

DRABBLE, Margaret. *A Writer's Britain. Landscape in Literature*. London: Thames and Hudson, 1979.

GAUGER, Annie. "Preface." *Kenneth Grahame: The Annotated Wind in the Willows*. Ed. Annie Gauger. New York: Norton, 2009, xix-xxxix.

HAMMOND Wayne G. and Christina SCULL. *The Lord of the Rings: A Reader's Companion*. Boston: Houghton Mifflin, 2005.

HARDYMENT, Christine. *Writing Britain. Wasteland to Wonderlands*. London: The British Library, 2012.

HUNT, Peter. "Introduction." *Kenneth Grahame: The Wind in the Willows*. Ed. Peter Hunt. Oxford University Press: Oxford, 2010, vii-xxxii.

KUZNETS, Lois R. "*The Hobbit* Is Rooted in the Tradition of Classic British Children's Novels." *Readings on J.R.R. Tolkien*. Ed. Katie de Koster. San Diego, CA: Greenhaven Press, 2000, 31-43.

LEWIS, Alex and Elizabeth CURRIE. *The Uncharted Realms of Tolkien*. Oswestry: Medea Publishing, 2002.

LEWIS, C.S. *On Stories and Other Essays on Literature*. New York: Harvest Books, 2002.

MENDELSON Michael. "*The Wind in the Willows* and the Plotting of Contrast." *Children's Literature* 16 (1988): 127-144.

MORGAN, Kathie C. "Waiting with Bated Breath: Intimations and Anticipation of Eternity Viewed throughough Children's Literature." *Faculty Publications and Presentations*. Lynchburg, VA: Liberty University, 2011.

SHIRLEY, Pat. *From the Riverbank to Middle-earth and Beyond*. Bloomington, IN: Trafford Publishing, 2013.

SPIRITO, Guglielmo. *Tra San Francesco e Tolkien. Una lettura spirituale del Signore degli Anelli*. Rimini: Il Cerchio, 2003.

WATKINS, Tony. "Cultural Studies, New Historicism and Children's Literature." *Literature for Children. Contemporary Criticism*. Ed. Peter Hunt. London: Routledge, 1992, 173-195.

"Reconstructing the Homeland: Loss and Hope in English Landscape." *Aspects and Issues in the History of Children's Literature* . Ed. Maria Nikolajeva. Westport, CT: Greenwood, 1995, 165-172.

Andrea Monda

Tolkien and Manzoni

Alessandro Manzoni died in Milan on 22nd May 1873, almost exactly one century before J.R.R. Tolkien's death, who was born in South Africa almost twenty years later, on 3rd January 1892. They never had the chance to meet, although it is likely that Tolkien heard Manzoni's name, as his work and fame travelled way beyond the English Channel.[1] We are not sure if the English writer had the chance to read the Italian novelist's masterpiece, but we are willing to assume that he would have certainly appreciated it. There are several parallels and points of contact between *The Lord of the Rings* and *The Betrothed*, Manzoni's most famous novel. In the following, I would like to take a closer look at a few of them.

History and Imagination

At the beginning and the end of his masterpiece, Tolkien includes a "Prologue" and some "Appendices" in order to provide a historical framework for his epic. These texts aim at establishing the historical nature of the main story, which is therefore presented as the description of an historical event, placed in a world meticulously described in great detail, from its flora to its fauna, its genealogies to its geographies, its social mores to its socio-economic system, be it the Shire or, more generally, Middle-earth. The reader does not move into a whimsical, mysterious and unstable world, but into a universe of which he knows the main coordinates thanks to the introductory texts given by the author. The long and detailed "Prologue", which may have confused more than one reader, provides a great deal of information regarding Middle-earth, the Hobbits, and especially about the pipe-weed (aka tobacco) consumed in this area. The reader is likely to feel as if he has opened a travel guide to an exotic and unknown (but still

---

1 Cf. Crosta 2014.

very real) land. To understand why Tolkien chooses to implement these paratextual features, we have to turn to a letter he wrote (and never sent) in 1956, addressed to the poet and ex-disciple W.H. Auden, in which Tolkien asserts: "I am historically minded. Middle-earth is not an imaginary world. [...]. The theatre of my tale is this earth, the one in which we now live, but the historical period is imaginary" (*Letters* no. 183). The stories of Bilbo, Frodo, and the Fellowship are all part of the larger framework of human history, as much as Renzo and Lucia's story is, and they thus agree with the rules of the genre of Historical Fiction, which Manzoni tried to revive.

Tolkien pretends to be merely the translator-cum-editor of a document that has ended up in his hands: *The Red Book of Westmarch*. It is based on the writings of mostly Bilbo and Frodo, with some additions by Sam Gamgee. This translation conceit presents the story of the War of the Ring as an account based on the eye-witness accounts that have been handed down through the millennia. This translation-conceit is also found with other authors, such as Jorge Luis Borges (1899-1986), who pretended that he, too, had merely "found" some of his texts. And so does Manzoni in his masterpiece.

There is, of course, imagination in both authors, and it unfolds into many and various colours. However, this always happens within the confines of a story – or, rather, history – that provides the framework to the plot designed by the writer. The frame for Manzoni is 7th-century Lombardy, that for Tolkien the end of the Third Age of Middle-earth. In this context we may quote Chesterton, who observed that the most interesting thing about a painting is its frame, which signifies the boundaries defined by the great artists for themselves.

History and the Stories

Manzoni, too, wrote a "Prologue" as well as an "Introduction" to his novel – yet these are only two parallels we can determine between the two narrators.

The first word in the "Introduction" of *The Betrothed* is "*L'Historia*" (literally, the History). As the narrator expands, it "can for real be defined as an eminent battle against time [...]." If time, *Krònos*, devours and annihilates everything in its never-ending motion, there is that one man – the historian – who opposes this process by positioning himself against the current, who creates a work with the help of memory, exhumation, and resurrection. The issue that Manzoni wants to stress is found in the adjective "eminent". It implies, in Manzoni's view, that history, as historical science, has always focussed on the narratives centred around eminent men, powerful empires, and the deeds of "great men". Such History would, of course, ignore a considerable part of humanity, distorting the narrative of human history in favour of "great" and exceptional individuals while neglecting the fact that "real" history is the product of small men with their small stories and their many frailties. Manzoni, with his novel, wants to emend this error in perspective by giving space to both levels of narration, History and the stories. In Manzoni, as well as in Tolkien, we find the double level of the small story that is entwined with great History. The two main protagonists of Manzoni's novel are Renzo and Lucia, two ordinary people who, after many twists and turns, will end up crossing the path of the great historical events of the sixth century and, as a result, end up wounded, tested, and also strengthened.

Similarly Tolkien's hobbits Bilbo and Frodo: they, too, interact with History and even influence the outcome of several of the great historical events. Bilbo, in the end, will be involved in the Battle of the Five Armies, and Frodo will be a pivotal figure in the defeat of Sauron.

The interesting thing is that Tolkien, following Manzoni's model, does not narrate the story "from the top-down", but "from the bottom-up". He does not give a voice to the *Historia*, but to the small chronicles that involve the Shire. The narrative matter has its origin in the History of Middle-earth, yet begins with the tale of the quiet (although "queer") Bilbo Baggins from the Shire. Sauron, the "legitimate" lord of the rings, is never seen by the reader. He always remains as a dark presence that fades into the background. So do the great kings and sovereigns of Middle-earth, from Elrond to Galadriel, Thranduil to Denethor and Théoden. These figures are never the main protagonists of the narration, but are of relevance only when crossing paths with the hobbits – whom Manzoni would have defined as "mechanic people of small businesses". This "humble" way, so full of picaresque humor and understatement, is the main path taken by Tolkien's epic, and also Manzoni's story unravels by following the events involving Renzo and Lucia. This fundamental characteristic has its origin in the Christian vision of history. This fact has stylistic consequences for the narratives.

History and Style

By the end of his "Introduction" to *The Betrothed*, Manzoni abandons the narrator-persona of the "eminent" historian with the courtly and solemn style, and starts injecting more life into his novel by writing in the language that defined it as "the ultimate" Italian novel. *The Betrothed* is considered to be the only work of Italian literature that, even from the point of view of the scholastic canon, can be compared to Dante's *The Divine Comedy*. It is of interest to see that, five centuries before Manzoni, the Florentine poet had adopted a similar stylistic strategy. Dante answered to Petrarca, who had suggested that he should write his poem in Latin, that he preferred the more "popular" option of the vernacular language. Manzoni, whose stylistic choice is intimately connected to the "philosophic" option, reflects on the meaning of the story. If it is necessary to tell the "small" story of the "mechanic people of small businesses", it does not make sense to do so applying the elevated style of "great" History, because content and style would clash. This does not mean, however, that the author should use a simple and crude language. On the contrary, Manzoni, in his attempt to rejuvenate the genre of the historic novel, feels the urge to "rinse the clothes into the Arno river", and subjects his expressive abilities to a never-ending effort of refinement.

Mutatis mutandis, Tolkien, bringing back the ancient (as well as obsolete) epic genre, makes good use of some of his vast and deep scholarly knowledge of ancient traditions and mythologies. His passion for languages and the ancient sources imbues the *Legendarium* with life. At the very moment when Tolkien gives shape to his masterpiece, he realises that it is necessary to dismiss the elevated and archaic tone of those legends, because at the centre of the story there are not the "eminent" Elves, but the hidden and humble Hobbits.

History, the Humble Ones, and Providence

Tolkien's Hobbits are the literary expedient that allows the English Catholic writer to express his vision of history. As mentioned before, the Hobbits are those whom Manzoni would have described as "mechanic people of small businesses." Yet it is these "small people" who enter into the tragic, tangled story of the "eminent" lords of Middle-earth – and bring it to fulfilment, providing a happy ending.

The essential element is that the solution of the tale, for both Tolkien and Manzoni, is essentially influenced by Providence and partakes in the divine Grace. In both novels, the actual main protagonist is a hidden one: divine Providence. It is a power that moves and directs everything toward the right destination by mysterious and surprising ways.

Much has been written on the subject of Providence, and we have to limit ourselves to those aspects that will allow the reader observe the similarities and analogies between Frodo and the Fellowship's journey and the one of Renzo and Lucia. Both Tolkien's Hobbits and Manzoni's couple are forced out of their homelands and thrown (as amateurs) into the big world. Yet these characters, though simple and apparently not equipped sufficiently, persist with exceptional tenacity and astonishing courage through all the trials they have to face. Furthermore, wherever they go, they bring about change and "small revolutions", mostly in the hearts of the people they encounter. In Tolkien, this happens in Lothlórien, Fangorn, Rohan, Isengard, Gondor, and even in Mordor. All these will never be as they were before the hobbits came along. In *The Betrothed,* to take just one example, we have the case of the Unnamed. Here we have a real "revolution" that exchanges the roles of the victim and the oppressor, so that the grim Unnamed will be the one to be scared of the trembling girl, and, to use the words of *Magnificat,* "he hath put down the mighty from their seat and hath exalted the humble and meek." In the end, the "bottom line" is the same in both novels, and it is the same as Maria's exclamation in the Gospel of Luke: *exaltavit humiles*. Renzo, Lucia, and the Hobbits, are the humble ones celebrated by the Bible, those simple men that "great" History, the one written by "eminent" men, will never talk about. Modesty is the real virtue of the Hobbits, who live in holes in the ground. These "little people", whose existence is literally down-to-earth, are indeed "humiles", from *humus* (land). This humility seems to be their main virtue, apart from the typical tenacity of those who keep their feet firmly on the ground and who love and appreciate life as such. This no-nonsense attitude prevents most Hobbits from giving it up as a sacrifice for a higher purpose. Here topics such as courage, fear, and also humour come in. Humour is actually closely connected to humility – probably even on an etymological level.

The Hobbits are small people who live in holes not unlike rabbits, and quite a few people have commented on the similarities between the two, not least since both either flee, or cower and tremble as soon as Big People approach. Yet the same small coward (half-)men are the ones who, eventually, will be capable of major endeavours worthy of the greatest heroes. Gandalf the Wizard takes a chance on them, a wager that will eventually result in the victory of the Free Peoples. Tolkien takes a chance on them because he loves them. He looks at them with the eyes of empathy and mercy as the way to true understanding. Tolkien and Manzoni both know the human heart, and know that courage is not lack of fear, but traversing and overcoming that very fear.

The subtle humour that characterises both Tolkien and Manzoni has its origin in this conflict between fear and courage, and from the subsequent merciful gaze. Pirandello writes in his essay *On Humour*:[2]

> The coward is ridiculous and comical when he is creating imaginary risks and dangers all by himself. However, a coward stops being comical and has real reasons to be scared when he, who would by natural inclination avoid even the smallest confrontation, is caught in a terrible conflict because, according to the demands of duty, he should accept the fight. In such a context, even a hero like Fra Cristoforo, who confronts his enemy in the latter's own house, will not be enough. Don Abbondio does not have the courage to do his duty, but then that duty is made most difficult by other people's malice and therefore mustering the courage to do one's duty is anything but easy. Indeed, to fulfill that duty would take a hero. (Pirandello 1960, 143)

Don Abbondio is quintessentially non-heroic (indeed he is the paradigm of cowardice) and the second part is referred only to Sam: "but the description could as well be referring to Sam, at the same time gun-shy and heroic". Starting with Don Abbondio, Pirandello begins an enlightening analysis:

---

2 Translation by the author.

Which side is the poet's sentiment on? Does he despise or sympathise with Don Abbondio? Manzoni has an abstract, most noble ideal of the priest's mission on earth, and he embodies that ideal in Federigo Borromeo. However, out of the humoristic attitude there comes reflection. The poet seems to suggest that this abstract ideal can incarnate only under very special circumstances, and that human weaknesses are many as well. Had Manzoni listened only to the voice of that abstract ideal, he would have depicted Don Abbondio in such a way as everyone would have hated or despised him. Yet the poet hearkens also to the voice of the human weaknesses. Due to the natural attitude of his soul, due to the life-experience that shaped that attitude, Manzoni cannot help splitting that concept of religious and priestly ideal and, between the burning flames of Fra Cristoforo and Cardinal Federigo, he sees 'don Abbondio's shadow, wary and submissive, grow long on the ground.' (Pirandello 1960, 140)

Thus the reader of Tolkien's epic, instead of seeing the flames of the battle between the various towers in Middle-earth, from Isengard to Barad-Dûr, will see instead the tiny Hobbits' shadows "stretching, wary and flabby". This is Tolkien's "Manzonian" humour, and it is this humour that "saves" these characters, from Sam to Don Abbondio (let's not forget that, eventually, he will be the one to celebrate the long-awaited nuptials between Renzo and Lucia). It also saves the actual novels that, just as Dante's poem, turn out to be "comedies" – and this is, perhaps, the reason for their timeless success.

Bibliography

MANZONI, Alessandro. *I promessi sposi*. Milan: Mondadori, 2002.

CROSTA, Alice. *Alessandro Manzoni nei paesi anglosassoni*. Bern: Peter Lang, 2014.

PIRANDELLO, Luigi. *Saggi, poesie e scritti varii*. Ed. Manlio Lo Vecchio-Musti. Milan: Mondadori, 1960.

Melissa Ruth Arul

The Yoke of Pride and Shame: Joseph Conrad's Lord Jim and J.R.R. Tolkien's Túrin Turambar

Pride has long been known to strongly influence and motivate a hero. In many instances it transcends and envelops other emotions, courting ruin and disaster.

Tolkien comments that heroic pride proves the downfall of Beorhtnoth in his fight against the Viking raiders. He states that "this element of pride, in the form of the desire for honour and glory, in life and after death, tends to grow, to become a chief motive [...] when it not only goes beyond need and duty, but interferes with it" (*HBBS*, "Ofermod"). Furthermore, Jane Chance (2001, 117) argues that "excessive pride is not truly indicative of heroism." This overarching heroic desire can lead to endangerment not just of the hero, but also of those around him. One motive for such excessive pride is to compensate that which dwells within them – shame.[1] Shame is the awareness of a lack within the self, what Michael Balint (1969, 14) calls "the basic fault" of the self. Friedrich Nietzsche (1882) defines liberation as "no longer being ashamed of oneself", an internal evaluation of the self. While the pursuit for greatness may be considered constructive, it is not necessarily always so. Trying to compensate for a deficit or an inadequacy by means of a hunger for power and perfection only becomes a case of denial. Thus, the underlying problem is not addressed and leads to a vicious cycle of overcompensation. Joseph Conrad's Jim and Tolkien's Túrin Turambar are men with a great sense of pride. Jim dreams of becoming a hero like those found in adventure novels, while Túrin, son of Húrin, knew nothing less, having grown imbibing the heroic spirit at his mother's breast.[2] Yet, it is this very sense of pride that leads the two to such misfortune and pain.

---

1 Cooper (2003, 10) states that "an inflated image of ourselves always has deep-rooted feelings of inferiority working behind the scenes."
2 See Honegger 2018 for a discussion of the problematic nature of Túrin's heroic personality.

Shame is an intense personal emotion. It is also very often employed as a social construct to regulate society. However, Christina Tarnopolsky (2010, 1) points out that "while it can function to help us negotiate our interactions with others in a decent and respectful manner, it can also cause us to turn away from such engagements, or to lash out against what gets uncovered in these interactions." Phil Barker (2003) agrees with the latter, arguing that shame is "often less constructive than guilt" as it is focussed inwards. This is unlike guilt, which concerns the outward action of a person, a sense of regret and accountability over a deed rather than the self of the person. The inward focus of shame is reflected in the actions of the shamed: blushing, covering of the face and avoidance of others. This can lead to a shamed person retaliating in defensive and aggressive behaviour, striking out deliberately to bring others down and subsequently uplifting oneself. Both Jim and Túrin, who are sensitive in nature and socially awkward, react negatively when shamed.[3] Jim blushes, while Túrin hides his face behind the Dragon-helm.[4] It can be argued that Túrin simply wears the helm as it is a family heirloom, but the fact remains that he only began to wear it when he started to worry about the safety of his family and his inability to do something about it. Soon, both men progress to alienating themselves from society and changing their names to stay incognito. Eventually, they resort to violence. Jim enters a scuffle with the Dane who made "some scornful remark at Jim's expense" (*LJ* 152), while Túrin, as a warrior, turns to violence more often to solve his problems, Saeros and Brandir being two examples at the receiving end of his wrathful retaliation.[5]

However, the two manage shame differently. Jim grapples with shame by running away from the emotion. He would "leave suddenly the seaport where he happened to be at the time and go to another" (*LJ* 10). He is subjugated by shame, shame of what he perceives as his inherent lack and shame in the eyes of the naval society. Túrin, meanwhile, wrestles shame by covering it with "the pride of his heart" (*S*, Qu.21). It is necessary for Túrin to be in command so that people see this side of him, and not that of his shame that frequently is the very consequences of his pride. Their differing approaches to handling

---

3 Jim has awkward outbursts of emotions throughout the novel, and Túrin is rough around the edges, a warrior who spends his time honing his sword rather than his social skills.
4 See Greaney (2000, 1-14) for a detailed study of Jim and the act of blushing.
5 Túrin throws a cup at a taunting Saeros and he slays Brandir in anger and denial.

the same emotion is likely due not just to differences in personality, but to circumstances as well. Túrin was a child born in war, unlike Jim, who was a child untested and belonging to "placid, colourless forms of men and women [...] as free of danger or strife as a tomb" (*LJ* 257). To Túrin, pain comes at an early age, beginning with the death of his sister Lalaith. Looking at a young Túrin, the servant Sador observes that "Grief is a hone to a hard mind" (*UT* II, "The Childhood of Túrin"). Like his mother Morwen, Túrin holds onto his pride as a shield against the trials of life.

Túrin's downfall, Jonathan Evans (2007, 544) observes, are his "repeated rash deeds and heedless rejection of advice, warning, pardon, and prophecy", which "result from character flaws centering upon prideful arrogance". With his strong personality, Túrin easily overrides the caution of others, thus entangling them in his doom. In Nargothrond, despite being warned by Gwindor, Túrin begins to "yearn for brave strokes and battle in the open" (*S*, Qu.21). Soon, persuaded by Túrin, "the Elves of Nargothrond forsook their secrecy and went openly to battle" and "thus Nargothrond was revealed to the wrath and hatred of Morgoth" (*S*, Qu.21), which will eventually lead to its downfall. When he arrives in Brethil and promises that a "new day is come" for him to "stay at peace", his warrior spirit asserts itself and before long he picks up his sword to fight the servants of Morgoth (*UT* II, "The Coming of Túrin into Brethil"). Again, because of his aggression and heedlessness, Túrin exposes Brethil to the dragon Glaurung. But why does Túrin constantly need to prove himself?

Paul G. Hiebert (1985, 212) succinctly states that "in true shame-oriented cultures, every person has a place and a duty in the society." While the culture of Middle-earth is not shame-oriented, it does explain how Túrin perceives himself and his role in society. Hiebert (1985, 212) carries on to say that in such a society "one maintains self-respect, not by choosing what is good rather than what is evil, but by choosing what is expected of one." This is never clearer than when the young Túrin, who is sent away to King Thingol in Doriath, objects since, as the heir of Hador, he "should stay in Hador's house to defend it" (*UT* II, "The Departure of Túrin"). However, Tom Shippey (2000, 252) points out that "some responsibility, to begin with "must be laid on Túrin's mother Morwen". It is Morwen who denies Túrin this privilege. It is a difficult decision for her to make but Morwen is like a sword whose steel has been tempered by hardship, and she remains unbending in what she believes to be the best course of action. This decision is not just a blow to Túrin's heart, but to his pride as well as this decision will leave him a houseless lord.

As shame is "a reaction to other people's criticism, an acute personal chagrin at our failure to live up to our obligations and the expectations others have of us" (Hiebert 2008, 212), there is thus a constant need for Túrin to prove himself as he never could as a child. In Túrin lingers a sense of dishonour as he believes he has not fulfilled his duty to his people. When he arrives in Dor-Lómin, his revenge on the Easterlings is excessive to the point that even his aunt Aerin rebukes him. In Doriath, Túrin does not rise to the taunting of Saeros until he makes a remark about the women of Hithlum. He takes up "a drinking-vessel and cast it in Saeros's face, and he fell backward with great hurt" (*UT* II, "Túrin in Doriath"). Even more tellingly, when Saeros attempts to ambush Túrin the following day, Túrin retaliates and cries out, "Morwen! […] now your mocker shall pay for his scorn!" (*UT* II, "Túrin in Doriath"). It is Morwen's face he sees in Saeros' taunts. Saeros has unwittingly hit a very sore spot in Túrin's psyche. Such boorish jokes as taking a jab at mothers or a man's womenfolk are not uncommon and especially widespread in patriarchal societies. It is likely that Saeros only does this to taunt him and has no intention of targeting Túrin's female relatives in general or Morwen in particular. However, for Túrin, it *is* very personal. It is, as Shippey (2000, 253) writes, "Túrin's major trauma – the image of a naked woman running." It is his mother and his kin that he has so far been unable to defend that he sees as the target of the taunt, so that it remains not just a general insult. It is this image that will lead him to wed his sister Nienor, and tragically, as Shippey (2000, 253) points out, all this leads back to pride.

Jim's pride is no less destructive but, unlike that of Túrin's, his is an inward spiral of self-destruction. When discussing Karen Horney's (1999) insight on the overvaluing and undervaluing of the self, Terry D. Cooper (2003, 113) suggests that "pride and self-contempt may both be part of one process, rather than polar opposites." The idealised self is a front to hide and safeguard the undervalued self. Reflecting on his upbringing, the narrator of Jim's life, Marlow, is amazed that Jim "should belong to […] [a family that would] "never be called upon to grapple with fate (*LJ* 257). This is a contradiction from the beginning of the novel when Marlow is quick to assure his listeners that many a commander has come from "these abodes of piety and peace" (*LJ* 10). Did Marlow see Jim as a person aside from the others? The answer is yes. Whether the choice was made consciously or not, placidity was a life-choice for Jim's family. For Jim, this environment would have been stifling and he turns to lofty dreams of literary heroes to escape his prison. The gentle love of his family with "their untroubled shapes" was not enough for Jim (*LJ* 260).

This is not to say that Jim did not care for them, he had after all "carefully preserved" (*LJ* 256) an old letter from his father, a display of sentimentality if nothing else. However, a young Jim sees himself "saving people from sinking ships [...] always an example of devotion to duty, and as unflinching as a hero in a book" (*LJ* 11). Donald Gutierrez (1987, 46) suggests that the traditional fate worse than death for men is "cowardice, and it can be especially grim if it is publically exhibited or exposed." Jim may have seen himself as a hero but dreams and reality are two very different things. When a young Jim is first confronted with danger, the "brutal tumult of earth and sky" held him in awe, holding him in place (*LJ* 13). When he decides to take action, it is too late and Jim is left with "the pain of conscious defeat in his eyes" (*LJ* 12). Unlike his literary heroes, Jim does not react decisively. Later, with youthful callousness, Jim dismisses the actions of "the bowman of the cutter – a boy with a face like a girl's and big grey eyes", who "was the hero of the lower deck", thinking his bragging was a "pitiful display of vanity" (*LJ* 13). Aside from feminising the bowman, he soothes his ego with the conviction that he would surely have performed better and indeed that he was destined to even greater deeds of heroism. This, however, is not the case as Jim discovers when disaster strikes the *Patna*. Unlike his literary heroes, Jim abandons ship along with his captain and other crew members, leaving the passengers of the *Patna* to their watery fate. Jim's family are people who do not rock the boat, and neither does Jim. He is slow to move in his first encounter with danger and was, on the *Patna*, confused and scared. Jim chooses to follow rather than to lead or stand apart. This choice haunts him to the end of his life.

Also interesting to note is Jim's ardent devotion to duty. He is well liked by his employers and all praise his work ethics. Jim lives for and by the approval of others. Yet, for all his romantic ideals, he lacks the courage to set himself apart from others. Jim knows this as he knows his family's inherent trait and it is likely that he views this as a lack within himself. Thus, he seeks to remedy this by hiding behind pride. George Panichas (2005, 10) argues that Jim may have stood trial to "separate himself morally from the captain and the engineers." While it may have been morally honourable to stand trial, the desire to do so was certainly driven by Jim's pride. Jim is never noted to have felt guilt or remorse for his irresponsibility. While guilt and shame can be bed partners, they are not, in fact, interchangeable. Guilt is a sense of accountability over an action. Judith Lewis Herman (2007, 162) says that "Shame is an acutely self-conscious state in which the self is 'split,' imagining the self in the eyes of the other; by contrast, in guilt the self is unified." Guilt is externalised, an emotion of what one has done or not. Michael Greaney (2002, 3) notes that it is shame that Jim experiences in his "humiliating failure to seize the opportunity for heroism of which he had dreamed for so long." Tolkien discusses this dilemma, stating that Beorhtnoth's *ofermod* originates from a "defect of character [...] not only formed by nature, but moulded also by 'aristocratic tradition', enshrined in tales and verse of poets [...] Beorhtnoth was chivalrous rather than strictly heroic" (*HBBS*, "Ofermod"). In the same manner, Jim stands trial *not* for his failure to fulfill his duty to look after the safety of his passengers, but rather for his failure to become the hero of his fantasies. Like Beorhtnoth, Jim's heroic desire takes precedence over the people under his care.[6] Jim's entire existence is founded on living up to his version of a hero; when failing again at the crucial point, this failure would influence his choices to the very end.

However, the two do not seem to realise that their actions have consequences that affect not just themselves, but also the people around them. Shippey (2000, 250) notes this as well, pointing out how "minor outbreaks of selfishness or carelessness mean more than they seem: snowballs leading into avalanches once more." Túrin's rashness eventually leads to the deaths of Beleg, Finduilas, and Gwindor, to name a few. Besides deserting his post and employers, Jim has a curious effect on a particular individual. Captain Bierly, when discussing Jim, speaks not just for himself but the naval community as a whole when he sug-

---

[6] Tolkien argues that Beorhtnoth "was responsible for all the men under him [...] It was wholly unfitting that he should treat a desperate battle with this sole real object as a sporting match" (*HBBS*, "Ofermod").

gests to Marlow that they "undertake to make the beggar clear out" (*LJ* 56). Michael Greaney (2002, 78) comments that the narrator Marlow

> transforms what might have been a painfully systematic study in the psychology of cowardice into something far more subtle, open-minded and open-ended. [...] Marlow recognizes that embarrassment is contagious, that the story of Jim's failure of nerve makes for desperately uncomfortable listening; accordingly, his version of the story is oblique to the point of evasiveness.

To Bierly and the naval community at large, Jim, who is considered a gentleman, should not be sitting in court "while all these confounded natives, serangs, lascars, quartermasters, are giving evidence that's enough to burn a man to ashes in shame" (*LJ* 56).

However, Jim believes that going to court is the only honourable option left to him. But by doing so, Jim exposes not only himself to the eyes of the world, he exposes the naval community as well. His presence in court is a source of shame to the naval community and their social standing. Jim's shame is reflected on them, exposing in turn, their dark secrets. This is later made evident by the suicide of Brierly. For all his contempt towards Jim, it is as though a window had been opened in Brierly's soul, forcing him to face the true worth of his own character.

While Marlow could find no fault in Brierly's career, it is insinuated that Brierly, in "holding silent inquiry into his own case" (*LJ* 49) found a lack in himself that he thought repugnant enough to throw himself overboard rather than to bear such a shame. When discussing Jim with Marlow, Brierly wishes that Jim "had flown into space like a witch on a broomstick" (*LJ* 42), like the skipper of the *Patna*. Is this a reflection of his own desire to escape if he had ever been found in a similar situation? Marlow suspects so. Brierly is not so much a mirror to Jim, but rather a "what if" exploration. After all, Jim too was making good headway in his career prior to the *Patna* incident. Very much like Brierly, "who had one of the best commands going on", and who, like Jim, "was acutely aware of his merits and of his rewards" (*LJ* 48-49). Brierly is a projection of what Jim would have become if not for the *Patna*, an "example of others who are no better than yourself, and yet make good countenance" (*LJ* 114). Knowing this, seeing it exposed to the world through Jim, Brierly finds it despicable. Despicable enough to throw himself overboard rather than to bear such a shame.

Based on Toni Massaro's study on shame (1999, 89), Tarnopolsky (2010, 1) notes that "as Greek tragedies and modern psychological case studies attest, it can even cause a person to commit suicide." We revisit Nietzsche's theory that the liberation of the self happens when one is no longer shamed in front of oneself. Death is a drastic solution to a shamed person who can find no recourse. It is the ultimate form of disappearing from society and the eyes of the world. Although Túrin's tale is influenced by the Finnish mythological poem *Kalevala*, Kullervo, whom Túrin is based on, is the only unsalvageable tragic character of the tale. Like a tragic Greek hero, a despairing and ashamed Túrin ultimately casts "himself upon the point of Gurthang" to compensate for all his mistakes and misjudgements (*S*, Qu.21). "Tolkien", Verlyn Flieger (2003, 102) states, "has made Túrin a paradigm of modern alienation, a self-exiled outsider driven by emotions he does not understand, wilful and conflicted, coming to painful self-awareness only at the end of his life." Túrin, at the point of total self-awareness, finds no escape; his pride and his family's curse have caught up with him. Death, an escape from living, is the only form of liberation he can find, much as Brierly did. Curiously, it is Jim who walks to his death with a pride akin to Beorhtnoth and his men, rather than Túrin, the warrior.[7] Answering "the call of his exalted egotism" (*LJ* 313), Jim is killed at the hands of the grieving Doramin. It is, as Watts (2000, 24) argues, a "vindication of pride and romantic ambition." Jim finds redemption for his lost pride in death, as he willingly forsakes the love of a "living woman to celebrate his pitiless wedding with a shadowing ideal of conduct" (*LJ* 313). Yet, both Conrad and Tolkien have similar views regarding excessive pride. While Jim may feel that he regained his lost pride in death, no one else around him acknowledges this fact. His lover Jewel rages against his choice and now lives a "soundless, inert life", and to Marlow Jim is as "inscrutable" as ever, darkly romantic and unreal (*LJ* 313). It is Túrin who, with all his faults and Morgoth's curse on him, is honoured after his death for slaying the dragon Glaurung.

---

7 Tolkien states that the "'northern heroic spirit' [...] would direct a man to endure even death unflinching, when necessary: that is when death may help the achievement of some object of will, or when life can only be purchased by denial of what one stands for" (*HBBS*, "Ofermod").

Bibliography

BALINT, Michael. *The Basic Fault: Therapeutic Aspects of Regression*. First published 1969. New York: Brunner/Mazel Publishers, 1979.

BARKER, Phil. "Guilt and Shame." *Beyond Intractability*. Eds. Guy Burgess and Heidi Burgess. Boulder, CO: Conflict Information Consortium, University of Colorado, 2003. Retrieved from http://www.beyondintractability.org/essay/guilt-shame.

CHANCE, Jane. "The Germanic Lord: Tolkien's Medieval Parodies." *Tolkien's Art: A Mythology for England*. Lexington, KT: The University Press of Kentucky, 2001, 111-140.

CONRAD, Joseph. *Lord Jim*. First published 1900. London: Penguin Popular Classics, 1994.

COOPER, Terry D. *Sin, Pride, and Self-Acceptance: The Problem of Identity in Theology and Psychology*. Downers Grove, IL: InterVarsity Press, 2003.

EVANS, Jonathan. "Pride." *J.R.R. Tolkien Encyclopedia Scholarship and Critical Assessment*. Ed. Michael D.C. Drout. New York: Routledge, 2007, 543-544.

FLIEGER, Verlyn. "Tolkien's Wild Men: From Medieval to Modern." *Tolkien the Medievalist*, Ed. Jane Chance. New York: Routledge, 2003, 95-105.

GREANEY, Michael. *Conrad, Language and Narrative*. Cambridge: Cambridge University Press, 2002.

"Lord Jim and Embarrassment." *Lord Jim: Centennial Essays*. Eds. Allan H. Simmons and John Henry Stape. Amsterdam: Rodopi, 2000, 1-14.

GUTIERREZ, Donald. *The Dark and Light Gods: Essays on the Self in Modern Literature*. Troy, NY: The Whitston Publishing Company, 1987.

HERMAN, Judith Lewis. "Shattered Shame States and Their Repair." *Shattered States: Disorganised Attachment and Its Repair*. Eds. Judy Yellin and Kate White. London: Karnac Books, 2012, 157-170.

HIEBERT, Paul G. *Anthropological Insights for Missionaries*. First published 1985. Grand Rapids, MI: Baker Book House, 2008.

HONEGGER, Thomas. "'We don't need another hero' – Problematic Heroes and their Function in Some of Tolkien's Works." *J.R.R. Tolkien: Individual, Community, Society: Proceedings of the 5th International Conference on Tolkien in Hungary (Budapest, 3-4 September 2015)*. Published in Hungarian as "Nincs szükségünk még egy hősre – Problematikus hősök és szerepük Tolkien egyes műveiben." *Közösség, társadalom – Tolkien Konferencia tanulmánykötet*. Kiadja a Magyar Tolkien Társaság. Eds. Kincső Rózsa Kiss, Ágnes Bonácz, and Andrea Nagy Egyén. Budapest: MTT, 2018. [see also academia.edu for the English version]

HORNEY, Karen. "Self-Hate and Self-Contempt." *Neurosis and the Human Growth: The Struggle Towards Self-Realization*. First published 1951. New York: Routledge, 1999, 110-154.

MASSARO, Toni M. "Show (Some) Emotions." *The Passions of Law*. Ed. Susan A. Bandes. New York: New York University Press, 1999, 80-122.

NIETZSCHE, Friedrich. *The Joyful Wisdom (Die fröhliche Wissenschaft)*. First published 1882. Translated by Thomas Common, eBooks@Adelaide, Adelaide: The University of Adelaide Library. Retrieved from http://ebooks.adelaide.edu.au/n/nietzsche/friedrich/n67j/index.html. Last updated March 6, 2014.

PANICHAS, George A. "Chapter 2: *Lord Jim*." *Joseph Conrad: His Moral Vision*. Macon, GA: Mercer University Press, 2005, 15-34.

SHIPPEY, Tom. "*The Silmarillion*: The Work of His Heart." *J.R.R. Tolkien: Author of the Century*. New York: Houghton Mifflin, 2000, 226-263.

TARNOPOLSKY, Christina H. *Prudes, Perverts, and Tyrants: Plato's Gorgias and the Politics of Shame*. Princeton, NJ: Princeton University Press, 2010.

WATTS, Cedric. "Bakhtin's Monologism and the Endings of *Crime and Punishment* and *Lord Jim*." *Lord Jim: Centennial Essays*. Eds. Allan H. Simmons and John Henry Stape. Amsterdam: Rodopi, 2000, 15-30.

Chiara Nejrotti

From Neverland to Middle-earth[1]

When Tolkien was just eighteen (1910), he went to see a show of *Peter Pan* and was so fascinated that he wrote in his diary, "Indescribable, shall never forget it as long as I live" (Carpenter 1977, 47-48).

Barrie managed to stage what seemed impossible to represent. Despite the difficulty of making his fantasy world credible, he managed to involve the spectators to the point that he attained *the suspension of disbelief* that Tolkien always considered fundamental. In fact, at the climax of the show, Peter Pan asked the public to clap their hands and repeat with him, "I believe in fairies", involving not only the children but also some of the adults.

The show had a profound effect on Tolkien as it reflected themes that resounded in his soul – above all the relationship between the real world and *Faërie*. Even if the fairies that live in Peter Pan's world are very different from the Tall Elves of Tolkien's *Legendarium*, the influence of the concept of diminiutive fairies is quite clear in Tolkien's early works. Dimitra Fimi[2] has shown how present and significant fairies were in late Victorian and Edwardian literature and how much Tolkien was influenced as a young writer. Before developing his own artistic and poetic vision, the author followed the styles of his contemporaries that characterized the representation of fantasy creatures, even if he later renounced them. The imaginary tale was used between the end of the 19th century and the beginning of the 20th century in contrast to the ruling positivism, reusing themes that were already dear to Romanticism. The young author was particularly fond of Francis Thompson's works, a Catholic poet of the second half of the 19th century, who portrayed a mystic vision of the natural world in his poetry that included the presence of fairy-like beings. According to Thompson, nature is a manifestation of God's spirit and the presence of living

---

1 I would like to thank Allison Rowe for translating my essay from the original Italian.
2 See Fimi 2008b, 10-26 and Fimi 2008.

spirits in it, like elves and fairies, is a partial manifestation of this spirit. Many men of letters, both Spiritualists and Christians (like Chesterton) considered the belief in fairies as a possibility of the restoration of the supernatural in a world that denied its existence, as it looked only towards instrumental reason and technical knowledge.

In 1915, in the same period that he wrote *Goblin Feet* – the most significant example of what is described above – Tolkien wrote *The Cottage of Lost Play*, that became part of the first version of his *Legendarium*. In the tale he talks about *Olòre Malle*[3] – the path of dreams – that linked the world of men to the Land of the Elves; however, only children could reach it in their dreams. At the end of the path there is the Children's House, where the children of the Fathers of the Fathers of Men could play freely. The Elves controlled the house to make sure the little ones were never in danger, but above all, they guided anyone who, in their dreams, was wandering lost in the Fairy Realm. In fact, if this happened, the children did not want to return to the world of Men – and if they did return, they would forever suffer from a destructive sense of nostalgia. In a later version, the children who were lost and stayed in the Enchanted Land were gathered in the Cottage of Lost Play, where they could listen to ancient stories and who, in turn, could then go to the children of Men, whispering to them stories in their dreams. Their mission was to go among children left alone and to dry their tears.

The description of the House the lost children were led to seems to be a personal revisit by the young writer of *Peter Pan in Kensington Gardens*. In Barrie's tale the London park becomes a mysterious and magical place, and after "Lock-Out Time" it turns into fairy territory. In the park, fairies built a house as a shelter for lost children and it was Peter Pan's job to find them and lead them to the magical residence, guiding them with the sweet sound of his pan flutes.

The link between dreams, children and Enchanted Lands also appears in a poem entitled, *You and Me*[4], quoted by Christopher Tolkien in his comment on the chapter and written during the same period. The personal involvement is clear: the blonde boy and the dark-haired girl, he himself and his adored

---

3 *BLT1* 18-19, 27.
4 *BLT1* 28-29.

Edith all go to the Land of Fairies in their dreams, where they play happily until one day they are denied access to the Garden and the House; by now they have grown up and, therefore, are no longer able to find the magic road. Only the innocence of the young is compatible with the enchantment of the fairy world; adult life is nothing more than a long exile. The description of the fairies present in the garden that surrounds the House is also similar to Barrie's ethereal figures dedicated to dance and song, that play with their child guests in an everlasting party-like atmosphere.

In *BLT2* there is another character that reminds one of some of Peter Pan's features: Tinfang (Warble), the Elf that plays the flute. He descends half from the Solosimpi – the Elves that loved the sea and song, the first version of the Teleri – and the other line of descent is from the spirits of the woods and valleys that create the following of Yavanna, creatures similar to those of the Little People found in the folklore of the British Isles, that Tolkien eliminated in later versions. Tinfang was given his name because of the sound of his flute and is considered strange but incredibly wise. He lets people merely get a glimpse of him, but the sound of his flute lingers in the air even after he has disappeared. His music contains powerful magic, in that it reaches the soul of those who hear it like an echo of a dream or of nostalgia. The character of Tinfang brings to mind the divine piper, Pan, who also appears in Kenneth Grahame's *The Wind in the Willows* (1908) in the chapter "The Piper at the Gates of Dawn". The sound of his flute transports Rat and Mole, the two main characters, to a dimension of absolute peace and happiness, without being in conflict with the sense of terror that the Sacred presence provokes in them. Pan's music generates a destructive nostalgia in their souls but, at the same time, it comforts them, making them feel loved and secure. The last gift the Sylvan god gives them is that of oblivion, so that the nostalgia doesn't become too intense and stop them from living a normal life.

The figure of the god Pan often recurs in English literature of the 19th century and receives a poetic veneration that is linked to the romantic and pantheistic theme of Nature as a living manifestation of the divine.

When the god is present, in fact, all of nature is brought to life and reveals itself in a triumph of shapes and colours. The animal protagonists of Graham's novel experience this, just like Peter Pan who has some divine characteristics, too. His presence means that on his island it is always spring, yet, when he goes away everything is locked in wintery ice.

If the best-known Elf flautist in English literature is Peter Pan, it is worthwhile investigating more deeply the characteristics of the boy who wouldn't grow up and those of Neverland, to see whether traces of them can be found in later works of Tolkien – and which themes the two authors share.

The figure of Peter Pan first appeared in *The Little White Bird*, published by Barrie in 1903. The following year the Scottish writer presented his work entitled *Peter Pan, or The Boy who Wouldn't Grow Up;* however, in 1906 his publisher decided to extract the six chapters pertaining to Peter from *The Little White Bird* and publish them as a tale in their own right with illustrations by Arthur Rackham, and this was given the title *Peter Pan in Kensington Gardens*. Finally, in 1911, the work was published as a novel with the title *Peter Pan and Wendy*. There are numerous differences between *Peter Pan in Kensington Gardens* and the better-known version, but the most significant are the age of the protagonist and the place where his adventures take place. Barrie (1906, 12) writes:

> His age is one week, and though he was born so long ago, he has never had a birthday nor is there the slightest chance of his ever having one. The reason is that he escaped from being a human when he was seven days old, he escaped by the window and flew back to Kensington Gardens.

Peter is, therefore, initially an infant, but comes across as psychologically pompous in that he is given the task of leading the souls of babies who had fallen from their prams to the House.

In this context it is not possible to fully develop the origins of the figure created by Barrie, but one can recognize some autobiographical characteristics. His brother, David, was killed in a tragic ice-skating accident when he was just thirteen and his mother never got over it. Barrie tried to substitute for his dead brother, even to the point of dressing like him, but was never able to draw his mother out of depression and this marked him for life. On top of this, he discovered his artistic vocation, something which seemed irreconcilable with the seriousness of the social background of his time, which is why he developed the idea that artists never grow up and that the best age is childhood and pre-adolescence.

Peter Pan is the child who rejects adult life, but he is also the child who died prematurely; for this reason he will never grow up and will, therefore, never lose his innocence.

From this point of view, Barrie's work can be seen as consolatory children's literature, addressing the issue of child mortality at a time when it was still widespread. In the same way one can quote *The Water-Babies* (1863) by Charles Kingsley[5] and *At the Back of the North Wind* (1871) by George MacDonald,[6] both written during the Victorian era. Returning to Peter Pan, in the first work dedicated to him, the characteristics his figure is assuming are gradually being outlined, going from a simple figure in a children's tale to becoming a true archetype. The young child learns from birds to live only in the present, without worrying about the future; he makes himself a pipe to imitate their song but he cannot distinguish play from reality and he would like to be like the other children in the park. Then he manages to reach the Gardens, where his adventures with the fairies begin. The crucial episode in Peter's story can be found in the chapter "Lock-Out Time", implying a double reference to the closure of the park, on the one hand, and on the other to the closure of the window of the nursery: when Peter decides to return home to his mother, renouncing the magic life of the park, he finds his bedroom window closed and another child has taken his place. He can no longer return home and thus becomes, as prohesied by the crow Solomon Caw, "Betwixt-and-Between". This definition appropriately expresses his liminal nature. He is a being who is on the border of what is human and what is not – a sort of spirit that can no longer access the human condition as he rejected to accept its implications, that is to enter into time and its consequent mortality. There is something incomplete in Peter which, on the one hand, makes him so fascinating, but on the other hand, expresses his alienation. When Captain Hook asks him: "Pan who and

---

5 Tom, an ill-treated and exploited little chimney-sweep, falls into a river and is turned into a Fairy by a water-baby. He then has various adventures which make him mature; the tone of the tale is often allegorical with the intent of expressing morals.
6 MacDonald was an author much loved by Tolkien. This novel is deep and tells the story of a child's meeting with the Lady of the North Wind, the Angel of Death. She shows herself to be kind and loving with the little boy who is not afraid of her – on the contrary, he loves her intensely, captured by her beauty. The whole tale can be interpreted as a poetic metaphor for a terminal illness which leads to a slow death, but the adventures of Diamond with the North Wind become a journey in which the reader joins the characters of the story, looking for Beauty and Truth, transcending appearances.

what art thou?", Peter replies, defining his *puer* nature: "I'm youth, I'm joy, I'm a little bird that has broken out of the egg" (Barrie 1911, 160).

From a psychological point of view the *puer* lives outside time, in an ideal world of his own. He is lively, brilliant, and inquisitive, he has an insatiable thirst for novelty but, at the same time, he is egocentric and impatient, impulsive, and inconsistent. He belongs to a world of adventure and pleasure where there is no place for hard work, suffering or sacrifice. The difference between good and evil is an abstract concept to him, he is amoral in the sense that he is pre-moral, and he follows the principle of pleasure, not that of reality. In such an existence any possible disappointment is denied – a *puer* simply changes his game. A similar world cannot exist, as a *puer* cheats himself. He closes his eyes to limitations that characterize human existence, thinking that in this way he can avoid it. However, in doing so he loses his Shadow that cannot integrate with his psyche.

Living eternally in the present, where events leave no trace, makes Peter seem to not need anything or anyone. When he is flying with Wendy and her brothers, he tends to forget about them; no thought troubles him for long. A great part of his charm lies in the fact that he is elusive, uncatchable, and always somewhere else; he is like fresh air, evasive with no shape or direction. The *puer* is always accompanied by the element of flight. As Barrie states, only those who are cheerful, innocent, and heartless can fly.

The desire to elude time, to vanquish death and gain immortality occupies a central position in all of Tolkien's work.[7] However, the immortality of the Elves does not exclude the effects of the passing of time; in fact, it highlights it. This is because their fundamental problem is that of wanting to preserve the past in a world – Middle-earth – that is subject to change and ageing. The longevity of the Elves, much envied by mortals, does not serve as a solution. The Elves remain prisoners of the Arda cycles, which themselves are subject to time, even if it passes really slowly and is calculated according to the years of the Trees of Valinor.

---

7 Arduini & Testi 2012.

Nothing remains of the carefree Elves that sang under the stars in *The Hobbit*, because in the tales of *Legendarium* they appear as tragic figures, and in *The Lord of the Rings* their wisdom derives from the pain and suffering of the long eras they have spent in Middle-earth.

The escape from death of the eternal child has no place in Tolkien's work, as he does not fear the responsibility of adult life and would not want children to never grow up, apart from preserving the simplicity of the heart in the evangelical sense. Tolkien himself assumed responsibility and matured quickly, both because of his personal life (linked to the death of his mother) and because he had to face the horrors of war. As a father, he loved children but no longer considered the taste for fantasy their prerogative. All the characters in his works are completely mature and do not regret the passing of an ideal childhood. However, the theme of the escape from time – and its consequent strain – remains central to Tolkien's poetry, just like the nostalgia for the Elsewhere. Faerie, the Land of Fairies, remains a constant sub-creation of Tolkien's, while assuming quite different aspects within his works during the course of his existence. Which aspects does Faerie have in common with Neverland where Peter Pan lives?

Neverland is aptly named, as it highlights its existence outside not only normal space, but also time. It is the place of fantasy par excellence, which anyone can enter, in both their dreams or daydreams. There are pirates and native Americans, next to fairies and mermaids. They adapt to the dreamer's taste and predilections, but the basic elements stay the same: adventure and magic. Wendy, John, and Michael have the chance to enter, following Peter, and experience extraordinary adventures. Yet in contrast to Peter, they also have the opportunity to go back home. In this sense it seems to be following the same path as indicated by Tolkien's last novella, *Smith of Wootton Major,* in which he describes the travels of a mortal in a spellbound country. However, at a certain point he is forced to renounce and give up his "passport to Faerie".

From being a resident of Kensington Gardens, a place which belongs to ordinary existence even if it is transformed at night, Peter has developed into the inhabitant of Neverland par excellence. Neverland is the land of imagination where you live a life of play and adventure in an eternal present, and where you never grow up or age. However, it is exactly for this reason that one cannot evolve or change.

Middle-earth, created by Tolkien, does not have the same features as Neverland. It is a place where time passes and leaves its trace, where people change and make decisions, where death exists. In spite of this, in Tolkien's work there are places that have the characteristics of Faerie, at least for mortals. They are the Undying Lands – the Land of the Valar and Tol Eressea.[8] Men (and Hobbits) cannot have access except under special circumstances, as happened with Frodo and Bilbo, in that they were Carriers of the Ring; but, above all, you cannot return from these lands. Even Earendil, who reached the borders of Valinor to beseech the help of the Valar against the Melkor, was given the responsibility of navigating the skies as a shining star, but he could not return to Middle-earth. After the fall of Númenor, the Undying Lands were removed from the circles of the world so they could no longer be reached, except by the Elves for whom they were destined. The Path of Dreams, that the young Tolkien had imagined could be taken, also disappeared and was replaced with a much darker and pessimistic vision, like the one expressed in *The Sea-Bell* and *The Last Ship*.[9] In both of them the bitter knowledge that it is impossible for mortal men to physically enter the Undying Lands is expressed. The terrestrial Paradise is lost forever, even though a way of entering has to remain open during life on earth, even if Man cannot live there – he can only catch a fleeting glance of it.

In the comment on *Smith* the Oxford Professor, by now elderly, returned to the question, trying to reconcile human space and time with that of Faerie. In the essay that accompanies the presentation of the tale, the author tries to give a reason for the proximity of the two worlds and how they can coexist. Each of them, he argues, occupies a different time and space, or in different ways. The question of a different sense of time is dealt with in depth and Tolkien maintains that a moment in the fairy realm would not be worth hundreds of years in our world; or rather he seems to think it is the other way round. Yet the protagonist in his tale goes away for a few days and carries out explorations

---

8 See Flieger 1997.
9 See *ATB*, 66 and 74.

and experiences adventures which would take months or years, just as happens in dreams.

In note F of the essay *On Fairy-stories* (*TOFS* 82-83), on the subject of the critique of the theatre as a fairy-like medium, Tolkien upheld the theory that it can base itself on the influence of fantastic events on human beings but is unlikely to be able to represent the actual fantastic in a credible way. In this context he does not refer to the performance of *Peter Pan*, which had fascinated him so much in his youth, but mentions another of Barrie's works, *Mary Rose* (1924), as a negative example to support his theory. The storyline centres around a young girl who was kidnapped by fairylike beings and returns to the human world many years later – but for her only a moment had passed. According to Tolkien, the limitation of Barrie's work is to be found in its inability to show anything about the creatures of Faerie or about their existence. All it is able to present is the negative influence of Faerie on human beings. This theme is present in many tales and traditions about the Little People. Yet the Professor maintains that in them, although the outcome may be very similar, the attention is placed on the description of the Land of the Fairies and its inhabitants or, at least, on the adventures a mortal can experience there.

In his commentary on *Smith of Wootton Major*, Tolkien insists on the need to consider the Elves and the Fairies as benign forces that help the human race. They help it to find oneself and the correct relationship with things and nature that surrounds a person, instead of seeing them as disturbing and almost diabolical elements. In this sense it is possible to see an analogy between the best features of Peter Pan, in that he is an expression of the imagination and of creativity, and the way Tolkien intended Fantasy to be perceived.

Even if the authors are profoundly different, both of them express a need that draws them close to each other and that is particularly evident in the literary and artistic production of their time, which is to escape from the close and enclosed world of everyday reality in order to access another dimension. The latter is not in opposition to the former, nor is it an indispensible complement; in this dimension even death can become "an extraordinary adventure" (Barrie 1911) and the time of mortals and that of Faerie can meet and mingle while retaining their own distinct identities.

Bbliography

Works by J.M. Barrie:
Mary Rose. London: Hodder & Stoughton, 1924.
Peter Pan and Wendy. London: Hodder & Stoughton, 1911.
Peter Pan in Kensington Gardens. London: Hodder & Stoughton, 1906.
The Little White Bird. London: Hodder & Stoughton, 1902.

Other works
ARDUINI Roberto, Cecilia BARELLA, Giampaolo CANZONIERI, and Claudio Antonio TESTI (eds.). *Tolkien e i classici*. Turin: Effatà Editrice, 2015.

ARDUINI, Roberto and Claudio Antonio TESTI (eds.). *The Broken Scythe: Death and Immortality in the Works of J.R.R.Tolkien*. Zurich and Jena: Walking Tree Publishers, 2012.

ARGENTIERI, Niccolò. *La più grande avventura: figure del tempo nelle storie di Peter Pan e Harry Potter*. Acireale: Bonanno Editore, 2013.

BARELLA, Cecilia. "In mezzo scorre un fiume. Tolkien e Grahame." *Tolkien e i classici*. Eds. Roberto Arduini, Cecilia Barella, Giampaolo Canzonieri, and Claudio Antonio Testi. Turin: Effatà Editrice, 2015, 189-200.

CARPENTER, Humphrey. *J.R.R. Tolkien: A Biography*. London: Allen&Unwin, 1977.

FIMI, Dimitra. *Tolkien, Race and Cultural History. From Fairies to Hobbits*. Basingstoke: Palgrave Macmillan, 2008.

"'Come sing ye light fairy things tripping so gay': Victorian Fairies and the Early Work of J.R.R. Tolkien Working with English: Medieval and Modern Language, Literature and Drama." http://www.nottingham.ac.uk/english/working_with_english/Fimi_31_05_06.pdf, 2008b (Accessed 11/01/08).

FLIEGER, Verlyn. *A Question of Time*. Kent, OH: The Kent State University Press, 1997.

FRANZ, Marie Louise von. *The Problem of the Puer Aeternus*. Toronto: Inner City Books, 2000.

GARTH, John. *Tolkien and the Great Wars*. London: HarperCollins, 2011.

GRAHAME, Kenneth. *The Wind in the Willows*. First published 1908. London: Puffins Classics, 2008.

GULISANO, Paolo and Chiara NEJROTTI. *Alla ricerca di Peter Pan.* Siena: Cantagalli, 2010.

HILLMANN, James. *Senex and puer.* Uniform Edition, vol. 3. New York: Spring Publications, 2006.

KINGSLEY, Charles. *The Water Babies.* London: Macmillan, 1863.

MACDONALD, George. *At the Back of the North Wind.* London: Strahan & Co, 1871.

MORGAN, Kathie. "Waiting with Bated Breath: Intimations and Anticipations of Eternity Viewed through Children's Literature." Faculty Publications and Presentations. Paper 187, School of Education, Liberty University, Lynchburg, VA 24502, 2011. http://digitalcommons.liberty.edu/educ_fac_pubs/187.

PENNAROLA, Cristina. *Frammenti di immortalità: Peter Pan di J.M. Barrie.* Florence: Atheneum, 1995.

TIMTCHEVA, Viara. *Le Merveilleux et la Mort dans Le Seigneur des Anneaux de J.R.R. Tolkien, Peter Pan de J.M. Barrie et L'Histoire sans fin de Michael Ende.* Paris: L'Harmattan, 2006.

Giampaolo Canzonieri

The Hobbit and the Puppet: Two Protagonists Journeying into Opposite Directions

An author who has to choose the subject for his own contribution to a collection of essays such as "Tolkien and the Classics" will most likely choose the "classic" he feels more congenial or, for whatever reason, particularly close to his own nature and feelings. It is, however, not always so and, in my own case, I chose the subject because I wished to include in this collection a novel that, despite certain undeniable flaws, is the most famous Italian children book in the world. The choice, I would like to add, was not made out of chauvinism but, I daresay, by the intent of giving justice to a work that, far beyond its intrinsic literary value, is so deeply rooted in the Italian cultural world[1] as to become the subject of a sort of "eternal return" that has it resurface in endless adaptations of all sorts.[2]

If one wants to find similarities between Collodi's and Tolkien's works, what comes first to mind is to compare *The Hobbit*, the first of Tolkien's works, and *The Adventures of Pinocchio*. The enormous and unexpected success of *The Hobbit* when published in 1937 is in fact comparable to the vast acclaim gained by the publication of *The Adventures of Pinocchio* in 1883 in Italy.[3] Before examining the two works, however, I would like to point out that while it is evident – for obvious reasons (he died in 1890) – that Collodi could have never had knowledge of Tolkien's works, there is unfortunately not one single hint that Tolkien had any awareness of Collodi's work either. It is definitely possible

---

1 For the deep "Italianness" of *Pinocchio* see Tosi & Hunt (2013, 45): "Pinocchio is, after all, impregnated with Italian history: this is a very Italian story about hunger and education at a time when [...] it was still not clear what it meant for a new nation [...] to have to share common values as citizens."
2 It will suffice to quote, among others, the "mythical" television version by Luigi Comencini, the controversial film version by Roberto Benigni, the refined editions illustrated by the lamented Benito Jacovitti and by Lorenzo Mattotti, and the recent animated cartoon by Enzo d'Alò.
3 In order to size up the extent of Pinocchio's success, we quote the intriguing coincidence that, besides being translated in dozens of languages, both works have also been translated into Latin: *Pinoculus, in latinum sermonem conuersus ab Henrico Maffacini*, Florence: Marzocco, 1950 and *Hobbitus Ille, ex Anglico sermone in Latinum conuersus* (sic) *a Marco Walker*, London: HarperCollins, 2012.

that a young John Ronald had read Pinocchio in his childhood years, since the work was first published in England in 1892, the year of his birth. However, as far as we know, he never mentions it and we have therefore no direct piece of evidence. It is unlikely he had never heard of it, and not only because of the animated film produced by Disney in 1940 – which he must have not been much interested in if we consider how little he valued Uncle Walt's productions – but also because of the unusual coincidence that the first English translation of *Pinocchio* was published by T. Fisher Unwin,[4] uncle and first employer of Stanley Unwin who, 45 years later, was to publish *The Hobbit*.

Be as it may, in the absence of first-hand evidence we can only analyse the literary world of the two authors and how it is reflected in the character and adventures of the wooden puppet and the burglar with hairy feet.

The first thing to take into consideration is the structure and nature of the two works *per se*. *The Hobbit*, on the one hand, is a fairy-story that will gradually transform into an epic, quite realistic in the frame of the Secondary World, in which it is firmly rooted, and developing within it and only in its dimension. In *Pinocchio*, on the other hand, we find the coexistence of elements of three different genres, fable, fairy-story and realism, that Collodi uses in accordance with his own needs without being too discriminative.[5] Thus we find the Fairy and the Land of Boobies,[6] introducing the *topoi* of the fairy-creature and the fantastic world typical of fairy-tales. Furthermore, we encounter talking animals teaching moral lessons of all sorts, typical elements of the fable genre, but we also find destitution and social marginalisation directly related to the harsh reality the author himself had experienced. Geppetto's more than realistic bites of hunger are a tangible example of the Primary World intruding into the fantasy world, and even more so are the Fox and the Cat, who are not merely comic antagonists but "people" who live at the margins of society and, if circumstances call for it, do not even shrink from committing murder in cold blood. The dog Melampo too is a character of realistic squalor, even

---

4 *The Story of a Puppet or The Adventures of Pinocchio*, translated by M. A. Murray.
5 Cf. Asor Rosa (2005, 28): "Therefore, from a strictly narratological point of view, the adventures of Pinocchio are a typical 'compromise' […] Characters are equally split between realistic and fantastic ones" (translation by Giampaolo Canzonieri).
6 "Land of Toys" or "Toyland" would have been far more correct, but that is how M.A. Murray (see note 4) translates it, so be it.

more so because he accepts the polecats' offer to betray his master in exchange for a miserable chicken, lacking even that tiny speck of *grandeur* that leads the Master of Lake-town to betray his citizens in exchange for a conspicuous treasure, or Grima Wormtongue – but here we are already in the great epic of *The Lord of the Rings* – to betray his king in exchange for the hand of a princess (whom he did even love, at least in his own way). Finally, Collodi positively defines the world of Pinocchio as *our* world when Pinocchio, recounting his counter-metamorphosis from donkey into puppet, commends his astonished "buyer" to St. Anthony, thus violating one of the foundation pillars of Tolkien's vision, who thought any direct reference to religion in a fantasy work to be "fatal" (*Letters* no. 131). Moreover, Collodi also makes good use of allegory, a trope Tolkien openly disliked and avoided for both *The Hobbit* and *The Lord of the Rings*.[7] In this respect it will suffice to mention the character of the Ape Judge – "of the gorilla tribe" (*Pinocchio* XIX) – who condemns Pinocchio in the most comic, albeit somewhat tragic, episode of the book. The Ape Judge is the clear representation of the vexing whimsicalities that those in power show towards the common citizen.

Also, when we consider the inner coherence of the story, the two authors are poles apart. If Tolkien, on the one hand, is constantly revising his work to make sure his stories will work with clockwork accuracy – distances, timing, lunar phases and every other possible detail – Collodi, on the other hand, does not pay any attention to these aspects and his writings are riddled with incongruities, contradictions, and plot holes that would have caused Tolkien many nights of insomnia. Pinocchio starts his first wayward flight even before his first day of school and yet, even if with some difficulty, he reads the epitaph on the tombstone of the Child with blue hair; Fire-eater's puppets, the Parrot and the Blackbird call him by name, though they have never seen him before; the Talking-cricket is hit by the hammer and "remained dried up and flattened against the wall" (*Pinocchio* IV) but reappears later on, alive and well, with no explanation whatsoever; "a thousand large birds" (*Pinocchio* XVIII) land on Pinocchio's nose, and, what is more, while he is inside a room. We could

---

7 See, among others, Tolkien's comments in *Letters* no. 203: "There is no 'symbolism' or conscious allegory in my story. Allegory of the sort 'five wizards = five senses' is wholly foreign to my way of thinking."

go on and on with additional examples, yet they should not be interpreted as a form of criticism towards Collodi – or at least they should not be seen as *objective* criticism. Quite simply, Collodi did not have a coherent "vision"[8] for his story, in this being totally different from Tolkien who, while writing *The Hobbit* between 1930 and 1936, was already developing the principles he organized between 1937 and 1939. He presented his ideas in his lecture given at St Andrews University, which was later published as "On Fairy-stories", the cultural *manifesto* of his approach to fairy-story and myth. Collodi was writing a "simple" children story, and was allowing himself great creative freedom, drawing its legitimation from that "simple" intention;[9] the fact that this alleged "simplicity" resulted in a classic that after 130 years is still so popular can only give him credit.

Now, if we compare the styles of the two authors, the contrast between them attenuates and, at the same time, is confirmed. If we refer to the first part of either work, we notice Tolkien as well as Collodi use an openly "childish" style. They indulge in directly addressing the readers, and – a curious circumstance – in the *incipit* they both use the same device to attract the readers' attention. Both describe something, the hobbit-hole in Tolkien's case, and the piece of wood in Collodi's text, by what *it is not*.[10] However, Tolkien will soon abandon the plain and somewhat paternalistic style of the beginning in order to gradually achieve a higher register. The change of style will lead him eventually to the epic, and in the course of this evolution, determined – one may think – by a subconscious choice, he will gradually abandon the use of addressing the reader directly,[11] a stylistic device he will later openly regret.[12]

---

[8] Cf. Asor Rosa (2005, 16): "It would therefore be vain to expect the genius in *Pinocchio* to be found in an illuminated and conscious attempt at a literary renovation of Fairy-story" (translation by Giampaolo Canzonieri).

[9] Cf. Asor Rosa (2005, 16): "book written to be published as a serial novel, thus widely enjoying the freedom granted by the fact it hadn't been necessary to write it, nor perhaps to conceive it in its entirety, before it started being published" (translation by Giampaolo Canzonieri).

[10] "Not a nasty, dirty, wet hole [...] nor yet a dry, bare, sandy hole with nothing in it to sit down on or to eat: it was a hobbit-hole, and that means comfort" (*H* I). "This wood was not valuable: it was only a common log like those that are burnt in winter in the stoves and fireplaces to make a cheerful blaze and warm the rooms" (*Pinocchio* I).

[11] Cf. Thomas 2000: direct addresses to the readers are frequent in the first thirteen chapters, but they are totally absent in the last six.

[12] Cf. *Letters* no. 163 to W.H. Auden: "[*The Hobbit*] was unhappily really meant [...] as a 'children's story', and [...] it has some of the sillinesses of manner caught unthinkingly from the kind of stuff I had had served to me [...]. I deeply regret them. So do intelligent children".

Collodi, on the other side, never had such afterthoughts, and even if at times he writes in an unexpectedly modern dark style, as it is the case for the description of Pinocchio's near death by hanging[13] or the mephistophelic "little, fat man" driving the wagon to the Land of Boobies,[14] he never abandons the juvenile language. Collodi's uniformity is consistent with the plot and, unlike what happens in *The Hobbit*, it maintains the same homogeneity with no particular sparks of inspiration. After all it could have not been otherwise, since from the very first page Collodi affirms that the book is intended for "little readers" (*Pinocchio* I), a dangerous limitation of readership that Tolkien would have avoided since, as he asserts in his Andrew-Lang-lecture: "If fairy-story as a kind is worth reading at all it is worthy to be written for and read by adults. They will, of course, put more in and get more out than children can" (*TOFS* 58). As a matter of fact, when addressing the reader, Tolkien always uses a generic "you" that does not leave out adult readers.

Let us now analyse the main characters, Pinocchio and Bilbo, the puppet and the hobbit. The contrast we have already pointed out increases until one becomes almost the mirror image of the other. The Bilbo we meet at the beginning of the story is a typical hobbit with peculiarities perfectly fitting the *aurea mediocritas* so much appreciated by the community of the Shire: "Well-to-do" and "rich" (*H* I), predictable – "you could tell what a Baggins would say on any question without the bother of asking him" (*H* I) – "respectable" (*H* I) – he had "never had any adventures" (*H* I). In one word, the perfect bourgeois conformist who is only concerned with the opinion of his peers. Pinocchio, by contrast, is poor as a church mouse; even before being carved out of the piece of wood – where he was held as a sort of Michelangelesque Prisoner – he succeeds in causing Geppetto and Master Cherry to come to blows, and he runs away at the first opportunity in search of adventure. Bilbo's bourgeois nature is the product of his upbringing, whereas Pinocchio's unruly temper has been an intrinsic part of his personality even before his own "birth"!

---

13 It is worth noting that Pinocchio "dies" with four coins under his tongue, very likely a reminder of the Greek tradition to place a coin under the tongue of the dead in order to enable them to pay Charon's passage over the river Styx.
14 See Pentucci 2012.

Is there one thing they have in common? I believe there is and, if we consider Pinocchio's nature, it is quite an unexpected trait. In the darkness of the Orcs' tunnels, Bilbo spares Gollum's life, which can be interpreted in hindsight as the flap of the butterfly's wings that will cause the crumbling of Sauron's reign. Also, in the midst of the daring breakout from the prison of the Elvenking, he still takes the time to put the keys back on the belt of the chief guard in order to "save him some of the trouble he is in for" (*H* IX). Likewise, Pinocchio offers himself to burn as firewood under the Fire-eater's spit in Harlequin's stead, and out of respect for the dead he does not tell the peasant about the late dog Melampo's betrayal. The rascal and the conformist both share deep feelings of pity, all the more meaningful because they express them in things both small and big. Yet these are only drops in the ocean. We have already pointed out the mirror image nature of the relationship between the two characters at their starting points. Even more astonishing than this initial likeness are the parallels as they appear in their respective ends. Each novel can be considered, in its own way, a coming-of-age story.[15] Yet while Bilbo Baggins undergoes the transformation from bourgeois to "hero",[16] Pinocchio proceeds in quite the opposite direction, developing from "hero" to bourgeois. The conformist Bilbo, who smokes his pipe in front of Bag End, gives way to a hobbit who "had lost his reputation" and is considered "queer" because of his "heroic" interlude (*H* XIX); Pinocchio, who misbehaves since being a piece of wood and abandoning Geppetto to see Fire-eater's puppets, becomes "a boy, like all other boys" and is "glad" to "have become a well-behaved little boy!" (*Pinocchio* XXXVI). The almost baffling melancholy that often accompanies the return of the hero is contrasted with the vaguely factitious happy ending, typical of the moral stories

---

15 On Pinocchio, however, there is no unanimity. Richter 2002, although he considers it mainly a "novel of childhood" ("Roman der Kindheit"), also affirms that it is "proposed as a 'coming-of-age novel'". A "novel of childhood" because "the main character is a child" and the epilogue "is marked by the 'becoming a man' of this child", "coming-of-age novel" because, even if it is about "the rebellion against being forced to become adults", it is meant at the same time to "contribute in transforming children into adult people". Pentucci 2012, by contrast, maintains that it does not come under the category of the "coming-of-age novel" because "the puppet never learns from his mistakes" and "doesn't find strength in himself but is led to emancipation by external agents" (translation by Giampaolo Canzonieri).

16 In Shippey 2012 the author describes what he judges to be the "turning points" in Bilbo's development: his crawling towards the Trolls, the finding of the Ring in the tunnels beneath the Misty Mountains, the fight against the spiders, the descent into the tunnel that leads to Smaug's lair, and the delivery of the Arkenstone to the besiegers of the Lonely Mountain. For the definition of Bilbo as bourgeois hero, see Shippey 1992, 66f.

intended for the readers' edification. Although we have indeed absolutely nothing against "good boys" and "good citizens", still we indulge in the unspoken wish that the roads of the Tuscany countryside may one day lead a Gandalf to Pinocchio's door.

Bibliography

Asor Rosa, Alberto. *"Le Avventure Di Pinocchio. Storia Di Un Burattino" di Carlo Collodi*. Torino: Einaudi, 2005.

Collodi (pseudonym of Carlo Lorenzini). *Le avventure di Pinocchio. Storia di un burattino*. Translation by Mary Alice Murray. *The Story of a Puppet or The Adventures of Pinocchio*. London: T. Fisher Unwin, 1892. https://en.wikisource.org/wiki/The_Story_of_a_Puppet (accessed 4/9/2018).

Pentucci, Maila. "Il paese dei balocchi: Pinocchio tra Paradiso e Inferno." *Altre Modernità* 7. Milan: Università degli Studi di Milano, Facoltà di Lettere e Filosofia, http://riviste.unimi.it/index.php/AMonline/article/view/2136 (accessed 4/9/2018), 2012.

Richter, Dieter. *Pinocchio, o Il romanzo d'infanzia*. Roma: Edizioni di Storia e Letteratura, 2002.

Shippey, Tom. *The Road to Middle-earth*. London: HarperCollins, 1992.

"Not Back Yet." *The Times Literary Supplement*, 21st December 2012.

Thomas, Paul E. "Some of Tolkien's Narrators." *Tolkien's Legendarium: Essays on The History of Middle-earth*. Eds. Verlyn Flieger and Carl F. Hostetter. Westport, CT and London: Greenwood Press, 2000, 161-181.

Tosi, Laura and Peter Hunt. "Pinocchio and Alice: The Power of International Fantasies and National Stereotypes." Paper given at the conference "I mondi meravigliosi del Fantasy". Venice: Università Ca' Foscari, in collaboration with Ateneo Veneto, 2013.

Simone Bonechi

Tolkien and the War Poets

"In a trench in the ground there lived a poet ..."

During the years from 1914 to 1918, many people in Great Britain were writing poems directly inspired by the ongoing war. Looking at the anthologies of Great War poetry, we can find texts by known and unknown poets, by women who had served at the front as nurses or protested against the war, but most of all we can find poems by *soldier-poets*: men who had experienced the war on the battlefields. These are the War Poets we will deal with here: poets who, collectively, have now reached the status of a classic in the annals of English literature, so much so as to be formally canonised in 1985, with the affixing of a plaque in the Poet's Corner of Westminster Abbey, bearing the names of sixteen of them: Richard Aldington, Lawrence Binyon, Edmund Blunden, Rupert Brooke, Wilfrid Gibson, Robert Graves, Julian Grenfell, Ivor Gurney, David Jones, Robert Nichols, Wilfred Owen, Herbert Read, Isaac Rosenberg, Sigfried Sassoon, Charles Sorley, and Edward Thomas.[1]

Julian Grenfell apart (the only career officer among them), they were all volunteers and almost all served as junior officers: only Jones, Gurney, and Rosenberg joined the ranks as privates. They all fought on the Western Front, which is the war theatre that went from the westernmost corner of Belgium along all the north-eastern frontier of France. Although the British Army was also fighting in other parts of the world, in Europe as well as in Africa and the Middle-East, it is the experience of the Western Front that has become the foundation of the literary memory of the Great War, that which is passed down in school programmes and has assumed the value of *collective memory* of the First World War in Great Britain.

---

1 Of these men, the only one not having served at the front is Wilfrid Gibson, who, after having repeatedly tried to enlist, finally entered the Army Service Corps Motor Transport in 1917, and spent the rest of the war in London.

With the exception of the commoners Gurney, Rosenberg, and Read and of the aristocrat Grenfell, they were scions of the professional classes and of the gentry, educated in public schools and universities. Therefore, they shared the same social background as J.R.R. Tolkien and his closest friends Christopher Wiseman, Geoffrey Bache Smith, and Robert Quilter Gilson, united in the spiritual and artistic brotherhood of the Tea Club and Barrovian Society (T.C.B.S.).

The war caught them, usually, in the flower of their youth: almost all were born in the 1890s; Binyon was the oldest, being 46 in 1914, Blunden the youngest, barely 18 when the war broke out. A few of them were beginning to make a name for themselves as poets, writers, or artists (Gibson, Thomas, Gurney, Rosenberg, Jones).

By 1912 most of these poets had published their works in the anthologies of *Georgian Poetry*, which gravitated around Georgianism, then the poetic vanguard of the literary scene. The typical Georgian style was deliberately anti-Victorian: it aimed to replace the vague sentimental rethoric of the Victorians with a direct, plain and realistic, sometime even brutal, diction. At the centre of this poetics is a rural England of small villages and lush nature; its patriotism is rooted in this little England: a country real and ideal at the same time, which the Georgian Poets felt being threatened by the advance of modernity.

Driven to join their country's army by a mixture of patriotism and the force of circumstances, their paths took different turns: Brooke, Grenfell and Sorley died in the course of 1915. Their texts therefore reflect a specific stage in war poetry, when idealisations and abstracions still prevailed on the plain and immediate depiction of war experience. The first two of the above named poets were immediately raised to the Olympus of the hero-poets, as symbols of the supreme self-sacrifice that the best of the English youth was offering on the battlefields, and of that innocence that was going to be shattered to pieces forever by the gradual unveiling of the brutal reality of the war – a reality which would have found its most famous witnesses in Owen and Sassoon.

In 1916, Blunden, Gurney, Rosenberg, and Tolkien came to France, in time for the "Big Push" on the Somme, Owen arrived in December. It is in this year that the war finally took on a massified, industrialised, and depersonalizing character, becoming that "vast machine of violence"[2] that shocked and oppressed the soldiers' imagination. It is the year of the great offensives and of the great slaughters, of the coming of the steel helmet, of the appearance of the first tanks on the battlefield. The heavy artillery bombardments were becoming more and more devastating; the warring parties tried to develop new and better weapons and tactics, and thus to break the murderous deadlock of the Western front. The earlier, improvised trenches of 1914 had by that time become a vast and impregnable fortified system: a world apart, where one experienced a kind of life uncomprehensible to those who were not part of it. In March, the British Governement introduced conscription for all able males: the time of enthusiastic volunteers had come to an end.

Having come down with trench fever, Tolkien left France on 9th November. His brief experience of the front (5 months) had been nonetheless enough to make him feel what he will later describe as the "animal horror" of trench warfare (*Letters* no. 61). Two of his dearest friends died in that same year: Rob Gilson and G.B. Smith were killed while doing service on the Somme in July and December. Other soldier-poets will die before the end of the war: Thomas in 1917, Rosenberg and Owen in 1918. For the survivors began the phase of re-elaboration, of interpretation and, also, of guilt. Hence the necessity to discharge themselves of the war experience, to pass on their own truths, to testify to the horrible reality of the war out of respect towards the fallen and their common homeland.

"Finding a voice for all kinds of pent up things": Art and War in the Young Tolkien

Young Tolkien considered himself a poet. His first poems, dating from 1910, celebrate nature and the beauty of its landscapes. But from the *humus* of his philological, mythological, and linguistic interests, the seeds of his personal mythology started to sprout. On 24th September 1914, he wrote the poem *The Voyage of Éarendel, the Evening Star*, which marks the first mention of the

---

[2] "The dethronement of the soft cap clearly symbolized the change that was coming over the war, the induration from a personal crusade in a vast machine of violence, that had come into the South, where vague victory seemed to be happening" (Blunden 2000, 53).

character of Éarendel. At the same time he was elaborating his "fairy language", Quenya. In December, the T.C.B.S. gathered for the "Council of London" to discuss projects of future endeavours. Tolkien recognised in this event the real beginning of his own artistic vocation, the decisive boost that allowed him to find "a voice for all kinds of pent up things" (*Letters* no. 5). In 1915 Tolkien reworked earlier poems, bringing them into the framework of his ripening unitary mythological vision. In July he wrote *The Shores of Faery*, where the Two Trees, Valinor, Taniquetil, and Eglamar first appear, and in November *Kortirion among the Trees*. In the introduction to this poem (undated, but probably contemporary to it) Tolkien explained that Kortirion was a city of the Fairies in the Lonely Isle after the wars with Melko and the ruin of Gondolin, built in memory of their ancient dwelling of Kôr in Valinor.[3]

Even before his coming to France, then, the main elemements of Middle-earth's mythology were taking shape. The probable effect that war had on its artistic evolution up to this moment was to accelerate and direct this process, emphasizing themes such as mourning and change, lost beauty and memory, and strengthening its instinctive inclination to translate reflections and emotions on a fantastic-mythological narrative plane.[4] On the stylistic level, the tones are elegiac, the focus definitely far from the immediacy of reality.

The impact that the months spent on the front had on him is closely connected with the parallel vicissitudes of the T.C.B.S. After arriving in France as part of a "little complete body" (*Letters* no. 5), Tolkien is in close contact with the other members, exchanging texts and reflections, in the conviction of having been called, each in his own way, although in connection with the others, to greatness. And that is why the death of Gilson and Smith will hit him so deeply: the breaking of the dream of common greatness forced him to review all his schemes, to re-evaluate the objectives of the T.C.B.S. ("Kindle a new light, or, which is the same thing, rekindle an old light in the world", "testify for God and Truth" (*Letters* no. 5), and will drive him to reverberate, in the new artistic voice that he was forging, that of his dead comrades.

---

3 See Hammond & Scull 2017, 54-82.
4 "A real taste for fairy-stories was wakened by philology on the threshold of manhood, an quickened to full life by war" (*TOFS* 56; Garth 2003, 71-88).

Back in England, Tolkien started writing the stories of the Eleves – in prose. The first to see the light is *Tuor and the Exiles of Gondolin*, or, simply, *The Fall of Gondolin*. Written between the end of 1916 and the first half of 1917, it is a story of war, of oppression, of threatened beauty, of dragons halfway between the mythical monster and the technological machine, of bitter fighting and glorious defeat, of ruin and hope. His mythology finally takes on the form of a battle between Good and Evil, and his Elves are definitively given the status of heroes. And the figure of Melko assumes now a clear cut shape: that of a technological tyrant at the head of countless armies and hordes of slaves who toil in the vast armories of his realm of terror.

"Beyond the Circles of the World": the Great War between Remembrance and Representation

Tolkien and the War Poets, then, start from similar backgrounds. They are restless young men, feeling the tensions of their times (the gradual encroachment of the countryside by the expanding cities, the levelling preponderance of the industrial *Machine*, the loss of values and beauty, and the problems of a changing society. They strive to solve these issues by rekindling "an old light" (*Letters* no. 5) by re-establishing the right values through the recovery of a plainer and more immediate language and, finally, by following antithetical artistic paths from all that had come before, opposing the inner and the irrational to the rigid and philistine Victorian positivism.

Once plunged into the war, the schemes through which they filtered reality were shattered traumatically. The experience of the trenches destroyed the positivist conception of a constant progressive march of a human civilization, spearheaded by the West. And the resolution of pre-war tensions and issues would not ultimately come from the free play of the changing factors present in pre-war societies, but from the explosion of all that preceded in the conflagration of the war, throwing every soldier (and the more so, the greater his education and therefore his preconceived schemes) into an unprecedented situation. The experience of war, of this war, thus becomes an unescapable matter of confrontation.

The War Poets react either by falling back on the ideal of rural life, seen as the antithesis and as a remedy against the destructive chaos of the trenches (Thomas, Gurnery and, after the war, Blunden), or by denouncing the horrors of modern warfare, and placing them in satirical contrast with the mystifications of politicians and propagandists (Sassoon). Furthermore, they focus their attention on the soldier's ordeal and on the pity it inspires (Owen), or they strip the war of all heroic aspects and reduce it to mere fact, described through the prism of one's individual sensitivity (Gibson, Graves, Sorley, Rosenberg). For all of them, it is the *here* and *now* that matters, the immediacy of reality, the break with the past, the impact with a brutal and massifying modernity.

Tolkien's point of view is radically different. His predilection for mythology, together with his deep religious faith, push him immediately towards the widest possible perspective, in which the *here* and *now* are dissolved in a timeless dimension. The War Poets' realism, irony, and pity are overcome and incorporated into a broader perspective.

Thus, while in post-war England the myth of progress is being replaced by the demistification and the retirement into the disoriented individuality of the Modernists, and by the myth of war experience[5] that is shared by War Poets and ex-servicemen alike, Tolkien proposes the new/old myth. This is shaped by his deep Christian convictions, imbued with an elegiac quality and permeated by a deep sense of the transience of human existence. In the reality of war in the trenches, he finds those timeless truths that he believed myth had always conveyed and, by a natural spiritual disposition, he is urged to express them in the same form. To the *Make it new!* of the Modernists, Tolkien opposes his *Make it old in the new context*. He creates something new, a "mythology for England" to re-actualise the ancient, to renew its life and meaning in a profoundly changed cultural environment.

His answer to post-war disenchantment and loss of bearings is, then, the recovery of a moral horizon in which definite and eternal values exist and can be recognised, provided you pose them beyond "the Circles of the World", beyond the history of a world corrupted by the Fall. He can thus accept and represent in

---

5 Its distinctive characteristics would be disillusion and bitterness, the celebration of suffering, sacrifice and comradeship, and a deep nostalgia for *the world of yesterday*.

his works loss, pain, incertitude, and the apparent lack of meaning of everyday events, as all these elements are confidently placed within a divine order that cannot be other than ultimately good. In Middle-earth's pre-Christian world, this kind of Christian hope is still only very vaguely hinted at, but there is already the possibility for everyone to recognise and experience the higher and timeless values of man's life.[6]

An example of this difference in perspective is the use of the term "pity" in Tolkien and Wilfred Owen. In the preface to a volume of his poems, Owen affirms:

> This book is not about heroes. English Poetry is not yet fit to speak of them. [...] Above all I am not concerned with Poetry. My subject is War and the pity of War. The Poetry is in the pity. [...] Yet these elegies are to this generation in no sense consolatory. They may be to the next. [...] All a poet can do today is warn [the children]. That is why the true [War] Poet must be truthful. (quoted in Hibberd 2003, 399)

The pity evoked here is the one that springs from the experience of horror, a human instinct detached form philosophical and religious references. The poet formalises it in his poetry as a testimony and warning for future generations.

Tolkien too uses the term "pity", particulary in the conversation between Gandalf and Frodo when Frodo says: "What a pity that he [Bilbo] did not stab the vile creature [Gollum], when he had a chance!" and Gandalf answers: "Pity? It was Pity that stayed his hand. Pity, and Mercy." (*LotR, FR*.I.2). The pity evoked by Tolkien is therefore compassion. It is a virtue, rather than mere instinct born out the experience of suffering, and is thus placed on a higher moral order. In this sense, Tolkien's pity does not serve as a warning, but as an example; it does not derive its authority from experience, but from being related to a truth trascending human vicissitudes.

Furthermore, what pushes poets like Sassoon to assume a fiercely ironic tone is the disconnection they feel between the experience of war and the civilians' complacency, who make use of a pompous and chauvinistic language, mocking the reality experienced by the soldiers. Tolkien also senses this dichotomy between "the utter stupid waste of war, not only material, but moral and spir-

---

6 See Stevenson 2015.

itual" and the false representation of "poets" and "propagandists", and affirms the primary value of direct experience (*Letters* no. 64). But we immediately perceive the gap in perspective that sets him apart from Sassoon: the latter puts everything on the emotional and political level, whereas Tolkien from the start frames the human events within an otherworldly perspective:

> If anguish where visible, almost the whole of this benighted planet would be enveloped in a dense dark vapour, shrouded from the amazed vision of the heavens! And the product of it all will be mainly evil – historically considered. But the historical version is, of course, not the only one. All things and deeds have a value in themselves, apart from their 'causes' and 'effects'. No man can really estimate what is really happening at the present *sub specie aeternitatis*. (*Letters* no. 64)

In this way, the themes of the poems of the War Poets such as the soldiers as images of the suffering Christ, the intense fellowship between comrades, the loving care of an officer towards his men, the horror of dismembered or putrified bodies, and the rape of nature are also themes that we can find in Tolkien's prose. However, in Tolkien they are transformed by the filter of the epic and lit "as from an invisible lamp" (*Letters* no. 328), by a perspective of hope substantiated in the happy ending. The tragic quest of Frodo and the Calvary of the journey to Mount Doom, the comradeship of the Fellowship of the Ring, the care of Aragorn for Merry and Pippin, the mutilations inflicted by the Orcs to the body of Háma and to the dead of the Pelennor, and, finally, the faces of the corpses in the Dead Marches and the devastated No Man's Land in front of Mordor, are all motifs that have their counterparts in Tolkien's experiences on the Somme in 1916.

After the war, Georgianism lost the centre of the cultural stage in favour of the nascent Modernism, whose horizon was now reduced to the inner man who lacks a set of values by means of which he could orient himself and interact meaningfully with society. The surviving soldier-poets, however, generally did not join the ranks of the movement. David Jones is the only one who, due to his style, can be called a Modernist. A Catholic convert, poet, and painter, expert in folklore, liturgy, and myths, Jones is, among the War Poets, the one who has greatest affinity to Tolkien. With his poem *In Parenthesis*, published in 1937, he attempts a re-mythologising of the conflict, intertweaving the realistic representation of the soldier's experience with references to Celtic mythology, the Bible, Nordic myths, and in general to the British epic-literary tradition, thus reintegrating the war into a long-term perspective and giving it a sense of continuity with the past.[7]

In this way, he can ask how men, who have lived for centuries in symbiosis with nature and its creatures, will be able to introject and imbue the inventions of modernity with the same magic:

> We who are of the same world of sense with hairy ass and furry wolf and who presume to other and more radiant affinities, are finding it difficult, as yet, to recognize these creatures of chemicals as true extensions of ourselves, that we may feel for them a native affection, which alone can make them magical for us. It would be interesting to know how we shall ennoble our new media as we have already ennobled and made significant our old – candle-light, fire-light, Cups, Wands and Swords, to choose at random. (Jones 1963, xiv)[8]

The strong consonances with Tolkien's affirmations of the ability of the fantastic imagination to recover the magical dimension inherent in the apparently humbler things are evident (*TOFS* 68-69).

Whereas Jones strives to *re-enchant* Modernity, Tolkien tends rather to oppose it polemically. But these are just two possible issues of the same sensibility and perception of the role of poetry in the face of the challenges posed by the experience of war and, more generally, by a world in rapid transition.

It is in this affinity, as well as in the re-echoing of the soldier-poets' themes referred to above, that we can find that "common matrix" that allows us to place Tolkien's work among the late fruits of the luxuriant tree of Great War literature.[9]

---

7 Jones 1963.
8 In the same preface, he calls the trenches "a place of enchantment" (Jones 1963, lvi), capable of profoundly affecting the imagination to those that experienced them.
9 See also Shippey 2001, 155-160.

Bibliography

Amerio, A. and M.P. Ottieri (eds.). *La guerra d'Europa 1914-1918 raccontata dai poeti*. Rome: Nottetempo, 2014.

Baldick, Chris. *The Modern Movement*. (The Oxford English Literary History. Volume 10: 1910-1940). Oxford: Oxford University Press, 2004.

Croft, Janet Brennan. *War and the Works of J.R.R. Tolkien*. Westport, CT: Praeger, 2004.

—— "War." *A Companion to J.R.R. Tolkien*. Ed. Stuart D. Lee. Chichester: Wiley Blackwell, 2014, 461-472.

—— (ed.) *Baptism of Fire: The Birth of the Modern British Fantastic in World War I*. Altadena, CA: Mythopoeic Press, 2015.

Egremont, Max. *Some Desperate Glory. The First World War the Poets Knew*. London: Picador, 2014.

Eilmann, Julian & Allan Turner (eds.). *Tolkien's Poetry*. Zurich and Jena: Walking Tree Publishers, 2013.

Garth, John. *Tolkien and the Great War. The Threshold of Middle-earth*. Boston and New York: Houghton Mifflin, 2003.

Jones, David. *In Parenthesis*. London: faber and faber, 1963.

Hammond, Wayne G. and Christina Scull. *The J.R.R. Tolkien Companion and Guide*. London: HarperCollins, 2017.

Hibberd, Dominic. *Wilfred Owen. A New Biography*. London: Phoenix, 2003.

Hibberd, Dominic and John Onions (eds.). *The Winter of the World. Poems of the Great War*. London: Constable, 2007.

Hiley, Margaret. *The Loss and the Silence. Aspect of Modernism in the Works of C.S. Lewis, J.R.R. Tolkien & Charles Williams*. Zurich and Jena: Walking Tree Publishers, 2011.

Lee, Stuart D. (ed.). *A Companion to J.R.R. Tolkien*. Chichester: Wiley Blackwell, 2014.

Longley, Edna. "The Great War, History and the English Lyric." *The Cambridge Companion to the Literature of the First World War*. Ed. Vincent Sherry. Cambridge: Cambridge University Press, 2005, 57-84.

Kendall, Tim (ed.). *Poetry of the First World War. An Anthology*. Oxford: Oxford University Press, 2013.

SANTANU, Das (ed.). *The Cambridge Companion to the Poetry of the First World War.* Cambridge: Cambridge University Press, 2013.

SHERRY, Vincent (ed.). *The Cambridge Companion to the Literature of the First World War.* Cambridge: Cambridge University Press, 2005.

SHIPPEY, Tom. *J.R.R. Tolkien: Author of the Century.* London: HarperCollins, 2001.

SIMONSON, Martin. "*The Lord of the Rings* in the Wake of the Great War: War, Poetry, Modernism, and Ironic Myth." *Reconsidering Tolkien.* Ed. Thomas Honegger. Zurich and Jena: Walking Tree Publishers, 2005, 153-176.

STEVENSON, Shandi. "Beyond the Circles of this World: The Great War, Time, History, and Eternity in the Fantasy of J.R.R. Tolkien and C.S. Lewis." *Baptism of Fire: The Birth of the Modern British Fantastic in World War I.* Ed. Janet Brennan Croft. Altadena, CA: Mythopoeic Press, 2015, 110-130.

TURNER, Allan. "Early Influences on Tolkien's Poetry." *Tolkien's Poetry.* Eds. Julian Eilmann and Allan Turner. Zurich and Jena: Walking Tree Publishers, 2013, 205-221.

With Light Step Through the Threshold: Female Characters, the Gothic, and the *meditatio mortis* in Tolkien and Poe

Although we do not have documentation testifying Tolkien's knowledge of Poe's works, the juxtaposition between the two authors is not so unusual if we consider that some critics have already singled out parallels between the American writer and the author of the *legendarium*. In her essay "'In the Perilous Realms': the Fantastic Geographies of Tolkien and Poe", Carol Marshall Peirce points out lexical and thematic similarities in the descriptions of imaginary landscapes, both idyllic or dark and ominous. As an example for idyllic landscapes she compares the Valley of the Many-Colored Grass in *Eleonora* to Lórien and for the dark and ominous ones she chooses to compare the gloomy landscape descriptions in the poem *Ulalume* to the description of Mordor. Peirce defines both authors as "mythmakers". Of course, their mythopoesis unfolds with different peculiarities: for instance, the star twinkling through the clouds inspires hope in Sam during his journey through the land of Mordor. Instead, the star in *Ulalume* deceives the wayfarer because it leads him to the tomb of his lost love, thus condemning him to despair.[1]

Anyway, both Tolkien and Poe are authors of manifold peculiarities, at ease in different kinds of fantasy genres ranging from what Todorov defines as "uncanny" to the "marvellous", up to the detective story genre as is the case for Poe. In order to avoid going adrift in the *mare magnum* of generic "fantasy" themes, I will focus on the importance of female characters in both authors, notably in Tolkien's *The Silmarillion* and in three of the short stories Poe has dedicated to women: *Eleonora* (1842), *Morella* (1840), and especially *Ligeia* (1838).

---

[1] Peirce (1986, 124) synthesizes well: "Poe (except in his detective fiction which does not pertain here) forever moves out of light into darkness, despair, and tragedy: there exists always the hope of beauty but the threat of oblivion. Tolkien, facing a world of darkness and of terror, a Götterdammerung, strives on toward light and toward the Eucatastrophe."

The aesthetic category of the Sublime is certainly a stylistic crossroads for many authors under the influence of Romanticism, here including Tolkien[2] and Poe. Nonetheless, their writings show stylistic differences that make the comparison somehow problematic. In fact, the style Poe adopts in the short stories we are going to analyse can be defined as "vertiginous". It is a narrative device he adopts in order to represent the subjective point of view of the main characters, whose state of mind is altered by the use of drugs or by neurosis: this state of delusion is rendered through the shifting of the attention from the overall picture, rather indefinite, to the most minute details, as if the world he describes is seen through a magnifying glass that continuously shifts the distance from the observed object, from the very close to the very far. It all results in an effect of estrangement. Ligeia is described with marvellous enigmatic clarity, a woman of the real world but of mysterious origins whose beauty is at the same time ravishing and eerie. Still, when her most devoted husband, the main character of the story, speaks about her, he admits he doesn't even remember her last name.

Tolkien's descriptions in *The Silmarillion* are, by contrast, evocative and solemn in a style suitable to myth, yet the characters are portrayed with precision and constancy of characteristics. This is particularly evident in Lúthien, an Elven maiden who lives in a fantasy "secondary world" but looks almost more real than Ligeia, who belongs to our world, the "primary" one.

By origin and knowledge both Lúthien and Ligeia enjoy a by far higher status than their husbands'. Their romantic "nocturnal" beauty is exalted in their descriptions: Ligeia is praised for her "raven-black", "glossy", "luxuriant" and "naturally-curling" hair. Lúthien's hair is described as "dark as the shadows of twilight". Ligeia's "large", "shining", "divine" black pupils have their counterpart in Lúthien's grey eyes, resembling the "starlit evening". They both are said to have very musical voices and one of their most seductive features is their gait. Their light and graceful steps enable them to glide unnoticed over the most precious

---

[2] See Eilmann's study *J.R.R. Tolkien: Romanticist and Poet* (2017) for an in-depth exploration of this aspect of Tolkien's work.

oriental carpets or through dark crepuscular clearings.³ We find the same characteristics in the descriptions of the *Belle Dame sans Merci*, the ballad by Keats after which Mario Praz titled the chapter he dedicated to fatal women⁴ in his essay on Romanticism.

It is important to underline that in most cases Poe's heroines radiate an ambiguous fascination, whereas, at least in Arda, we almost never find feminine beauty associated with wickedness.⁵ The overlapping of these two semantic fields occurs only in one case, the famous passage of Galadriel's temptation, when the Elven princess imagines, just for a short moment, her transformation through the power of the Ring into a beautiful and terrible queen. In this respect it is no coincidence that the vision is described under the sign of the Sublime:

> In place of the Dark Lord you will set up a Queen. And I shall not be dark, but beautiful and terrible as the Morning and the Night! Fair as the Sea and the Sun and the Snow upon the Mountain! Dreadful as the Storm and the Lightning! Stronger than the foundations of the earth. All shall love me and despair!⁶

With the exception of this fleeting vision the negative feminine loses its quality of beauty and seduction: the repulsive shape of the spider soon appears under the guise of Ungoliant and its brood.

However, this does not mean that Tolkien's female characters are not for some other aspects under the influence of the darker themes of gothic Romanticism.

Undeniably Poe owes much to the Gothic genre, which goes from the pre-Romanticism of the late 1700s to the late Victorian Age, even if at times he recurs to it with ironic undertones. As for Tolkien the influence of the Gothic genre is filtered by the vast cultural baggage of the man of letters. However,

---

3 The light gait is also an attribute of various "vampire women" – one for all is Carmilla by Le Fanu (1872). As the 19th century is proceeding towards Decadentism, the vampire woman almost upstages the male vampire. Lúthien is a totally positive character, deprived of moral ambiguities, however it is quite peculiar that she covers herself with a skin of a giant bat to come to Morgoth's presence, and Huan discovers her while she was "flying like a shadow surprised by the daylight under the trees" (*S* 173). Of Ligeia is said that "she came and departed as a shadow" (Poe 2004, 160).
4 Keats' poem reads: "I met a lady in the meads, full beautiful – a faery's child, her hair was long, her foot was light, and her eyes were wild." Eyes, hair, and gait, and also the voice singing "a faery's song".
5 In *The Fall of Arthur* and *The Lay of Aotrou and Itroun* Tolkien presents seductive and morally questionable female characters, but these "fatal women" are direct descendants of pre-existent traditions and legends Tolkien brings back to life. However, he chooses to keep them out from his "secondary world".
6 *LotR*, FR.II.7.

unlike writers who confine themselves to a slavish adhesion to the canon, Poe and Tolkien reshape it in accordance to their own poetics, taking some of its stereotypes and overturning them in an original way.

Just to dwell on the same subject, Poe's women are alternatively victims and torturers: Morella, who was not so much loved as a wife, dies of consumption but ends up reincarnating in her daughter, who will inflict on her father/husband a posthumous vengeance; Eleonora, a sort of "ghost bride", will give up her rights over her husband from beyond the grave, one of the few happy endings in Poe's short stories. Ligeia, in particular, succumbs to the long tortures of a mortal illness but she returns in a sort of extreme vampirism at the expense of her husband's second wife. She not only takes her blood but she also takes possession of her body in which she is reborn to a second life, under the incredulous and adoring gaze of her husband.

Many of the Gothic elements in *The Silmarillion* can be found in the story of Lúthien Tinúviel, especially in its central part about the incursion against Sauron's fortress to free Beren and the descent to Angband to take possession of the Silmaril.

In this episode Tolkien makes use of the Gothic *topoi* of "damsels in distress" and gloomy fortresses and reverses them. The maiden Lúthien enters the dungeon of her own will and comes out of it triumphant as the lady of the castle. After defeating Sauron with the help of Huan the wolfhound, she turns to the defeated villain, taunts him for the loss of his power and makes him surrender the key of the castle. Unhesitatingly, she puts on a horrid bat-skin just in the same way as her lover Beren wears the skin of the werewolf, almost in spite of the monsters that persecute her. Finally, she willingly submits herself to the sight of the most dreaded of all villains, Morgoth,[7] trusting her own power that, for once, is not that of Light, typical of Tolkien's positive female

---

7 In the version of Lúthien's story in *The Lay of Leithian* when she wears the skin of Thuringwethil Lúthien's sensuality is more explicit: "About her slender shoulders hung / her shadowy hair, and round her clung / her garment dark, where glimmered pale / the starlight caught in elvish veil. / Dim dreams and faint oblivious sleep / fell softly thence, in dungeons deep / an odour stole of elven-flowers / from elven-dells where silver showers / drip softly through the evening air" (*LB* 297). Later on the carnality of Morgoth's desire is rendered with revealing words: "And who would not taste the honey-sweet lying / to lips, or crush with feet / the soft cool tissue of pale flowers, / easing like gods the dragging hours? / A! Curse the Gods! O hunger dire, / O blinding thirst's unending fire! / One moment shall ye cease, and slake / your sting with morsel I here take!" (*LB* 300).

characters, but the power of her slumber-inducing singing, a far more subtle allusion to her capacity not so much of seducing, but rather of neutralising or in this case even "devirilizing" the antagonist.[8] Certainly, the character of Lúthien does not possess any hint of the morbidity typical of Poe's heroines. However, she shows elements of physicality that redeem Tolkien's representation of the feminine from the stereotypes of the passive angel-like woman some critics have stigmatised. Cami D. Agan, in her essay "Lúthien Tinúviel and Bodily Desire in the Lay of Leithian" analyses this "physical" aspect of Lúthien, for example when she uses her body to triumph over Morgoth, or saves Beren by sucking the venom out of his wounds, or casts spells by means of her hair. Lúthien's body undergoes various metamorphoses before the final one, the transformation that will affect the very essence of the physical life, the one ontologically related to mortality.

It is worthwhile noticing that the theme of metamorphosis is present in both authors if we consider that also Ligeia and Morella undergo supernatural physical transformations. Todorov writes about it as one of the themes that characterize fantasy literature since its beginnings, because it spontaneously highlights "the transgression of the separation between matter and mind" (Todorov 1975, 113), an important factor from the point of view of transcendence that will lead us to the next point we are going to analyse.

***

Up to this moment the comparison between the two authors has proceeded along parallel tracks under the dazzling light of the sublime and the livid hue of the Gothic.

One more theme allows us to deepen our analysis beyond the "external" analogies, that is the analogies connected with literary *topoi*, and examine the affinities between the guiding sources of inspiration for the two authors. The theme is death and the otherworldly destiny of the soul. Its presence in Tolkien's work

---

8 The same thing happens, although in a less blatant way, in the episode of the failed abduction attempted by Celegorm and Curufin, forced to a shameful flight on the back of a single horse.

is like a karstic river that flows underneath, to resurface recurrently both in the narrative and theoretical writings. The theme is also of paramount importance in Poe, especially in *Morella* and *Ligeia*, and to a minor extent in *Eleonora*. In the famous (or should I say "notorious" because of the strong criticism it received) essay on poetics, "The Philosophy of Composition" (1846), Poe identifies the sad, melancholic aspect of poetry, the one related to death, as the most compelling subject matter, especially when it is accompanied by the theme of beauty, and therefore he concludes that "the death of a beautiful woman is unquestionably the most poetical topic in the world" (Poe 2004, 680).

What interests Poe is not simply the poetic artifice: the dying women of his short stories, each one in her own way, open the doors of an otherworldly metaphysical dimension seen through the eyes of the author that Todorov defines the "explorer of the limits".[9]

Tolkien's lifelong attempts to give his secondary world consistency in all its aspects led him to face the question of death, a theme he elaborates in accordance to the different races living in his universe: he envisages the reincarnation for Elves whereas for Men he imagines that after their death their souls leave towards a place nobody is allowed to know apart from Ilúvatar, creator of Arda.

Thanks to this special gift Ilúvatar has given them, the human race is set free from the bond that ties them to the world during their lifetimes, as well as from the seriality of the Elven existence. However, this is a mysterious and definitive *exitus* and the fear of the unknown gives the evil Morgoth (and later his successor Sauron) the opportunity to represent death as a curse rather than a gift. Besides, when Tolkien was writing "Athrabeth Finrod ah Andreth" (finished in 1959) he seems to have come to the conclusion that death, intended at least as separation from *fëa* (soul) and *hröa* (body), is not the natural condition for Men but rather the consequence of an ancient, obscure Fall.

Hence a man in Tolkien's secondary world can look at the afterlife with the same sense of mystery and apprehension as the characters of the real world

---

9 "It must be understood, however, that this fascination with death is not the direct result of some morbid impulse; it is the product of an overall tendency which is the systematic exploration of the limits to which Poe devotes himself" (Todorov 1990, 96).

described by Poe. Where are then the differences and similarities between the two authors?

First of all we notice that some of Tolkien's female characters are essential for his *meditatio mortis*. In the philosophical dialogue "Athrabeth" it is a woman, the wise Andreth, who exposes her ideas on mortality from the point of view of Men, while Finrod presents the Elvish perspective.

From the point of view of the narration, and starting from the beginning of the *legendarium*, it is a woman, Míriel, the first Elf who is said to have willingly abandoned life after giving birth to Fëanor. Her death leaves her husband Finwë, who later remarries, in dismay and even the Valar are disconcerted by that event. As for Poe's Eleonora, the young woman, who dies after having exchanged vows of eternal love with her lover, grants him forgiveness from the afterworld for having betrayed her memory. Likewise, Míriel's soul learns of Finwë's new marriage and accepts it[10] even if it entails that she will have to wait until Finwë's death before being able to rejoin her own body.

Another complex issue, the reincarnation of the Elves in their children's bodies, has a parallel in Poe's *Morella*. In fact, Morella dies giving birth to a baby girl who from the first years of her life shows an extraordinary resemblance in appearance and personality to her dead mother. The father, who was not much in love with his wife, adores his daughter instead. He waits years before giving her a name[11] – and when this happens it is the name "Morella" that comes to his lips; the child girl answers in a whisper "I'm here" and then falls lifeless to the ground: her mother's grave is found empty and she is buried in it. It may only be a coincidence but, in a more intensified way, *Morella* reminds us

---

10 The Valar debate at length on Míriel's decision to let herself die and later on Finwë's intent to marry again. Mandos recognizes the legitimacy of Finwë's request but in order to avoid possible conflicts or bigamy decides that Míriel's soul will linger in the Halls of Mandos (the debate is contained in *MR* 234-250). In Poe's story the main character is released from his vow to the departed Eleonora by a voice that whispers him in the night: "Sleep in peace! [...] thou art absolved, for reasons which shall be made known to thee in Heaven, of thy vows unto Eleonora" (Poe 2003, 90). We can say that in Finwë's case the reader and the main characters are simultaneously informed on the reasons of the decision.
11 The little girl of the story is baptised and receives the name that will seal her identity with that of the deceased mother when she is ten. It is interesting to notice that the tenth year of life of the Eldar children is also crucial because it is when they select their Chosen Name, chosen in accordance with what characterizes the personality of each one of them (*MR* 215).

of the paradoxical family relations that could have ensued if Tolkien had not abandoned the idea of the Elves' reincarnation in their offspring.

As for the theme of death, in Tolkien's mythology the most important character is Lúthien, the immortal Elven princess who implores the Vala of Fate for the return to life of her perished spouse Beren, a Man, so that she could be reunited with him and eventually share the same mortal destiny. The story of Beren and Lúthien is of key importance in *The Silmarillion*, to such an extent that Tolkien reprises it in *The Lord of the Rings* when Arwen gives up her Elven immortality to remain by Aragorn's side.

The barrier between life and death in Poe's stories is emblematically infringed upon by Ligeia. This mysterious woman, adored by her husband for her intelligence and charisma, reveals to him on her deathbed the existential sentence mankind is condemned to and she does it by means of a poem, *The Conqueror Worm*: here life is compared to a grotesque tragedy where men are represented as mimes on a stage, who run around vainly under the eyes of weeping, powerless angels until a monstrous crawling creature appears and devours them.

Certainly the idea that the world is a land "contaminated" by evil is also present in Tolkien and this pessimistic concept is well enunciated in the expression "the long defeat". The expression is used by Galadriel when she describes the strenuous but hopeless battle against an evil that, because of the "marring of Arda", is destined to return in endless renewed shapes even when it seems to have been defeated.

Ligeia takes leave from her husband repeating a phrase that can be defined as the *leitmotif* of the story: "Man doth not yield him to the angels, nor unto death utterly, save only through the weakness of his feeble will" (Poe 2004, 166). With due caution, suggested mainly by the ironic detachment Poe sometimes seems to display towards the tumultuous matter of his fictional *rêveries,* we can place this determination to overcome death within the frame of the spiritualistic currents that became popular in America in the first half of the 19th century and were known to Poe thanks to his acquaintances.[12]

However, maybe the "rational" Poe as well as the "visionary" Poe, to apply the terms coined by his biographer Julian Symons, cast an inquisitive and poetic eye over the threshold more out of the urge to explore the limits rather than to look for answers consistent with a certain belief or doctrine. Poe, "verbal landscapist of death" (Davidson 1957, 115), returns from his metaphysical explorations with impressions that make him compare death to a dream, a suspended reality where the perception of the first-person narrator prevails over objective evaluations.

On the other hand Tolkien, in compliance with his Christian faith, is inclined to deliver a message of hope in the afterlife, the most famous example being the words pronounced by Aragorn to Arwen at the moment of their farewell.[13] Even more meaningful in relation to Lúthien and Arwen's choice is Finrod's vision in "Athrabeth", when he foresees that Men will have a fundamental role in Arda Reconstructed and its recreation after the end of times since they have been destined to "infiniteness" by their mortality,[14] which gives no circular seriality to their destiny.

Therefore, even if just for a short while, the two heroines seem to cross their light steps through the threshold separating life from the afterlife, both pushed to opposite directions by the same force, Love: Ligeia breaks the barriers of mortality by means of an ambiguous resurrection into her rival's body; Lúthien crosses the threshold the other way, giving up the prerogatives of a limitless life and choosing human mortality to share with her beloved Beren.

---

12 In particular he was attracted by the spiritualism of the poetess Sarah Helen Whitman, with whom he had a tormented relationship. The theme of afterlife also surfaces in the poetry-prose *Eureka* (1848), one of the most peculiar of Poe's works for the odd blend of scientific theories with lyrical and poetic elements.

13 "In sorrow we must go, but not in despair. Behold! We are not bound for ever to the circles of the world, and beyond them is more than memory. Farewell!" (*LotR*, Appendix A: "Annals of the Kings and Rulers" I.5).

14 "This, then, I propound, was the errand of Men, not the followers but the heirs and fulfillers of all: to heal the Marring of Arda, already foreshadowed before their devising; and to do more, as agents of the magnificence of Eru: to enlarge the Music and surpass the vision of the World!" (*MR* 318).

Bibliography

AGAN, Cami D. "Lúthien Tinúviel and Bodily Desire in the Lay of Leithian." *Perilous and Fair. Women in the Works and Life of J.R.R. Tolkien*. Eds. Janet Brennan Croft and Leslie Donovan. Altadena, CA: Mythopoeic Press, 2015, 168-188.

ARDUINI, Roberto and Claudio TESTI (eds.). *The Broken Scythe. Death and Immortality in the Works of J.R.R. Tolkien*. Jena and Zurich: Walking Tree Publishers, 2012.

CESARANI, Remo. *Il fantastico*. Bologna: Il Mulino, 1996.

CROFT, Janet Brennan and Leslie DONOVAN (eds.). *Perilous and Fair. Women in the Works and Life of J.R.R. Tolkien*. Altadena, CA: Mythopoeic Press, 2015.

DAVIDSON, Edward H. *Poe: A Critical Study*. Cambridge, MA: Harvard University Press, 1957.

DROUT, Michael D.C. (ed.). *J.R.R. Tolkien Encyclopaedia*. New York: Routledge, 2007.

EILMANN, Julian. *J.R.R. Tolkien: Romanticist and Poet*. Cormarë Series 36. Zurich and Jena: Walking Tree Publishers, 2017.

FLIEGER, Verlyn. *Splintered Light. Logos e language in Tolkien's Works*. Kent, OH: Kent State University Press, 2002.

FOREST-HILL, Lynn. *The Mirror Crack'd. Fear and Horror in JRR Tolkien's Major Works*. Newcastle: Cambridge Scholars Publishing, 2008.

HAYES, K.J. (ed.). *The Cambridge Companion to E.A. Poe*. Cambridge: Cambridge University Press, 2004.

KEATS, John. *Selected Poems*. London: Penguin Books, 2007.

LOVECRAFT, Howard P. *Supernatural Horror in Literature & Other Literary Essays*. Rockville, MD: Wildside Press, 2011.

PEIRCE, Carol Marshall. "'In the Perilous Realm'. The Fantastic Geographies of Tolkien and Poe." *Poe and Our Times: Influences and Affinities*. Baltimore: The Edgar Allan Poe Society, 1986, 124-136.

POE, Edgar Allan. *The Selected Writings of Edgar Allan Poe*. Ed. G.R. Thompson. New York: Norton & Co., 2004.

The Raven and Other Writings. New York: Aladdin Paperbacks, 2003.

PRAZ, Mario. *La carne, la morte e il diavolo nella letteratura romantica*. Florence: Sansoni Editore, 1976.

PUNTER, David. *The Literature of Terror: A History of Gothic Fictions from 1765 to the Present Day*. London: Longman, 1980.

SHIPPEY, Tom. *The Road to Middle-earth.* London: HarperCollins, 2005.

Roots and Branches: Selected Papers on Tolkien. Zurich and Berne: Walking Tree Publishers, 2007.

SYMONS, Julian. *The Tell-Tale Heart: The Life and Works of Edgar Allan Poe.* London: HarperCollins, 1978.

TODOROV, Tzvetan. *Genres in Discourse.* Cambridge: Cambridge University Press, 1990.

The Fantastic: A Structural Approach to a Literary Genre. Ithaca, NY: Cornell University Press, 1975.

VAX, Louis. *Les chefs-d'oeuvre de la littérature fantastique.* Paris: Presses Universitaires de France, 1979.

Tom Shippey

William Morris and Tolkien: Some Unexpected Connections

The influence of William Morris on Tolkien has been frequently recognised. There is a long entry on him in Scull and Hammond's *Reader's Guide* to Tolkien,[1] another by Michael Perry in Michael Drout's *Encyclopedia*.[2] In the very first letter in Humphrey Carpenter's collection of Tolkien's letters, written to his fiancée Edith in 1914, Tolkien says that he is trying to turn a section of the Finnish *Kalevala* into "a short story somewhat on the lines of Morris romances" (*Letters* no. 1). This would eventually become "The Tale of Kullervo" and one of the three "Great Tales" of the *Silmarillion*. My copy of *The Roots of the Mountains* says on the front cover "A Book that Inspired J.R.R. Tolkien", and in his collection *Tales Before Tolkien*, Douglas Anderson included another Morris short story, "The Folk of the Mountain Hall".[3] Jessica Yates has produced a bibliography of works discussing Morris's influence on Tolkien which contains nearly 70 items.[4] We know also that when Tolkien received a college prize in 1914, what he bought with the money included three works by Morris.[5] Many years later, in 1941, he lectured on Morris's poem of *Sigurd the Volsung*.[6] And the very useful list of books known to have been owned by Tolkien, prepared by Oronzo Cilli, includes eleven works by Morris.[7]

Nevertheless, and in spite of all this, I think that Morris's connections with Tolkien, and his effect on Tolkien, have still been underestimated. The reason for this, in a way, is the two authors' similarity, their originality, and, strangely, their popularity. Neither author fits neatly into the consensus view of literary history constructed and taught by my former colleagues in university departments of English studies. They have both suffered (in this very limited area)

---

1 Scull & Hammond 2006, 598-604.
2 Perry 2007, 437ff.
3 Anderson 2003, 120-132.
4 Yates, "William Morris's Influence on J.R.R. Tolkien: Bibliography", unpublished.
5 Scull & Hammond 2006, 599.
6 Scull & Hammond 2006b, 249.
7 Cilli 2019. I am most grateful to Oronzo for sending me this in advance of publication.

from the work and the attitudes of the people Tolkien called "misologists": literary scholars opposed to philology and anxious to promote "modernism" at the expense of "medievalism". It is one of life's ironies (which Tolkien would have been much amused by) that modernism now seems hopelessly out-of-date, while medievalism, in the shape of TV series like *Game of Thrones*, has become as popular as Tolkien. I will try, therefore, in this paper to correct some misapprehensions, and also offer some new connections.

The first connection is a very odd one, which I cannot yet explain. Years ago a former colleague of mine at the University of Birmingham, an Icelandic scholar called Ben Benedikz, told me about his aunt Sigrid.[8] It seems that during one of his trips to Iceland in 1871 and 1873, Morris had received hospitality from one of my friend Ben's family. Now, one of the pieces of advice given by the god Odin in an Old Norse poem declares that friendships should be kept up: "To his friend a man should be a friend, / and repay gifts with gifts." This applies to guest-friendship, as it is called, and the relationship is hereditary. It was therefore natural that when, nearly 60 years later, Ben's aunt Sigrid wanted to go to England, her family should contact Morris's daughter May, and that Sigrid should go to her. Sigrid accordingly, then about 19 or 20, arrived at Oxford station, and was collected in a pony-trap – a small carriage pulled by one horse – and taken to the Morris home at Kelmscott House.

Sigrid, however, did not like it at all! I forbear from repeating in print what she said about the Morris household, but Kelmscott House was isolated, neither lady could drive a car, and Sigrid found it uncongenial. So, quite soon, May Morris arranged for Sigrid to go and live with the Tolkiens in the city, in North Oxford, in Northmoor Road. It seems that aunt Sigrid did not like this much either. Probably in those days unchaperoned young ladies had little social life wherever they were, and Sigrid also complained that Professor Tolkien "always wanted to talk Icelandic!"

The interesting question, though, is why May Morris thought of passing her guest on to Tolkien. Had Tolkien perhaps had some correspondence with her? Or did she know that Tolkien, though a Professor of Anglo-Saxon, also took a

---

8 Private communication, see also Benedikz 2008, 11ff.

keen interest in Icelandic? But at any rate, we do know that there was a personal connection of some kind between the Morris family and the Tolkien family.

What of the literary connection? And now I come to the failures of literary history, as I was taught in my youth at Cambridge, and as is still the case. It is well known that in the last decade of his life Morris published a set of seven original romances, which I list as follows: *The House of the Wolfings* (1888), *The Roots of the Mountains* (1889), *The Story of the Glittering Plain* (1890), *The Wood Beyond the World* (1894), *The Well at the World's End* (1895), *The Water of the Wondrous Isles* (1896), and *The Sundering Flood* (1896).

These have been called by the editor Kirchhoff (1976, 11) "the least understood body of major Victorian fiction." There is one little set of essays about them, published in highly amateurish form by the William Morris Society. I borrowed a copy from the library of Washington University in St. Louis. It had never previously been borrowed in 20 years, and the pages were still uncut: no-one had ever read it! Within that little volume the editor Frederick Kirchhoff noted that in the preceding fifteen years there had been more published on Morris's single poem, "The Defence of Guenevere", than on all seven romances combined.

If you look in the indexes of major works on Morris, you will soon see how sketchily the romances are treated. Philip Henderson's biography does not mention two of them, and seems not to know that *The House of the Wolfings* is a full-length work.[9] E.P. Thompson's 850-page study gives them 8 pages (Thompson 1955, 781-89) and asks at the end: "Had Morris gone soft in the head? [...] It may be that the world will be too busy for many years to turn back to these fairy-stories: there is little in them from which it can learn" (Thompson 1955, 789).

There is a reason for this dismissal, which is political. Morris, besides being a very successful capitalist, was also a socialist. His biographers, left-wing like most academics, highly approve of this. But the truth is that Morris became tired of the Socialist movement, and of the Socialist League which he had helped to found and of which he was the main financial supporter. About 1889 he resigned as Treasurer, and started writing romances instead. To people like E.P. Thompson,

---

9 Henderson 1967.

whose biography of Morris is subtitled "Romantic to Revolutionary", going back from being a revolutionary to being a romantic again was a betrayal. In any case, according to the canons of literary criticism, ever since Don Quixote the novel has been the main literary form, and the romance a sub-literary one, long superseded. At any rate, among literary critics.

Of course, the truth is very different. The 1890s were the age of what some now call "the New Romancers", people like Conan Doyle, inventor of Sherlock Holmes, Bram Stoker, creator of Dracula, Robert Louis Stevenson, H.G. Wells, as well as Rider Haggard and later John Buchan, whom Tolkien very much appreciated. None of these were on the syllabus in Cambridge in my youth, and they still are not: though of course they remain immensely popular outside the academic world.

As for Morris, it is astonishing how well-received his romances were. *The Glittering Plain* (1891) was reprinted at least seven times before 1912. In Paul Fussell's excellent book on *The Great War and Modern Memory* he notes that, "There was hardly a literate man who fought between 1914 and 1918 who hadn't read [*The Well at the World's End*] and been powerfully excited by it in his youth" (Fussel 1989, 135). In the same work Fussell cites Hugh Quigley's memoir *Passchendael and the Somme*, where Quigley wrote:

> The ghastly canal at Ypres [...] is like the poison pool under the Dry Tree in [*The Well at the World's End*], around which lie bodies with 'dead leathery faces ... drawn up in a grin, as though they had died in pain ...' [It was all happening in] a land of horror and dread whence few return, like that country Morris describes in *The Well at the World's End*. (Quigley, quoted in Fussel 1989, 137)

C.S. Lewis was one of the soldiers who had read Morris's work: he bought his copy in 1917 just before leaving for the front.[10] War memoirs are full of references and allusions to the book: the soldiers thought its images well described the "land of horror and dread" in which they found themselves. Tolkien's Dead Marches reflect memories of the Somme, but Thiepval and Ypres also stirred memories of William Morris, as Tolkien declared:

---

10 See Fussel 1989, 136.

> The Dead Marshes and the approaches to the Morannon owe something to Northern France after the Battle of the Somme. They owe more to William Morris and his Huns and Romans, as in *The House of the Wolfings* and *The Roots of the Mountains*. (*Letters* no. 226)

Soldiers thought romance was much more realistic than, say, the society novels of Henry James.

This is true of Morris's poems as well. John Garth (2003, 105ff.) has noted the strange ambition of Tolkien and his friends to emulate the Pre-Raphaelite Brotherhood of Morris and his friends, and to kindle a new light, for England, through poetry. What in the world were they thinking of? And why did Tolkien persist, all through the 1920s, in writing long narrative poems like *The Lays of Beleriand*? Everyone knew – in my youth, in Cambridge – that the day of the long narrative poem had passed by, and that the future belonged to ironic, allusive, difficult poetry, like T.S. Eliot's *The Waste Land*.

But my teachers at Cambridge were wrong, even about literary history. In Victorian times there had been an immense market for long narrative poems like Morris's *The Earthly Paradise* (1868-70), Tennyson's retelling of the King Arthur story in his *Idylls of the King* (1859-85), or Robert Browning's *The Ring and the Book* (1868-69). Claudio Testi (2018, 47) has reminded us recently how "polyphonic" Tolkien's writing is: "In this respect we can compare the *Legendarium* to the polyphonic novel that, according to Bakhtin, was introduced by Dostoyevsky." Tolkien's writing is indeed polyphonic, stories told by different voices at different times, both in *The Lord of the Rings* and in *The Silmarillion*, but (whatever Bakhtin may have thought) there was a model for Tolkien long before Dostoevsky. A more likely model here, for Tolkien, is surely Browning's 21,000-line poem, the story of an Italian murder trial in 1698, in 12 books, told by 10 different characters. This too was being eagerly read in the trenches in Word War 1.[11]

So, in writing his *Legend of Sigurd and Gudrun*, Tolkien may well have been hoping to emulate Morris's extremely successful poem *The Story of Sigurd the Volsung* (1876). In writing *The Fall of Arthur*, he surely was responding both to Tennyson's *Idylls of the King* and Morris's own "Defence of Guenevere" (and

---

11 See again Fussel 1989, 163.

other Arthurian poems, 1858). As for *The Lays of Beleriand*, one model for them (again a polyphonic one) must have been Macaulay's once more enormously popular and well-known *Lays of Ancient Rome* (1842).

If I have laboured this point, please excuse me. It is out of a kind of indignation. When I was young, I was never told about any of this, and all the works I have mentioned have been in effect "airbrushed" out of literary history. As, of course, so often has Tolkien! Also, I was taught carefully about "the Great Tradition" of English literature. But there was and there is Another Great Tradition! Both in poetry and in prose.

But I will turn now from indignation to matters of more detail – though I fear that indignation will continue to overcome me – and although I will come back to the poetry I will start with the romances of the 1890s. As I have said, there are seven of these, and I divide them into a heroic group, which is set in pagan times (the first three to be published), and a romantic group, where the characters live in a medieval Christian world (the remaining four).

I have discussed the first two of these before (*Wolfings* and *Mountains*),[12] and the point I have made is, very briefly, that these are romances inspired by the achievements of comparative philology, of which Morris was very well aware – unlike his later editors and commentators. In brief again, the characteristic activity of comparative philologists was reconstruction. First they reconstructed words from extinct languages: elsewhere I have explained that the Italian word *cinque* and the English word "five", despite their total dissimilarity, derive from the same extinct source, which must have been a word like **pinpe*.[13] We can trace their history through regular changes, instanced in early records. Not only did philologists reconstruct extinct words, however, they reconstructed whole extinct languages, and went on to reconstruct whole extinct societies.

That is what Morris was doing in *The House of the Wolfings* and *The Roots of the Mountains*, and both could actually be called historical novels: they contain no dates and their geography is not ours, but we can still work out when and

---

12 Shippey 2007, 115-136.
13 See Manni & Shippey 2014, 24.

where they were set, again by comparison with early records – like *The Saga of Heidrek the Wise*, first edited in 1960 by Christopher Tolkien, which includes the poem on "The Battle of the Goths and Huns", on which Christopher wrote in detail elsewhere.[14]

But this was not understood, then or since – except, I am sure, by Tolkien. May Morris, who edited her father's works, like Christopher, did not, I am afraid, understand her father as well as Christopher understood his. In her introduction to *The Roots of the Mountains* she wrote:

> In HW and in RM my father seems to have got back to the atmosphere of the Sagas. In that it is part metrical, part prose, the Wolfings may be held experimental, but in this tale of imaginary tribal life on the verge of Roman conquest – a period which had a great fascination for the writer, who read with critical enjoyment the more important modern studies of it as they came out – the personages have none of the severity of the early world, more of the Saga-born impression of Fate moving the pieces on the board. The place too of the Wolfing tribes and of the Burgdalers and Silverdalers – *the wonderful land about the foot of the Italian Alps* – had a great hold on his imagination […] (M. Morris 1912, xv)

I'm afraid much of this is wrong. There is very little of the sagas in these tales. Morris did indeed read "important modern studies" and clearly used for instance the new philological edition of Jordanes' *History of the Goths*. But – though Trento, where this paper was originally delivered, was the wrong place to say so – I fear *The Roots of the Mountains* cannot have been set even in Morris's imagination at the foot of the Dolomites: the romance describes the first clashes of Goths and Huns, and these took place in reality, as Christopher Tolkien has indicated, far to the east of Trento, probably in the Carpathian mountains, not the Dolomites.

There is much more history in these works than May realised. But she and Morris's later commentators did not know that, or want to know that. May indeed told a story about a German professor:

> I am reminded here, by the by, of the German professor who, after the Wolfings came out, wrote and asked learned questions about the Mark, expecting, I fear, equally learned answers from our Poet who sometimes dreamed realities without having documentary evidence of them. (M. Morris 1912, note to p. xxv)

---

14 C. Tolkien 2010 and C. Tolkien 1953-57.

This unknown German professor has been repeatedly cited, for instance by Thompson, who quotes with approval Morris's alleged reply, "Doesn't the fool realize [...] that it's a romance, a work of fiction – that it's all LIES!" (Thompson 1955, 676). But the German professor was only responding to Morris's efforts of reconstruction. I cannot help thinking that mentioning him scornfully is a characteristic "misologist" reaction, there to tell the lazy and linguistically challenged that they need think no further. I'd add that Morris was an extremely learned man in early Germanic languages. During his career he translated (with Eirikur Magnusson) ten major sagas as well as *Heimskringla* from Icelandic and *Beowulf* (with A.J. Wyatt) from Old English. I was recently given a paper to read on that latter topic which censured Morris for mis-translating, based on a comparison with a modern translation: in every instance the modern translation was wrong and Morris was right.

However, I will not labour the point about Morris's philology, and Tolkien's, any further. Instead I will ask what effect Morris's later romances may have had on Tolkien, and here I will make a very speculative suggestion.

We know that Tolkien had no clear plan for *The Lord of the Rings*. He continually underestimated how much he had to write, and did not seem to know how the plot would develop. It seems to me – and this is the very speculative suggestion – that a turning point came at what is now p. 424 of *The Treason of Isengard*. There Christopher quotes a little note by his father, setting out some linguistic parallels:

> Language of Shire = modern English
> Language of Dale = Norse (used by Dwarves of that region)
> Language of Rohan = Old English
> 'Modern English' is *lingua franca* spoken by all people ...

What this note does is explain why the dwarves have names taken from Old Norse, which is not a dwarvish language, but is related to both Old and Modern English. What it also did was give Tolkien licence to reconstruct an early Germanic society, just like Morris's. It was, essentially, Anglo-Saxons + horses. And though their language and poetry were Anglo-Saxon, that is Old English, what the Riders most resemble, I would suggest (and here I make amends for having rejected the Dolomites) is the ancient Lombards, as described not by

Jordanes but by another barbarian historian, Paul the Deacon, in his *History of the Lombards*.

At exactly this point in *The Lord of the Rings*, though – just before the Riders of Rohan appear – I'd suggest that Tolkien once again started to draw on Morris. One of the main and repeated features of Morris's later romances is what I have called their sense of "wavering uncertainty" (Shippey 1980, x). In *The Well at the World's End* Ralph is cautioned by one maiden against the Wood Perilous, which he has to cross to reach the Burg of the Four Friths. In the Wood he meets an armed company who offer to escort him there. But then he meets a second armed company, and rescues a lady from them, who cautions him against the Burg, inhabited by robbers and murderers, and directs him to Hampton instead. Still in the Wood, though, the first maiden reappears and says Hampton is inhabited by the Fellowship of the Dry Tree, robbers and reivers. Another passer-by directs him back to the Burg, but when he gets there they have a Dry Tree themselves, which is a gallows.

Who is telling the truth? In the same way, in *The Wood beyond the World* Ralph finds himself in a kind of "quadrille of eavesdropping" (Shippey 1980, xiv), with the hero, Walter, torn between a Lady and a Maiden, a King's Son and a Dwarf, all talking privately, and all contradicting each other to poor Walter. It is, Walter concludes, "a house of guile and lies" (Morris 1980, 67). But actually there must be a right side and a wrong side there. Probably the Maiden is the one to trust, not the Lady, because the Maiden at least admits she is a liar.

This, it seems to me, is very similar to the situation at the start of *The Two Towers*. Aragorn and Legolas and Gimli, have gone well out of their way in Wilderland, and are moreover not at all sure what they ought to do, or ought to have done. Merry and Pippin are likewise lost, and unsure whether or not to enter Fangorn Forest. Moreover, there are two wizards at large in the Forest, one of them being Saruman and the other Gandalf: not easy at this point to tell apart.

Who does Gimli see at the end of the chapter "The Riders of Rohan"? Gimli thinks it must have been Saruman, and since he is sure that Gandalf is dead, and Éomer has told them that Saruman walks the wood, that seems a reasonable suggestion. Aragorn, however, points out that the figure Gimli saw was wearing a hat, like Gandalf, not a hood, like Saruman; and Legolas points out in the next chapter, "The White Rider", that the horses dragged their pickets "as horses will when they meet a friend." Later on in that chapter another wizard appears, wearing Saruman's white robes, so that Gimli initially and reasonably takes him to be Saruman as well. This time, however, the wizard is definitely Gandalf. Gandalf nevertheless confirms that the first sighting must have been Saruman: "You certainly did not see me ... I must guess that you saw Saruman."

But if so, as Aragorn noted, why was Saruman wearing a hat? And surely, as Legolas pointed out, the friend the horses sensed was Shadowfax? Hasufel and Arod indeed reappear with him at the end of the chapter. On the whole, the evidence suggests that Gimli was wrong both times, both times seeing Gandalf and taking him for Saruman. But why would Gandalf deny that? Who *did* Gimli see the first time? If it was Saruman, and this is only Gandalf's "guess", what was he doing? Fangorn at this point is very like one of Morris's intensely confusing woods, the Wood Perilous, the Wood beyond the World.

Galadriel is also in some ways a Morrisian character, for Éomer regards "the Lady of the Golden Wood" as a sorceress, a net-weaver: dangerous but attractive females are a regular feature of the Morris romances, like the Witch, in *The Water of the Wondrous Isles*, and the rescued Lady, in *The Well at the World's End*. They are hard to tell from the attractive but benevolent women like the Maiden in several romances, and Habundia, the fairy-woman of the woods, again in *Wondrous Isles*, a character very like Galadriel. It is not entirely inappropriate for Gríma Wormtongue to describe Lothlórien as "Dwimordene", which we might translate as "valley of illusion", a meaning which furthermore fits Éomer's description of Saruman as "dwimmer-crafty, having many guises". On the other hand the Nazgûl steed, which Éowyn calls a "dwimmerlaik", is not an illusion at all. It is perhaps in the nature of the word and the concept that we cannot even be sure what is illusory.

I note finally the related Scottish expression, "in a dwam", usually taken to mean a state of semi-consciousness, but in my experience used also of a person who is just not responding, perhaps because he is in a state of paralysed uncertainty. That seems to be very appropriate for Aragorn, Legolas and Gimli. At this point in the story they are by no means paralysed, but they are quite unsure what to do or what to think, partly because they are not sure what is real and what is illusion. Have they met Gandalf wearing Saruman's colours, or seen "dwimmer-crafty" Saruman with hat and staff like Gandalf? Speaking for myself, even after many readings I am not sure what to think about what has been seen or not seen in Fangorn Forest. It is "Dwimmerland" indeed.

Finally, if coincidentally, it is at this point too in Tolkien's story that Shadowfax appears as a character. The name of Ralph's horse in *The Well at the World's End* is Silverfax, and the first thing that is said about Shadowfax is, "By day his coat glistens like silver […]."

What I'm suggesting is, then, two things: first, that at the start of *The Two Towers* we find ourselves in a scenario very reminiscent of Morris's later romances; and second, that at just about the same point Tolkien worked out how to bring into his story the element of social reconstruction so prominent in Morris's earlier romances. If both these suggestions are accepted, one could accordingly argue that the influence of Morris at this point was not only important: it was pivotal, a moment of breakthrough.

Two more similarities, one of which I can make very quickly. Characteristic of Morris's later romances is a "figure of eight" structure. In *The Water of the Wondrous Isles* (the second-longest of Morris's romances) the heroine, Birdalone, is stolen from her mother by a witch and brought up in the witch's cottage in the wood of Evilshaw. She escapes in a magic boat; reaches a series of wondrous isles; and on one of them is rescued from the witch's sister by three damsels, who beg her to send their lovers to save them. She reaches the castle of the three lovers, who duly sail off and rescue their ladies. Birdalone retires to support herself by working in the City of the Five Crafts but then comes back successively to the knights' castle, the magic boat, the wondrous isles, the witch's cottage, and, finally, the town from which she was kidnapped, where in the end she lives in peace with her lover. One could say the same of *The Story of the Glittering Plain*. And of course of *The Lord of the Rings*, noting also the sub-title of *The Hobbit*, "There and Back Again".

But the last thing I have to say goes rather deeper into Tolkien's psychology, and so must be especially speculative. The most recurrent element in Tolkien's writing is surely its sense of loss, separation, and above all yearning. It is there in his occasional poems, from beginning to end. "The Nameless Land" (1927), gives us a vision of the land across the Sea. In "The Happy Mariners" (1920), the mariners reach the land across the Sea. In "Firiel" (1934) a mortal maiden refuses to sail with the elves across the Sea, and remains to die in Middle-earth. In "Looney" (1934), by contrast, a mortal returns from the land of the elves across the Sea, but never recovers. In "Imram" (1955), a mortal again returns from across the Sea to die in Middle-earth. In "King Sheave" (written c. 1936),[15] a mortal dies but returns across the Sea. While the poems offer several variations on the shared theme, the shared emotion is yearning, regret, and in the end resignation.

The early poem "King Sheave" moreover develops a legend of one who came to Middle-earth from across the Sea, as a kind of redeemer, and who, unlike the characters in the poems just mentioned, is allowed to leave Middle-earth and return to his homeland, but only in death. The theme gives special power to the very end of *The Lord of the Rings*, when Sam accompanies Frodo to the ship which will take him (like King Sheave) to Valinor, but then – like Firiel – goes back to wife and family, saying only "Well, I'm back." It has been called "the most heartbreaking line in all of modern fantasy" (Swanwick 2001, 45), and I agree.

The sense of yearning also accounts for Tolkien's long fascination with the theme of "the lost road", which once allowed passage to the land of immortality, but which no longer exists – except, in legend, for the occasional fortunate exception. Of which number, Tolkien knew, he could not be one.

The wish for escape is, however, as we all know, strongly nuanced, because taking the last ship, or the lost road, means inevitably, leaving Middle-earth. And that too will be a loss. As Haldir the elf says in *The Fellowship of the Ring*, the elves may still, at the end of the Third Age "pass to the Sea unhindered and leave Middle-earth for ever." But that is a choice which he regrets: "Alas

---

15 See *LR* 77-98, for poem and commentary.

for Lothlórien that I love! It would be a poor life in a land where no mallorn grew. But if there are mallorn-trees beyond the Great Sea, none have reported it" (*LotR*, FR.II.6).

The compromise solution, I feel, lies in the idea of *le paradis terrestre*, a medieval image made popular by a medieval English writer, Sir John Mandeville. He had heard that, somewhere unexplored, the Paradise from which Adam and Eve had been expelled was still present on Earth. So one might have immortality and mallorn-trees as well! And in my opinion, Lothlórien is Tolkien's image of that place, *le paradis terrestre* itself. But, as I am sure readers will have guessed already, where is that theme used before Tolkien? Obviously, in Morris's most popular poem, now very rarely read, *The Earthly Paradise*.

One major element in that poem was discontent with industrial England, and this is the very start of it:

> Forget six counties overhung with smoke,
> Forget the snorting steam and piston stroke
> [...]
> And dream of London, small and white and clean,
> The clear Thames bordered by its gardens green
> (Morris 1905, 3, lines 1-6)

Compare the start of *The Hobbit*: "One morning long ago in the quiet of the world, when there was less noise and more green [...]" (*H* I).

The other element was yearning for a different land, Morris again:

> A nameless city in a distant sea,
> White as the changing walls of faërie
> [...]
> There, leave the clear green water and the quays
> And pass betwixt its marble palaces
> (Morris 1905, 3, lines 17-22)

Compare Tolkien's poem of 1923, "The City of the Gods":

> A sable hill, gigantic, rampart-crowned
> Stands gazing out across an azure sea
> Under an azure sky, on whose dark ground
> [...]
> Gleam marble temples white, [...]
> (*BLT 1* 136)

Morris's work, I would suggest, focused Tolkien's mind on the idea of an earthly paradise, not in the East where Mandeville located it, but in the West, across the sea, and now inaccessible to us. Moreover Morris's poem must surely have given Tolkien a hint, or a model, for the idea framing *The Book of Lost Tales*. The frame of Morris's poem is like this:

> Certain gentlemen and mariners of Norway, having considered all that they had heard of the Earthly Paradise, set sail to find it, and after many troubles and the lapse of many years came old men to some Western land, of which they had never before heard: there they died [...] (Morris 1905, 3, "Argument" to Prologue)

But first they tell their stories, and hear the stories of the far land. Compare Tolkien's opening to *The Book of Lost Tales*:

> Now it happened on a certain time that a traveller from far countries, a man of great curiosity, was by desire of strange lands [...] brought in a ship even as far west as The Lonely Island [...] (*BLT 1* 13)

And there, of course, he hears the tales, which are the "true tradition" of the fairies, and become the *Silmarillion*.

Finally, I have only to say that the theme of loss and yearning increasingly animates Morris's later romances. The first two, as I've said, are in a way historical novels, set in a real world and a real history and geography (even if his critics have not appreciated them in that way). The third of them, *The Story of the Glittering Plain*, still takes place in a pagan world, in which the hero Hallblithe journeys to the Land of the Undying – a word-for-word translation of the pagan Old Norse expression *Odainsakr*, and comes back again. But the tone of it is set by his first encounter, with three strangers, who say they seek "the Land of Living Men", and call out desperately, "Is this the Land? Is this the Land?" The main character Hallblithe tells them cheerfully, that it isn't:

> Here men die when their hour comes, nor know I if the days of their life be long enough for the forgetting of sorrow; but this I know, that they are long enough for the doing of deeds that shall not die. (Morris 1979, 3)

So, he tells them, be cheerful, enjoy life! But they ignore him and ride on, crying out sadly: "This is not the Land! This is not the Land!!"

The next three are all in their way quest-stories, but the last of the seven again brings up forcefully the theme of separation. It is called *The Sundering Flood*, and the central idea of it is the love-story between Osberne and Elfhild, a man and a maiden, in love with each other, but separated by a river which they cannot cross. It would not take much to add to this the idea that Osberne is a man, but Elfhild is an elf: and there you have, in essence, the stories of Beren and Lúthien, or Aragorn and Arwen, who cannot overcome the fact that their destinies are different. In Tolkien, more so than in Morris, *Amor non vincit omnia,* love does not conquer all.

Summing up, I have argued that Morris gave Tolkien, or perhaps I should say more temperately, suggested to Tolkien the themes of:
- the philologically reconstructed early society
- the value of the long narrative poem
- the figure-of-eight structure, "there and back again"
- the terrestrial paradise
- the sense of unfulfilled yearning
- the theme of separation which in Tolkien lasts even beyond death
- and the framing narrative of wanderers telling tales in a long-lost city.

Perhaps the question that remains is – and here I return to my own theme of indignation – why have Morris and Tolkien been so popular, but so critically disparaged? I have tried to answer that question as regards Tolkien several times, but for Morris?

The answer must be that he is simply not easy to read. He used an unnatural high diction. He did not choose successful verse-forms. He composed poetry too easily. His romances are mysterious, but too few of the mysteries are even explained. They are also shapeless. Unlike Bilbo and Frodo, his heroes and heroines do not grow in the course of the narrative. Nor do they have that unflinching focus – on Smaug, on the Ring – which Tolkien learned.

Nevertheless, if Tolkien had not invented hobbits – if we knew him only from *The Book of Lost Tales, The Lays of Beleriand, The Silmarillion* – the resemblance between Tolkien and Morris would be much closer and more readily recognised. I have suggested also that at a critical moment in the development of *The Lord of the Rings*, it was the memory of Morris's romances which helped to unlock Tolkien's inspiration.

Bibliography

Primary Sources

Morris, William. *The Story of the Glittering Plain*. First published 1890/91. Reprinted. London: George Prior, 1979.

—. *The Earthly Paradise*. 4 volumes. First published 1868-1870. Reprinted. London: Longmans Green, 1905.

—. *The Wood beyond the World*. First published 1894. Reprinted. London: Oxford University Press, 1980.

Secondary Sources

Anderson, Douglas (ed.). *Tales Before Tolkien: The Roots of Modern Fantasy*. New York: Ballantine, 2003.

Arduini, Roberto and Claudio A. Testi (eds.). *Tolkien and Philosophy*. Zurich and Jena: Walking Tree Publishers, 2014.

Benedikz, B.S. "Some Family Connections with J.R.R. Tolkien." *Amon Hen* 209 (January 2008).

Cilli, Oronzo. *Tolkien's Library: An Annotated Checklist*. Edinburgh: Luna Press, forthcoming 2019.

Drout, Michael C. (ed.). *J.R.R. Tolkien Encyclopedia: Scholarship and Critical Assessment*. New York: Routledge, 2007.

Fussell, Paul. *The Great War and Modern Memory*. First published 1975. Reprinted. London and New York: Oxford University Press, 1989.

Garth, John. *Tolkien and the Great War*. London: HarperCollins, 2003.

Haber, Karen (ed.). *Meditations on Middle-earth*. New York: Byron Preiss Books, 2001.

Henderson, Philip. *William Morris: His Life, Work and Friends*. London: Thames and Hudson, 1967.

Kirchhoff, Frederick (ed.). *Studies in the Late Romances of William Morris*. New York: William Morris Society, 1976.

Manni, Franco and Tom Shippey. "Tolkien Between Philosophy and Philology." *Tolkien and Philosophy*. Eds. Roberto Arduini and Claudio A. Testi. Zurich and Jena: Walking Tree Publishers, 2014, 21-72.

Morris, May. "Introduction" to *The House of the Wolfings*. Volume 14 of *The Collected Works of William Morris*. London and New York: Longmans Green, 1912, xv-xxix.

Perry, Michael W. "William Morris." *J.R.R. Tolkien Encyclopedia: Scholarship and Critical Assessment*. Ed. Michael D.C. Drout. New York: Routledge, 2007, 439-441.

Scull, Christina and Wayne G. Hammond. *The J.R.R. Tolkien Companion and Guide: Reader's Guide*, London: HarperCollins, 2006.

The J.R.R. Tolkien Companion and Guide: Chronology. London: HarperCollins, 2006b.

Shippey, Tom. *Roots and Branches: Selected Papers on Tolkien*. Zurich and Berne: Walking Tree Publishers, 2007.

"Goths and Huns: The Rediscovery of the Northern Cultures in the Nineteenth Century." *The Medieval Legacy: A Symposium*. Ed. Andreas Haarder. Odense: University of Odense Press, 1982. 51-69. Reprinted in Tom Shippey. *Roots and Branches: Selected Papers on Tolkien*. Zurich and Berne: Walking Tree Publishers, 2007, 115-136.

"Introduction" to William Morris. *The Wood beyond the World*. First published 1894. Reprinted. London: Oxford University Press, 1980, v-xix.

Swanwick, Michael. "A Changeling Returns." *Meditations on Middle-earth*. Ed. Karen Haber. New York: Byron Preiss Books, 2001, 33-46.

Testi, Claudio A. *Pagan Saints in Middle-earth*. Zurich and Jena: Walking Tree Publishers, 2018.

Thompson, E.P. *William Morris: Romantic to Revolutionary*. London: Lawrence and Wishart, 1955. Revised edition. New York: Pantheon, 1976.

Tolkien, Christopher (ed. and trans.). *The Saga of King Heidrek the Wise*. Reprinted. London: HarperCollins, 2010.

"The Battle of the Goths and Huns." *Saga-Book of the Viking Society* 14 (1953-57): 141-163.

Yates, Jessica. "William Morris's Influence on J.R.R. Tolkien: Bibliography." unpublished work.

Walking Tree Publishers
Zurich and Jena

Walking Tree Publishers was founded in 1997 as a forum for publication of material related to Tolkien and Middle-earth studies.

http://www.walking-tree.org

Cormarë Series

The *Cormarë Series* collects papers and studies dedicated exclusively to the exploration of Tolkien's work. It comprises monographs, thematic collections of essays, conference volumes, and reprints of important yet no longer (easily) accessible papers by leading scholars in the field. Manuscripts and project proposals are evaluated by members of an independent board of advisors who support the series editors in their endeavour to provide the readers with qualitatively superior yet accessible studies on Tolkien and his work.

News from the Shire and Beyond. Studies on Tolkien
Peter Buchs & Thomas Honegger (eds.), Zurich and Berne 2004, Reprint, First edition 1997 (Cormarë Series 1), ISBN 978-3-9521424-5-5

Root and Branch. Approaches Towards Understanding Tolkien
Thomas Honegger (ed.), Zurich and Berne 2005, Reprint, First edition 1999 (Cormarë Series 2), ISBN 978-3-905703-01-6

Richard Sturch, *Four Christian Fantasists. A Study of the Fantastic Writings of George MacDonald, Charles Williams, C.S. Lewis and J.R.R. Tolkien*
Zurich and Berne 2007, Reprint, First edition 2001 (Cormarë Series 3), ISBN 978-3-905703-04-7

Tolkien in Translation
Thomas Honegger (ed.), Zurich and Jena 2011, Reprint, First edition 2003 (Cormarë Series 4), ISBN 978-3-905703-15-3

Mark T. Hooker, *Tolkien Through Russian Eyes*
Zurich and Berne 2003 (Cormarë Series 5), ISBN 978-3-9521424-7-9

Translating Tolkien: Text and Film
Thomas Honegger (ed.), Zurich and Jena 2011, Reprint, First edition 2004 (Cormarë Series 6), ISBN 978-3-905703-16-0

Christopher Garbowski, *Recovery and Transcendence for the Contemporary Mythmaker. The Spiritual Dimension in the Works of J.R.R. Tolkien*
Zurich and Berne 2004, Reprint, First Edition by Marie Curie Sklodowska, University Press, Lublin 2000, (Cormarë Series 7), ISBN 978-3-9521424-8-6

Reconsidering Tolkien
Thomas Honegger (ed.), Zurich and Berne 2005 (Cormarë Series 8), ISBN 978-3-905703-00-9

Tolkien and Modernity 1
Frank Weinreich & Thomas Honegger (eds.), Zurich and Berne 2006 (Cormarë Series 9), ISBN 978-3-905703-02-3

Tolkien and Modernity 2
Thomas Honegger & Frank Weinreich (eds.), Zurich and Berne 2006 (Cormarë Series 10), ISBN 978-3-905703-03-0

Tom Shippey, *Roots and Branches. Selected Papers on Tolkien by Tom Shippey*
Zurich and Berne 2007 (Cormarë Series 11), ISBN 978-3-905703-05-4

Ross Smith, *Inside Language. Linguistic and Aesthetic Theory in Tolkien*
Zurich and Jena 2011, Reprint, First edition 2007 (Cormarë Series 12),
ISBN 978-3-905703-20-7

How We Became Middle-earth. A Collection of Essays on The Lord of the Rings
Adam Lam & Nataliya Oryshchuk (eds.), Zurich and Berne 2007 (Cormarë
Series 13), ISBN 978-3-905703-07-8

Myth and Magic. Art According to the Inklings
Eduardo Segura & Thomas Honegger (eds.), Zurich and Berne 2007 (Cormarë
Series 14), ISBN 978-3-905703-08-5

The Silmarillion – Thirty Years On
Allan Turner (ed.), Zurich and Berne 2007 (Cormarë Series 15),
ISBN 978-3-905703-10-8

Martin Simonson, *The Lord of the Rings and the Western Narrative Tradition*
Zurich and Jena 2008 (Cormarë Series 16), ISBN 978-3-905703-09-2

Tolkien's Shorter Works. Proceedings of the 4th Seminar of the Deutsche Tolkien Gesellschaft & Walking Tree Publishers Decennial Conference
Margaret Hiley & Frank Weinreich (eds.), Zurich and Jena 2008 (Cormarë Series 17), ISBN 978-3-905703-11-5

Tolkien's The Lord of the Rings: Sources of Inspiration
Stratford Caldecott & Thomas Honegger (eds.), Zurich and Jena 2008 (Cormarë Series 18), ISBN 978-3-905703-12-2

J.S. Ryan, *Tolkien's View: Windows into his World*
Zurich and Jena 2009 (Cormarë Series 19), ISBN 978-3-905703-13-9

Music in Middle-earth
Heidi Steimel & Friedhelm Schneidewind (eds.), Zurich and Jena 2010 (Cormarë Series 20), ISBN 978-3-905703-14-6

Liam Campbell, *The Ecological Augury in the Works of JRR Tolkien*
Zurich and Jena 2011 (Cormarë Series 21), ISBN 978-3-905703-18-4

Margaret Hiley, *The Loss and the Silence. Aspects of Modernism in the Works of C.S. Lewis, J.R.R. Tolkien and Charles Williams*
Zurich and Jena 2011 (Cormarë Series 22), ISBN 978-3-905703-19-1

Rainer Nagel, *Hobbit Place-names. A Linguistic Excursion through the Shire*
Zurich and Jena 2012 (Cormarë Series 23), ISBN 978-3-905703-22-1

Christopher MacLachlan, *Tolkien and Wagner: The Ring and Der Ring*
Zurich and Jena 2012 (Cormarë Series 24), ISBN 978-3-905703-21-4

Renée Vink, *Wagner and Tolkien: Mythmakers*
Zurich and Jena 2012 (Cormarë Series 25), ISBN 978-3-905703-25-2

The Broken Scythe. Death and Immortality in the Works of J.R.R. Tolkien
Roberto Arduini & Claudio Antonio Testi (eds.), Zurich and Jena 2012 (Cormarë Series 26), ISBN 978-3-905703-26-9

Sub-creating Middle-earth: Constructions of Authorship and the Works of J.R.R. Tolkien
Judith Klinger (ed.), Zurich and Jena 2012 (Cormarë Series 27),
ISBN 978-3-905703-27-6

Tolkien's Poetry
Julian Eilmann & Allan Turner (eds.), Zurich and Jena 2013
(Cormarë Series 28), ISBN 978-3-905703-28-3

O, What a Tangled Web. Tolkien and Medieval Literature. A View from Poland
Barbara Kowalik (ed.), Zurich and Jena 2013 (Cormarë Series 29),
ISBN 978-3-905703-29-0

J.S. Ryan, *In the Nameless Wood*
Zurich and Jena 2013 (Cormarë Series 30), ISBN 978-3-905703-30-6

From Peterborough to Faëry; The Poetics and Mechanics of Secondary Worlds
Thomas Honegger & Dirk Vanderbeke (eds.), Zurich and Jena 2014
(Cormarë Series 31), ISBN 978-3-905703-31-3

Tolkien and Philosophy
Roberto Arduini & Claudio R. Testi (eds.), Zurich and Jena 2014
(Cormarë Series 32), ISBN 978-3-905703-32-0

Patrick Curry, *Deep Roots in a Time of Frost. Essays on Tolkien*
Zurich and Jena 2014 (Cormarë Series 33), ISBN 978-3-905703-33-7

Representations of Nature in Middle-earth
Martin Simonson (ed.), Zurich and Jena 2015, (Cormarë Series 34),
ISBN 978-3-905703-34-4

Laughter in Middle-earth
Thomas Honegger & Maureen F. Mann (eds.), Zurich and Jena 2016
(Cormarë Series 35), ISBN 978-3-905703-35-1

Julian Eilmann, *J.R.R. Tolkien – Romanticist and Poet*
Zurich and Jena 2017 (Cormarë Series 36), ISBN 978-3-905703-36-8

Binding Them All. Interdisciplinary Perspectives on J.R.R. Tolkien and His Works
Monika Kirner-Ludwig, Stephan Köser, Sebastian Streitberger (eds.), Zurich and Jena
2017 (Cormarë Series 37), ISBN 978-3-905703-37-5

Claudio Testi, *Pagan Saints in Middle-earth*
Zurich and Jena 2017 (Cormarë Series 38), ISBN 978-3-905703-38-2

Music in Tolkien's Work and Beyond
Julian Eilmann & Friedhelm Schneidewind (eds.), Zurich and Jena 2019 (Cormarë
Series 39), forthcoming

Sub-creating Arda: World-building in J.R.R. Tolkien's Works, its Precursors, and Legacies
Dimitra Fimi & Thomas Honegger (eds.), Zurich and Jena 2019 (Cormarë Series 40),
ISBN 978-3-905703-40-5

"Something has gone crack": New Perspectives on J.R.R. Tolkien in the Great War
Janet Brennan Croft & Annika Röttinger (eds.), Zurich and Jena 2019 (Cormarë
Series 41), forthcoming

Tolkien and the Classics
Roberto Arduini, Giampaolo Canzonieri & Claudio A. Testi (eds.), Zurich and Jena
2019 (Cormarë Series 42), ISBN 978-3-905703-42-9

Beowulf and the Dragon

The original Old English text of the 'Dragon Episode' of Beowulf is set in an authentic font and bound in hardback as a high quality art book. Illustrated by Anke Eissmann and accompanied by John Porter's translation. Introduction by Tom Shippey. Limited first edition of 500 copies. 84 pages. Selected pages can be previewed on: http://www.walking-tree.org/beowulf

Beowulf and the Dragon
Zurich and Jena 2009 , ISBN 978-3-905703-17-7

Tales of Yore Series

The *Tales of Yore Series* provides a platform for qualitatively superior fiction that will appeal to readers familiar with Tolkien's world:

The Monster Specialist

Sir Severus le Brewse, among the least known of King Arthur's Round Table knights, is preferred by nature, disposition, and training to fight against monsters rather than other knights. After youthful adventures of errantry with dragons, trolls, vampires, and assorted beasts, Severus joins the brilliant sorceress Lilava to face the Chimaera in The Greatest Monster Battle of All Time to free her folk from an age-old curse. But their adventures don't end there; together they meet elves and magicians, friends and foes; they join in the fight to save Camelot and even walk the Grey Paths of the Dead. With a mix of Malory, a touch of Tolkien, and a hint of humor, The Monster Specialist chronicles a tale of courage, tenacity, honor, and love.

The Monster Specialist is illustrated by Anke Eissmann.

Edward S. Louis, *The Monster Specialist*
Zurich and Jena 2014 (Tales of Yore Series No. 3), ISBN 978-3-905703-23-8

Tales of Yore Series (earlier books)

Kay Woollard, *The Terror of Tatty Walk. A Frightener*
CD and Booklet, Zurich and Berne 2000, ISBN 978-3-9521424-2-4

Kay Woollard, *Wilmot's Very Strange Stone or What came of building "snobbits"*
CD and booklet, Zurich and Berne 2001, ISBN 978-3-9521424-4-8

Information for authors

Authors interested in contributing to our publications can learn more about the services we offer on the "services for authors" section of our web pages.

http://www.walking-tree.org/authors

Manuscripts and project proposals can be submitted to the board of editors (please include an SAE):

Walking Tree Publishers
CH-3052 Zollikofen
Switzerland

e-mail: info@walking-tree.org

Walking Tree Publishers, Zurich and Jena, 2019

www.ingramcontent.com/pod-product-compliance
Lightning Source LLC
Chambersburg PA
CBHW070727160426
43192CB00009B/1341